Dolomites

Book 2: Centre and East

Florian Fritz and Dietrich Höllhuber

SUNFLOWER BOOKS

First edition © 2023
Sunflower Books™
PO Box 36160
London SW7 3WS, UK
www.sunflowerbooks.co.uk

All rights reserved. No part of this publication may be reproduced, stored in a retrieval system, or transmitted by any form or by any means, electronic, mechanical, photocopying, recording or otherwise, without the prior written permission of the publishers.

ISBN 978-1-85691-542-7

Important note to readers

This book is a translation from guides originally published in Germany (see Publisher's note on page 6). We have tried to ensure that the descriptions and maps are error-free at press date. The book will be updated, where necessary, whenever future editions permit. It will be very helpful for us to receive your comments (sent to info@sunflowerbooks.co.uk, please) for the updating of future editions — and for our online update service.

We also rely on those who use this book — especially walkers — to take along a good supply of common sense when they explore. Conditions can change fairly rapidly due to storm damage. Explore *safely,* while respecting the beauty of the countryside.

Cover photograph: the Drei Zinnen/Tre Cime di Lavaredo from the east, above the Paternsattel/Forcella di Lavaredo (Walk 30)

Translated from *Dolomiten/Südtirol Ost* by Dietrich Höllhuber (and revised edition by Florian Fritz) and *Dolomiten Wanderführer* by Florian Fritz, text and maps ©2006, 2009, 2015, 2018, 2020 Michael Müller Verlag, Erlangen, Germany

Photographs: 21, 27, 30, 31, 32, 33, 47, 48, 50, 54, 56-7, 59, 60-1, 63, 64, 65, 66-7, 68, 72-3, 74-5, 78, 84-5, 88, 90-1, 99, 104, 105, 111, 112-3, 152-3, 162-3, 164 (Florian Fritz); 25, 42, 83, 93, 94-5, 97, 100 (both), 102, 120, 125, 127, 128, 130, 132, 139, 150, 154-5, 158, 166, 170-1, 177, 180 (Dietrich Höllhuber); 176 (Eisacktal Tourist Board); 18, 178 (i-stock photo); 5, 28-9, 34, 37, 71, 81, 106-7, 115, 117, 118, 121, 122-3, 134, 137, 140-1, 142, 144-5, 146, 149, 151, 160-1, 167, 168, 175, cover (Shutterstock)

Sunflower Books is a Registered Trademark.
A CIP catalogue record for this book is available from the British Library.
Printed and bound in England by Short Run Press, Exeter

Contents

Preface	5
Publisher's note	6
Introduction	8
When to go	8
Travelling to the Dolomites	9
By air • By train • By car	
Getting around the area	10
By car • By bus • By train • By cycle	
Where to stay	13
Hotels • Farmhouse holidays • Mountain huts, youth hostels, campsites	
Cuisine	14
Practicalities A-Z	16
Climate and weather • Communications • Festivals, customs and events • Information • Maps • Medical care • Money/banks • Opening times • Shopping and souvenirs • Sports	
Short historical summary	24
Walking in the Dolomites	27
Walking areas • Weather and best times to walk • Flora • Fauna • Equipment and food • Emergencies and emergency phone numbers • Planning your walks and getting to them • Waymarks and signposts, grades, maps, GPS	
1 Grödner Tal/Val Gardena	36
● Walk 1: From St Christina/Santa Cristina to St Jacob/San Giacomo church	46
● Walk 2: Over the alms of Col Raiser	48
●❗ Walk 3: From Col Raiser to Pic and then to St Christina via the Seurasas alms	51
●❗ Walk 4: To Seceda via Raschötz/Rasciesa and the Panascharte/Forcella Pana	55
●❗ Walk 5: From Wolkenstein/Selva to the Stevia Hut	58
● Walk 6: From Wolkenstein/Selva into the Langental/Vallunga	62
● Walk 7: From the Ciampinoi lift to the Sellajoch/Passo Sella	65
●❗ Walk 8: Circuit round Langkofel/Sassolungo	69
● Walk 9: From Seceda to the Regensburger Hut/Rifugio Firenze and Wolkenstein/Selva	74
●❗ Walk 10: From the Grödner Joch/Passo Gardena to the Pordoi Joch/Passo Pordoi via the Sella massif	76
●❗ Walk 11: Pisciadù Hut and Lake	80
●❗ Walk 12: Two-day hike from the Grödner Joch/Passo Gardena to Piz Boè and the Boè lift	82
●❗ Walk 13: From the Grödner Joch/Passo Gardena through the Langental/Vallunga	84

●●● Symbols indicating grading of the walks: see page 35

4   Dolomites, Book 2: Centre and East

- Walk 14: Circuit on the Seiser Alm/Alpe di Siusi from Mont Sëuc   89
  Walking tips: ● to Wolkenstein/Selva on the Luis Trenker Promenade and the old railway; ● Mont de Sëura to the Rifugio Comici; Col Raiser to the Regensburger Hut/Rifugio Firenze; *Cycling tip:* from the Seiser Alm down into Gröden by mountain bike

2 Gadertal/Val Badia   92
- Walk 15: Seres and the Valley of the Mills   103
- Walk 16: High-altitude hike from the Holy Cross Hospice to Stern/La Villa   106
- Walk 17: From the Capanna Alpina to the Scotoni Hut and Lake Lagazuoi   110
- Walk 18: Pisciadù Waterfalls   114
- ●❗ Walk 19: From Stern/La Villa to the Fanes group   116
- Walk 20: Across the Sennes to the Seekofel Hut   119
- Walk 21: Wengen/La Valle and the 'viles'   122
  Cycling tips: from St Martin towards Brixen/Bressanone; Fanes and Sennes by mountain bike

3 Fassatal/Val di Fassa   124
- Walk 22: From the upper station of the Ciampedié lift to the Paolina Hut   136
- Walk 23: From Mazzin to the Vajolet Hut via the Antermoia Hut   138
- Walk 24: The Bindelweg/Viel dal Pan   140
  Walking tip: ● Val Contrin; *Walking and cycling tip:* ● from Penìa to Pozza and Moèna

4 Val di Fiemme/Fleimstal   142
- Walk 25: Laghi di Colbricon   146

5 Primiero Valley   147
- ●❗ Walk 26: Round Pala di San Martino   151

6 Agordino   154
- ●❗ Walk 27: From the Falzàrego Pass to Lagazuoi   162
- Walk 28: From the Falzàrego Pass round Averau and Nuvolau   166
- Walk 29: Under the walls of Civetta   168
  Walking tips: ● stroll through the 'viles'; ●❗ Col di Lana

7 Ampezzo   170
- Walk 30: Round the Drei Zinnen/Tre Cime di Lavaredo   177
  Walking tip: ● Monte Piana from the Bosi Hut

8 Cadore   179

Index   182

Fold-out area map   *inside back cover*

Preface

In 1788 the head of the Department of Mineralogy at the Ecole des Mines in Paris, Deodat de Dolomieu, visited the southern Tyrol to explore the mountains. At that time there was no special name for these steep-sided, isolated mountains with their brightly coloured rock. In those days hardly anyone was interested in the new sciences of mineralogy and geology; most people believed that God had created the world 6000 years earlier — why worry about exactly *how* it came about?

Dolomieu found petrified tropical corals and other fossils at a height of 3000 metres, which told him that these mountains were once under the sea. Above all, he found a stone that, after his scientific studies were published, was named for him: dolomite. In dolomitic rock the calcium in the original limestone sediment from the sea bed or coral reefs is transformed to incorporate magnesium. Gradually the term 'Dolomites' began to appear in the scientific literature when this part of Tyrol was discussed, and it finally filtered down to common use.

The dramatically sited Christomannos eagle (see Walk 22)

Up to 240 million years old, these coral reefs rose from the sea bed in an almighty upheaval some 65 million years ago. These tectonic events, coupled with ongoing erosion from glaciers, snow, rain and wind have created deep valleys which today make a first-class holiday base. The Dolomites are a mecca for walkers, mountain bikers, climbers, skiers and paragliders. But you don't have to be an *aficionado* of any of these sports to enjoy the fresh air in the upper valleys, the healthy mountain setting and home-made cooking, visits to working alms or taking a lift up to the high peaks.

Publisher's note

Sunflower's original guide to the Dolomites, published in 2010, was translated from a German *general* guide, with 35 long and short walks. The Preface above is taken from that book, authored by the late Dietrich Höllhuber. His guide was updated by Florian Fritz, who has since written a purely *walking* guide. We're very fortunate to have these authors, who both started walking and climbing in the Dolomites in their teens; their enthusiasm shines through on every page.

Sunflower always wanted to offer readers more walks in the fabulous Dolomites, so we've put both books together — giving a total of 70 long and short walks. But because we wanted to keep all the other information in the general guide (everything from history to cuisine, from town plans to lift opening times and prices), this called for *two* books. To keep both guides to the same size and with an equal number of walks in each, we've split the guides in a rather unorthodox way — not in the usual east/west division.

The 'chapters' in **Book 1** cover **the north** (areas along the SS49 and Rienz/Rienzo River) **and west** (regions east of the A22 motorway/SS12 and Eisack/Isarco River). Those in **Book 2** cover areas more 'inland' of these roads: **Gröden/Val Gardena, Gadertal/Val Badia**, and regions further **east and south**. *Neither guide takes in the Brenta Dolomites west of the A22 motorway.*

The way we have split the guides has resulted in certain anomalies: for instance, walks to the Drei Zinnen/Tre Cime di Lavaredo feature in *both* books: they are approached from the north (from Sexten/Sesto) in Book 1 and from the south (from Lake Misurina near Cortina) in Book 2. There are several similar overlaps: *the walks are based on where you leave your transport — either to start the walk itself or to take a lift to a mountain station to begin.*

The format in these introductory guides is a bit different from the usual Sunflower style: instead of car tours, each 'chapter' covers a specific holiday area (see fold-out maps), with information about the towns and villages — from the 'sights' to lift opening times and prices. The **35 long and short walks** are described, with maps, following each chapter. But there are also dozens of other **detailed walking and cycling 'tips'** and suggestions for more of the authors' favourite hikes in each chapter — which you can follow using the relevant Tabacco 1:25,000 map (see page 35).

While it is usual for English-language guide books about the Dolomites to use **Italian place names**, you won't find these names taking precedence 'on the ground'. Italian is the main language in the Val di Fiemme/Fleimstal, Primiero, Agordino and Cadore; Ladin in the Fassatal/Val di Fassa, Buchenstein and Ampezzo. German is so widely spoken in South Tyrol (where a good many of these walks are based) that even Italians may use German place names (many of the Italian names were created under Mussolini: the original, German, names were simply translated into Italian). Signposting usually gives both names (or three, in **Ladin** areas). Since the maps in this book were produced in Germany, with **German place names**, we generally use these names in the text, but always show the Italian name when the place is first mentioned — or we list *all three* names, if the village is Ladin (see page 40). The Index of course lists all names.

Those of you unfamiliar with the area may be puzzled by the German word '**alm**', which can be used in several contexts. An alm is a mountain pasture above tree line, usually with a 'hut' (German 'Hütte', Italian 'Malga'), often used for dairy farming. Many of the 'huts' welcome visitors, selling fresh milk and cheese … and enticing meals.

Finally, please take into account that Dietrich and Fritz were/are very strong hillwalkers, completely at home in this mountainous environment. It would certainly be wise to build in *plenty of additional time* for these walks, until you feel at home following in their footsteps! And of course, we advise you *never to walk alone.*

Introduction

The Dolomites — a UNESCO World Heritage Site since 2009 — are located just south of the Austrian border, between the Eisack/Isarco Valley to the west and the Sexten/Sesto and Piave valleys to the east. The southern boundary lies on a line that curves roughly northeast from Trento to Belluno.

When to go

The whole Dolomites, whether it be the northern Pustertal/Val Pusteria or the southern Cadore, have a continental alpine climate. **Summers** are hot and dry, especially in the valleys. Only in areas affected by the famous 'Adriatic lows' is there significant rainfall. On the highest terrain it can freeze up and snow even in high summer! **Autumn** comes late and is mostly dry, perfect for outings. Unfortunately, most hotels in the Dolomites close by the middle or end of September; if you plan to come after this, be sure to book ahead and remember that *many lifts may be closed.* By mid-December all the lifts are open again, and Dolomiti Superski — the largest collection of lifts and runs in the world — is in full swing. **Winter** precipitation is not very high in the Dolomites, so the pistes must be carefully (and often

---

UNESCO World Heritage Dolomites

The nine most important areas of the Dolomites have been part of the UNESCO World Heritage since 2009. More than 231,000 hectares of mountainous land in the provinces of Belluno, South Tyrol, Pordenone, Trento and Udine were placed under its protection. The universal value of the Dolomites was justified by the extraordinarily varied mountain formations, the enormous importance for geological science (the wealth of fossils from the Triassic Era), and its 'sublime, monumental, lush and colourful landscape'. This means that cultural elements are also included in the justification, because landscape is not just nature: man has shaped it very significantly.

The protected areas of the Dolomites are:
- Pelmo, Croda da Lago (Belluno)
- Marmolada (Belluno, Trento)
- Pale di San Martino, Pale di San Lucano, Dolomiti Bellunesi, Vette Feltrine (Belluno, Trento)
- Dolomiti Friulane e d'Oltre Piave (Belluno, Pordenone, Udine)
- Northern Dolomites (Belluno, South Tyrol)
- Puez-Geisler (South Tyrol)
- Schlern-Rosengarten, Latemar (South Tyrol, Trento)
- Bletterbach (South Tyrol)
- Dolomiti di Brenta (Trento)

The province of Belluno has 41.2% of the core zone, South Tyrol 31% of the core and 51.8% of the buffer zone. Trento, Pordenone and Udine have only smaller areas (14.6/10.7/2.5% of the core and 8.9/16.9/6.5% of the buffer zone respectively).

very artistically) prepared. Sunny days are far more frequent than they are north of the Alps, and the view from the top of many ski slopes takes in about half the range. **Spring** begins late, no earlier than April/May in the valleys and June higher up — that's the time to explore the Dolomites on foot! Read more about the weather on pages 28-30.

Getting to the Dolomites
By air
There is an airport in the Dolomites, at Bozen/Bolzano, but as of press date there are no flights from the UK. The three airports handiest for the Dolomites are Innsbruck to the north and Verona and Venice to the south — with onward travel by rail, bus or car taking about two hours. Other gateways are Milan or Bergamo (onward travel about four hours), Treviso (onward travel under three hours) or Munich (four hours away). To see some flight suggestions, log on to South Tyrol's website: www.suedtirol.info.

Travelling by train is comfortable, but, unfortunately, quite a long-drawn-out affair from the UK

By train
The Dolomites *can* be reached by rail from London St Pancras International in under 24 hours, but at least two changes of train will be involved (with a change of *station* as well). If your heart is set on going by train, details can be found at www.bahn.de (German railways), www.trenitalia.it (Italian railways) or trainline.com.

The main railway stations in the Dolomites, served by the fast Eurocity trains, are at Trento, Bozen/Bolzano, and Brixen/Bressanone. From these stations there are direct bus services to the northern and western holiday areas in the range. Only the far south-eastern side of the Dolomites, near Belluno, is more quickly reached by train from Padua or Venice. The Franzensfeste/Fortezza station is where you should change for trains to the northern areas near the Pustertal/Val Pusteria; these stop at Bruneck/Brunico, Toblach/Dobbiaco and Innichen/San Candido.

For copious details about rail connections — including any of the few remaining **motorail** possibilities (unfortunately most have closed), log on to www.seat 61.com, a cornucopia of train information.

By car
Driving to the Dolomites is an option recommended for those who enjoy the flexibility and freedom of having their own

transport. After crossing the English Channel by tunnel or ferry (there are also ferries from Hull and Rosyth in Scotland to Zeebrugge) it is an easy drive of about 12 hours on the Continent's excellent motorways. (For an overview of the route, motorway tolls and approximate fuel costs, log on to www.viamichelin.com.)

The best approach to the Dolomites is via the A22 motorway over the Brenner Pass. This gives quick access to the western and northern parts of the range, and there are exits at Brixen/Bressanone, Klausen/Chiusa, Bozen/Bolzano and Trento, from where you can head east and south on good roads. (Other motorways which you might use if you are only visiting the southern and eastern Dolomites include the very busy A4 linking Milan and Venice. From Mestre near Venice the less-travelled A27 gives access to Belluno, with a good national road, the SS51, continuing to Cortina.)

In addition to your passports, be sure to have a valid **UK photocard driver's licence** (if you do not have a *photocard* licence, you will need an international driving permit). You must also have a **vehicle registration document** and **green card insurance** (guaranteeing that you have third party cover). If you are involved in an accident, all three documents will be required.

You will also need a **GB sticker**, **spare bulbs**, **warning triangle**, and a fluorescent yellow jacket for each person in the car. If you have a new or valuable car, it is worth getting special vehicle recovery insurance for the trip, offered by all automobile clubs and insurers. This covers the costs of transporting the vehicle to the nearest garage, getting you and your car back home, the cost of sending spare parts, any accommodation costs incurred, etc. Not all insurance contracts are the same, so read the small print!

Do contact your motoring insurer or log on to www.gov.uk before travelling, to check for any late Brexit-related changes!

Getting around the area
By car

Naturally the same rules apply in the Dolomites as north of the Brenner Pass, although Italians drive more on instinct than by 'rules'. But on the whole respect for motoring laws is better in the north of the country than in the south ... so you can pretty much rely on traffic halting at red lights!

Roads in the Dolomites demand the utmost concentration. When holiday traffic is heavy, you'll be crossing the more difficult passes at a snail's pace.

The **speed limit** on **motorways** for cars and motorbikes is 130km/h (80mph), for cars with trailers 80km/h (50mph), for caravans above 3.5t 100km/h (60mph). Motorbikes under 150ccm are not allowed. On **main roads** the speed limit for cars and motorbikes is 110km/h (70mph), for cars with trailers 70km/h (45mph), for caravans above 3.5t 80km/h (50mph). On **secondary and minor roads** the speed limit for cars and motorbikes is 90km/h, for cars with trailers 70km/h, for caravans above 3.5t 80km/h.

Dipped headlights are mandatory when driving, *even in daylight*.

At **red lights**, you are allowed to turn right if no traffic is approaching from the left.

Introduction: Getting around the area 11

Frequently seen traffic signs
Baccendere i fari: put on your lights;
attenzione: caution;
deviazione: detour;
divieto di accesso: entry forbidden;
lavori in corso: works in progress;
parcheggio: car parking;
rallentare: slow down;
senso unico: one way;
strada senza uscita: one-way street;
tutte direcioni: all directions;
uscita veicoli: caution: vehicle exit;
zona a traffico limitado: limited vehicle access;
zona disco: parking only with disc;
zona pedonale: pedestrian zone.

Seat belts must be worn in both front and rear seats, and an appropriate harness is obligatory for children aged 3-12.

The permitted **alcohol level** is 0.5mg/l; this means that you cannot drink more than one glass of wine without risking going over the limit. Motorists driving over the limit will have their licences revoked for two weeks to three months and pay high fines. If you have an **accident** the car will be impounded (these rules apply to foreigners as well as Italians).

There are **emergency** phone boxes at 2km intervals along the motorways. Private emergency services are not allowed. The service vans of the ACI (Italian Automobile Club) can be reached 24 hours a day on ℭ 116 but, since they will not always speak English fluently, speak slowly and carefully.

For **full information about** driving to and in Italy, see www.italia.it.

Petrol prices are about the same as in surrounding Continental countries. For lead-free ask for *senza piombo;* super = *super* and diesel = *gasolio;* octane and quality are the same as in other Continental countries.

Petrol stations are only open 24 hours on the motorways; on main roads and in towns and villages they are usually *closed* from 20.00-7.00 and from 12.00-15.00 as well as *all day Sundays.* More and more petrol pumps are fitted with credit card automats which also take euro notes.

Charging stations for electric cars are steadily increasing on the motorways and in towns. At the Brenner Pass there are many dispensers for varying marques of car; in towns there are often special parking places with charging stations. Many hotels — and not just the high-priced ones — have charging points in their garages, some even offer rental of high-powered electric cars.

By bus
Buses in the three Dolomites provinces of South Tyrol, Trentino and Belluno are a fast, economical and reliable way of getting about — as long as you aren't trying to travel on a Sunday, when many of the smaller places are not served by bus.

On all three traffic networks (see below) you can buy tickets when boarding the bus, in the office of the bus operator, or at local shops and kiosks (usually tobacconists). Buying a ticket on boarding is significantly more expensive.

Both individual tickets and passes are on offer; the latter are good for all buses and also the trains. The ticket or pass must be validated on boarding, or you will face a hefty fine.

Some of the operators offer **free (or very cheap) bus travel for skiers and hikers** in winter, even serving isolated hotels and the valley stations of the lifts. In a very few cases (like the Lake Karer/Carezza area), this is also true in summer. Ask at the operators' offices for information.

SAD (www.sad.it) is the bus operator in **South Tyrol**, with its offices in Bozen/Bolzano, from where a good number of their orange-red and green buses also depart. Other centres are in Brixen/Bressanone and Bruneck/Brunico. SAD also travels to some places outside South Tyrol, for instance to the Fassa Valley in Trentino (from Bolzano) and Cortina d'Ampezzo in Belluno (from Toblach).

The two other operators are **Trentino Trasporti** (www.ttspa.it) in **Trentino** and **Dolomitibus** (www.dolomitibus.it) in **Belluno**.

By train

The Brenner railway line and the railway in the Pustertal/Val Pusteria offer good services for those based at Bozen/Bolzano, Brixen/Bressanone, Bruneck/Brunico and Toblach/Dobbiaco or

> **Mobilcard and other guest cards**
>
> If you plan to use buses and trains to any extent, you will come to appreciate a **Mobilcard**. You can get them for the whole South Tyrol region — for all buses and trains and even some ski lifts (1 day for 15 €, 3 days for 23 €, 7 days for 28 €; see www.mobilcard.info). Cards must be validated whenever you travel. They are available from tourist offices or automats in local train stations.
>
> Or you can buy a **Museum Mobilcard** offering the same transport options but including free entrance to almost all South Tyrol's 128 museums: 3 days 30 €, 7 days 34 €.
>
> Accommodation providers sometimes give their guests free **local mobile cards** — of which there is such a confusing variety that it's best to search the web beforehand.
>
> For **cyclists** there's the **Bikemobil Card** (1 day for 25 €, 3 days for 30 €, 7 days for 35 €).
>
> For those exploring the whole range, there's the **Dolomiti Super Summer Card** (see page 22).

Bus station at Bozen/Bolzano

Innichen/San Candido. Trains travel almost hourly every day from Innichen to Franzensfeste/Fortezza via Toblach and Bruneck. From there you change to trains for Brixen, Klausen and Bolzano as well as Auer and Neumarkt. For information see www.trenitalia.com.

Since many stations are unmanned, buy tickets at automats or from *bus* drivers. Only when there is no automat can you pay on the train. In Italy train tickets **must always be validated** before you board the train, otherwise you may be subject to a high fine. Single tickets — unless they are passes — are only good for a bus *or* a rail journey; they are *not* interchangeable.

By cycle
Because of the strenuous gradients, the Dolomites are not suited for long-distance cycling. But they *are* ideal for mountain bikes. Almost all **trains** will accept mountain bikes (see www.trenitalia.it for more information). Carriages for bikes are at the start or end of the train. One-day tickets cost about 6 €. All **bus** companies will take bikes *if there is room* (not usually the case on weekends).

Where to stay
Hotels
The number of rooms in hotels, *pensions,* apartments and farmhouses in the Dolomites is huge.

South Tyrol has an especially large choice. Prices are pretty much the same throughout the Dolomites — and on the high side overall. The most economical places to stay are in South Tyrol.

Accommodation standards are quite high whatever the category: all hotel rooms have bath or shower, WC, telephone, TV (usually satellite), hairdryers, internet (usually free, but it may not work very well in individual rooms). Most have mini-bars as well. A balcony, usually flower-filled, is standard, except in historical houses and the small houses where individuals rent out private rooms. A common feature of many 3-4 star hotels is a very luxurious 'wellness centre', with saunas, whirlpools, in- and outdoor swimming pools, gym equipment and solaria.

In many places, especially *pensions,* three nights is the **minimum stay**. In high season you will also be expected to take half-board terms. Room and breakfast is generally only available in low season.

Unless you are using a travel agent or booking a package holiday, surf the web to find a place that appeals to you. Most of the sites have an English version with e-mail facility, should you have any questions. You can then **book the accommodation** on the web, or by phone or letter.

While **seasonal opening** varies, **high season** in all the provinces is from the 4th week in July until the 3rd week in August, and from Christmas to 6 January; in skiing areas only, also from February to mid-March.

Hotels in the **family-friendly group** (usually 3-5 stars) take special care of the children, with playgrounds or playrooms and sometimes special programmes for kids. Log on to www.familien hotels.com (English pages).

There are also 3-4 star **hotels for walkers** and their families, with equipment hire, mini-bus for walk access, guided walks, walk

'libraries' with maps and guides. See www.wanderhotels.com (English pages).

Farmhouse holidays

Farmhouse holidays *(agriturismo)*, while less common in Trentino and Belluno, are possible in many areas of South Tyrol, where they are known as *Buschenschank*. For details log on to the relevant website: www.roterhahn.it.

Mountain huts, youth hostels, campsites

Mountain huts are reserved for mountain climbers and are not included in any list of accommodation *unless* they are run as guest houses for tourists. In summer, from 20 June to 20 September, virtually all mountain huts are open, and many stay open until mid-October or later. The tourist boards know all the opening dates and will supply lists on request.

Youth hostels are in short supply. The provinces in the Dolomites don't appreciate tourists who don't spend! Exceptions are the lovely youth hostel in the old Grand Hotel in Toblach/Dobbiaco, the hostel in Bolzano and some church centres like the Kassianeum in Brixen.

Campsites are also very thin on the ground, with just one place in South Tyrol — in Völs. For what there is, log on to www.camping.it.

Cuisine

Food in the Dolomites is a unique combination of Tyrolean, Imperial Viennese and Italian cooking. On top of that you have the pleasure of Tyrolean wines, from the dry white Sylvaners from the Eisack/Isarco Valley to the elegant Pinot Noir from the lower Etsch/Adige.

Broadly speaking, the Dolomites can be divided into three culinary regions where either dumplings, potato-based gnocchi or pasta predominate. In South Tyrol, even in the Ladin areas, dumplings dominate: bacon dumplings with sauerkraut and little dumplings in the soup. In Trentino's Fassa Valley the preference is for gnocchi, like the spinach-green *strangolapreti* ('priest chokers' — though no one knows how it came by this name). This is also true in the formerly Austrian Buchenstein and the Ampezzo Valley with Cortina. South of the old Austrian border, in Belluno province, pasta comes second only to polenta, the thick maize porridge.

This Italo/Tyrolean/old Austrian 'fusion' is at its most interesting in South Tyrol, where there are the most high-class restaurants, but in other provinces it also attains high standards. So traditional eating in the Dolomites is very simple: there are dumplings or the ravioli-like 'Schlutzer' or polenta, and with it maybe bacon or a soup with dumplings or little dumplings. Bacon and smoked sausages are available everywhere, although 'bacon' here means something different from what you would find in Germany, Austria or Switzerland (see below).

Dolomites specialities

Bacon *(Speck)* is made by stripping the hind legs of fat then soaking the meat in a bath of salt with cabbage. After this it is cold-smoked over juniper wood and stored for a long time. This makes the bacon extremely tender, with a mild flavour. In Tyrolean style this is cut into thick chunks and, once on the table, cut again into rashers and served on bread with a glass of

Introduction: Where to stay/Cuisine

> **Buschenschank and Törggelen**
>
> 'Törggelen' has almost become synonymous with the culinary way of life in South Tyrol. The meaning itself comes from the word 'Torggel', or wine press, and 'törggelen' means going to taste the new wines at the vintner's. Naturally this is best done with a little food on the side!
>
> In the autumn people walk up to the high ground, where the sun seems to linger longer, and the vintners open their premises for a short time — offering wine-tastings and home-cooked titbits. Traditionally this took place between saints' days — St Martin (11 November) and St Catherine (25 November) but, like all other customs today, the period has been stretched and now lasts from late October to the end of the year!
>
> A bouquet above the entrance draws attention to the fact that the 'Buschenschank' is now open. The new wine ('Nuie') to be tasted is displayed in the farmer's room or on a table in front of the house ... together with 'Schlachtschüssel' (cooked bacon, liver sausage and fresh blood sausage), roasted chestnuts, 'Speck', 'Krapfen' and perhaps a strong barley soup with dumplings and cabbage. Even if the vineyard is accessible by car, it's the walk (or cycle ride) that 'makes' the day's outing.

'Speck' appetizer in Cortina

red wine for the *merende* (the equivalent of a very hearty English afternoon tea). Done in the Italian way it is (like all other hams) cut paper-thin and served as an appetiser. Unfortunately it is still legal to call packaged bacon 'Südtiroler Speck' — so if you are buying it in a shop, *beware*; better still, buy it direct from the farmer. (For an interesting treatise on South Tyrolean bacon, see www.recla.it/en!)

There are various **local cheeses** from the Alpine pastures. The local cheese is often grated over pasta; from Trentino, for example, there's the very good, parmesan-like *grana* cheese. In the Val di Fassa and Val di Fiemme/Fleimstal they make the strong-smelling *puzzone*, covered with a light ochre skin. *Ziger* is a cone-shaped fresh cheese with chives; widely available in South Tyrol, it is eaten on black bread with vinegar, oil and onions.

All **desserts** in the Dolomites hark back to Austrian days: strudel, especially apple strudel, *Kaiserschmarrn* — Austrian pancakes with raisins, the famous *Sachertorte*, and buckwheat gateau with red berry filling. You can also expect to find *Zelten*, a fruit bread, and from Trentino a gingerbread biscuit with lots of lemon and orange zest. *Krapfen* are a Ladin speciality — an elongated deep-fried doughnut with poppy seeds.

Practicalities A-Z

Climate and weather

The Dolomites encompass several climate zones, from the mild climate of western Lombardy in northern Italy (with an average annual temperature above 10°C) to the hard mountain climate (average annual temperature about 0°C). Few settlements lie above the upper sub-alpine border (1600m) and none at all in the alpine zone. For full details of climate and weather, see under 'Walking' on pages 28-30.

> **Weather forecasts on the web**
> *South Tyrol:* www.provinz.bz.it/wetter (in English); other weather forecasts at www.datameteo.com (also in English).

Communications

In almost all tourist centres there are **post offices** and (card) **telephone kiosks** (buy cards from tobacconists). The **post** is slow and expensive: *posta prioritaria* is recommended, as it is a bit faster, although more expensive. Many towns and villages have **internet points**; more are added every year, and several villages have free hot spots. Take your **mobile/smart-phone**: there is an excellent network of masts — and ever fewer public phone boxes. **Television** is pretty well confined to programmes in Italian or German, but most 3- and 4-star hotels and apartments have satellite television receiving news from Sky, the BBC or CNN.

For **telephone information** in Italy call ❰ 12, for outside the country ❰ 186. When making **international calls** from Italy to the UK preface the number with 0044; to North America with 001. Calling from outside the country to Italy, preface the number with 0039 and *include the zero* from the area code (eg for a number in the Bolzano area call 0039/0471 + the number).

The general **emergency service** (including helicopter ambulance) is ❰ 118; **police** ❰ 112; **fire department** ❰ 115; **breakdown/vehicle recovery service (ACI)** ❰ 116. Other emergency numbers, specifically for walkers, are on page 33.

Festivals, customs and events

Even without the events organised by the tourist boards, there is always enough to see and do in the Dolomites. One sees people in local costume in the farmers' markets or on Sundays going to church. The brass bands and 'Schützen' (see opposite), with their attendants, gather together at church festivals, processions, annual fairs, the many pilgrimages and the autumnal transhumance with decorated cattle.

The following festivals and events take place annually throughout the Dolomites:

Prozesso alle Streghe, a folk festival in remembrance of the witches' trials (Cavalese, 1st week in January);

Hay-sleigh and **horse-drawn sleigh races** (Stern/La Villa, February);

Good Friday processions in most places that have a church;

Corpus Christi processions take place on the Sunday after Corpus Christi, since Corpus Christi is not a holiday in Italy;

Oswald von Wolkenstein Ride, mock historical battles on the Seis plateau, end May/early June (see Walk 17, page 128 in Book 1);

Sacred Heart Festival in June, with processions in many places. In the evening eye-catching fires are lit on the surrounding mountains, showing, for instance, the flaming heart symbol surmounted by a cross;

International Choirs Festival (in the Hochpustertal/Alta Pusteria;

Jazz Festival (in Bruneck/Brunico, July);

Estate Musicale di Fiemme, a festival of classical music, choirs, jazz and operettas (in the Val di Fiemme/Fleimstal, July/August);

I suoni delle Dolomiti spread among the mountains in Trentino during July and August — music from classical and chamber to jazz and pop. A highlight is the 'Sunrise in the Dolomites' concert held on Col Margherita, starting with a cable car ride to the col at 3am;

Gustav Mahler Weeks (in Toblach/Dobbiaco, mid-July to mid-August) — classical music by Mahler, who lived and composed here during three summers, but also by others;

Festa delle Bande: brass-band

Schützen

'Schützen' were Tyrolean citizens charged since the early 16th century with the protection of the homeland. They played an important role in 1797, when Napoleon's troops invaded. Associations of Schützen still exist, and members see themselves in the true sense of the word as 'defenders of the homeland' and as followers of the first defenders of Tyrol.

But there are not only Schützen in South Tyrol: everywhere in the old Austrian parts of the Dolomites you will see a growing number of Schützen at all possible festivals.

Schützen association websites are mostly in German, but if you key the word into an advanced search in English, there are some interesting references.

Passo Giau, backed by the rock bastion of Ra Gusela, and with 'alpenrosen' in the foreground — a rhododendron species

festival (in Cortina d'Ampezzo, August);

Ascension Day (15th August), holiday processions throughout the Dolomites, with various guilds and associations (including Schützen) in traditional costume; especially noteworthy at pilgrimage churches dedicated to the Virgin Mary, like Maria Weissenstein near Deutschnofen;

Palio della Sloiza: folk festival when the hay is cut, with traditional sledges (in Primiero, end August);

Folk music and folk-dancing day: in the folk museum at Dietenheim (September);

Spectaculum, a three-day Middle Ages festival (in the streets of Bolzano and at Runkelstein Castle, September);

Almabtrieb/Desmontegada are the German/Italian words for the annual transhumance in the autumn, when the cattle come back down from their alpine pastures. This festival is celebrated in many places, but is especially interesting when the goats are brought down in Cavalese on the 3rd of September;

Harvest: a procession giving thanks for the harvest (many places, on the first Sunday in October)

Speckfest in Villnöss/Funes, early October, samplings of difference bacons, music

Kuchlkirchtag in Brixen/Bressanone with guided culinary walks; also **Kuchlkastl** in Völs/Fiè, a culinary folk festival on Schlern/Sciliar (both in October);

Leonhard-Ritt, a religious procession featuring riders on horseback, horse-drawn carriages, etc (in St Leonhard/San Leonardo in the Abteital/Val Badia on the second Sunday in November);

Krampus Day (5 December) and the **Krampus Lauf** in Toblach/Dobbiaco (see page 47 in Book 1);

Christmas markets in Bozen/Bolzano, Brixen/Bressanone (the oldest) and other places, in the style of German and Austrian Christmas markets (in December).

Information

Tourist boards outside South Tyrol all have the abbreviation

APT (Azienda Promozione Turistica) or IAT (Ufficio Informazioni Assistenza/Accoglienza Turistica). Websites for the various tourist boards are shown at the top of each chapter. Naturally you can also consult the **Italian Tourist Board** (www.italia.it or www.italiantourism.com), but they usually have less local information to offer than the bodies mentioned above.

There are excellent **internet sites and apps** for the Dolomites and South Tyrol — right down to room rentals, sports opportunities, government departments and public places. *Most of the sites have English pages.*

www.suedtirol.info is the official site of the South Tyrol Tourist Board — very informative and user-friendly.

www.suedtirolerland.it has wide-ranging information about accommodation and leisure activities.

www.suedtirol3d.it offers delightful panoramas to inspire you or to remind you of your visit when you're back home.

www.naturparks.provinz.bz.it, info about the nature parks in South Tyrol.

www.trenitalia is the official site of the Italian railways.

For **smartphone** users there is an ever-increasing number of apps, some more useful than others.

Sentres is a very comprehensive outdoor databank with walks and cycle tours of all grades; great for planning.

Südtirol to go is an app where you can check all public transport. Available in English, but some pages only in Italian, German or Ladin.

ArchApp (South Tyrol) gives an overview of the most interesting architecture in South Tyrol. It's especially useful if you're touring the area by car.

Other apps are mentioned in the book where appropriate and, unless otherwise specified, all are free.

Maps

Free maps from tourist offices are only useful for general orientation. Many commercial touring maps leave off the less-visited south of the range. An exception is **Michelin**'s 1:400,000 Regional Map 562 ('Italy Northeast'). The map of South Tyrol published by Tabacco (1:160,000) shows almost all the Dolomites and is good for touring by car and motorcycle, or for planning long-distance treks. Excellent large-scale maps (scale 1:25,000) are produced by the same publisher; see page 35.

Medical care

Before travelling, you may wish to get a Global Health Insurance Card (**GHIC**) which gives you the right to free emergency healthcare. For more information, log on to gov.uk.

You are also strongly advised to take out **travel insurance** which includes health cover since, for instance, mountain rescue will not be covered by a GHIC.

In case of illness, do *not* go to the doctor first, but to the USL (Unità Sanitaria Locale; the local medical centre), which is specially set up to deal with tourists. They will send you to a doctor or hospital. Since the opening dates and times of the USLs vary enormously, we have not given them in this book; check at the tourist office when you arrive — or look in the town halls, where opening hours are posted. If you are treated by a registered doctor with a private practice (thus not at the medical centre or a hospital), you will usually be expected to pay, then claim it back on your travel insurance when you return home.

Pharmacies and doctors open or on call at night and on weekends are posted at the town hall and on the doors of pharmacies. They are also listed in the daily newspapers like *Dolomiten* in South Tyrol.

The only **hospitals** in the area covered by this book are at Bolzano, Brixen/Bressanone and Bruneck/Brunico. People suffering serious accidents or illnesses are often flown by air rescue to Trient/Trento or Innsbruck for treatment.

Money/banks

The euro (€) is the local currency. Almost every town and village has an automatic bill dispenser (if you hold the appropriate debit card); the relevant charge on your card will be upwards of 5 €. If you make withdrawals with a credit card, reckon on a surcharge of about 3%. All Cirrus, Maestro and Visa credit cards — with or without chip — should be accepted.

Opening times

In South Tyrol many shops used to be closed on Saturday afternoons, but that has been changing in the last few years. **Banks** are usually open Mon-Fri from 08.00-13.00/14.30-15.30; post offices Mon-Fri from 08.15-13.00.

Shopping and souvenirs

Shopping, usually confined to rainy days, can be quite fun on good days, if it's combined with an excursion or a walk. Products from the farms are the best souvenirs to take home (see 'Dolomite specialities' on page 14).

Traditional handicrafts, including wood carvings, fabrics (like loden wear), embroideries, *Speck*, wine and schnapps are the best-loved gifts. More fanciful would be a bouquet of dried flowers, a reverse painting on glass, a book about local cuisine…

Loden wear: This attractive dress never goes out of style, so it's always a good investment. It's worth shopping around: prices are cheaper in Toblach/Dobbiaco, for example, than in Bolzano.

Fabrics and lace: Good places to buy hand-made linen or cotton/linen tablecloths are in the Pustertal/Val Pusteria (for instance, shops in Bruneck/Brunico). In the upper Tauferer Ahrntal/Valle Aurina you can also get pillow lace (for instance in Prettau/Predoi).

South Tyrolean *Speck* (see page 14) is world-famous and available in all good-quality food shops. Avoid all packaged *Speck*; buy it from the farmer who has smoked it himself, to get the best, old-style quality — mild and tender.

Mushrooms: Italians go mad for the dried porcini mushrooms *(Boletus edulis),* also called ceps. Specialist purveyors (like 'Tutto Funghi' in Bruneck/Brunico) guarantee fine-quality produce.

Cheeses: Cheese from the alpine pastures is a good choice, especially the semi-hard and mature cheeses. The products of the Sexten/Sesto and Toblach/Dobbiaco dairies are especially recommended.

Sports

In both summer and winter the Dolomites are an ideal destination

Practicalities A-Z

for sports enthusiasts. In summer the landscape is perfect for walking, long-distance hiking, climbing and mountain biking. With the first snows, the landscape changes to a paradise for skiing, snowshoe walking and snowboarding. It's a wonder people aren't tripping over each other, but there's such a choice of sports that this only seems to happen in a few places.

The classic Dolomite sport of mountain climbing has now threaded out into many different strands, since **walkers, mountain climbers, rock- and free-climbers** not only all have different goals but different equipment. Whatever your choice, there's an excellent network of walking routes and many climbing 'gardens' and climbing walls.

A special feature of the Dolomites is the *via ferrata* (literally 'iron road'). There are many of these protected climbing trails: iron grips, pegs and cables enable those who are not technical experts to scale walls that would

Attractive group of farmhouses in Insom (Walk 3)

Dolomiti Superski

'One ski pass, 12 ski areas, 1200km of pistes' — that's Dolomiti Superski's advertising slogan. It offers the largest selection of lifts and pistes anywhere.

One of their pistes (Gran Risa in Stern/La Villa) counts among the most interesting, fastest and most popular in the world. Names like Wolkenstein/Selva, St Ulrich/Ortisei, Stern/La Villa, Plose, Kronplatz/Plan de Corones, Cortina d'Ampezzo (1956 Olympics), Canazei, Val di Fiemme/Fleimstal (FIS World Cup/Nordic Championships 2003) make winter sports enthusiasts' hearts beat faster. The Sella Ronda, which circles the Sella group, and the Marcialonga, the Nordic marathon in the Val di Fiemme, have attained mythical status. Most places have taken snowboarding and cross-country snowshoe walking to heart.

The **Dolomiti Superski pass** encompasses almost the whole of the range (with the exception of the western Brenta Dolomites and the Adamello group). The pass isn't exactly cheap and is only worth buying if you want to travel to more than one of the ski centres mentioned here or if you are staying in a place from where various ski resorts are easily reached — for instance in Brixen/Bressanone, with the nearby Eisack/Isarco Valley, Gröden/Val Gardena, and the Seiser Alm/Alpe di Siusi or Bolzano, with its good connections to almost all areas.

The pass encompasses **12 skiing regions**: 1 Cortina d'Ampezzo; 2 Kronplatz/Plan de Corones; 3 Hochabteital/Alta Badia; 4 Grödnertal and Seiser Alm/Val Gardena and Alpe di Siusi; 5 Fassa Valley and Lake Karer/Lago di Carezza; 6 Arabba; 7 Hochpustertal/Alta Pusteria; 8 Fleimstal/Val di Fiemme and Obereggen; 9 San Martino di Castrozza and the Rolle Pass; 10 Eisack/Isarco Valley; 11 Tre Valli (Moèna, Lusia, Falcade); 12 Civetta.

Anyone who is visiting the whole range should consider the **Dolomiti SuperSummer Card** (www.dolomitisupersummer.com), which offers discounted rates on more than 100 lifts (ascents reduced 20%, descents 35%). And if you are planning a longer stay or visiting several times during the season, it may even be worthwhile considering a season ticket costing about 350 €, since the price of single tickets mounts up faster than you think!

Ski pass offices are in all towns and villages where they may be used, often at the lower lift stations.

For **information** and up-to-date prices and concessions see www.dolomitisuperski.com.

---

usually only be the province of Grade IV climbers or beyond. But you still have to have a helmet and other equipment — and, naturally, experience in Alpine terrain. For information contact the AVS (the South Tyrol Alpine Association; www.alpenverein.it). Only a couple of walks in our two-book guide involve a *via ferrata* — and they would be categorised as 'easy' by *via ferrata* standards.

Walking is covered on pages 27-35.

Fishing is allowed in the many clear watercourses in the range. Licences for foreigners are easily obtained from tourist offices or

Practicalities A-Z

even tobacconists. Private fishing areas are marked in Italian with *Divieto di pesca* or *Pesca privata*.

The only people who come to the Dolomites to **swim** are those who like indoor hotel swimming pools. Actually, that's even becoming a pleasure now in the 4-star hotels, with their 'wellness' areas, saunas, whirlpools, etc. Whoever wants to swim 'naturally' can do so in Lake Vahrn near Brixen/Bressanone or in Völs/Fiè. Or in one of the many ice-cold mountain lakes — very refreshing, if you can stand it!

The lack of level terrain is a hindrance to building **golf courses**, but there are a couple in the area covered by this guide — at Deutschnofen/Nova Ponente and Reischach (Bruneck/Brunico).

The strong up-currents which characterise weather in the Dolomites (especially on fine mornings before noon) make the range a superb meeting place for **paragliding**. The best starting points are the mountain stations of the lifts or nearby places, like on Plose above Brixen/Bressanone or the Spitzbühel Hut on the Seiser Alm/Alpe di Siusi. For South Tyrol you can get up-to-date information at www.paragliding.it.

Cycling and mountain biking are two of the top sports in the Dolomites. **Cyclists** on racing bikes swarm along the major roads, especially around the Sella group. Mountain bikers are competing more and more with walkers, and there are some fine cycle routes for families. Since you can take your bike with you on the bus anywhere in the Dolomites (provided there is room), you can cover long distances without having a car at your disposal. **Cycle hire** is available almost everywhere. Many tourist boards hand out free MTB guides and maps and/or offer biking guides.

The network of old mountain roads dating from the First World War, originally built as mule tracks, is an Eldorado for mountain bikers. These roads are generally only moderately steep, most are very well maintained, and they are closed to all motor traffic.

The Dolomites are not very suitable for **horse-riding**, which is mostly concentrated in the outlying wooded mountains and on the large plateaux like Seis/Siusi. In the valleys north of the Pustertal/Val Pusteria there are some riding stables which specialise in trekking; more information on this from the Tauferer Tal Tourist Board: www.tauferer.ahrntal.com. For South Tyrol you can get information about riding stables and farms with horses from the Tourist Board (www.suedtirol. info). If you like Haflinger horses, contact the South Tyrol Haflinger Breeders' Association, www. haflinger-suedtirol.com.

Every tourist centre has **tennis courts**, and you can rely on all 4-star hotels having them.

Winter sports — like **snow-shoe walking** and **hiking** — are becoming ever more popular: February is now considered high season; accommodation must be booked well in advance. The mountain lifts and pistes, as well as the region's ski runs are managed in cooperation with Dolomiti Superski (www.dolomitisuperski. com). There is now an impressive network of **winter walking trails** — perhaps with a cosy inn as the focal point.

Short historical summary

From about 12,000 BC: After the Ice Age the first hunting expeditions in the area of the Dolomites.

From about 5000 BC: First Stone Age farming settlements in the wide valleys, soon followed by cattle husbandry on the mountain slopes (for example at the Seiser Alm/Alpe di Siusi or the alm south of Croda da Lago).

About 3500 BC: Ötzi, the man from the Schnalstal north of Merano, dies on a high mountain pass. When he was found in 1999, he had metal objects and goods that came from far away (flint from Monte Lessini near Verona).

From about 500 BC: Celtic invaders populate areas around the Eisack/Isarco and Etsch/Adige valleys.

16/15 BC: Roman Legions under Drusus conquer the area now known as Trentino-South Tyrol; incorporation in the province of Raetia; Romanisation of the Celtic population.

493-526: Rule from Verona under the Goth Theoderich I, otherwise known as 'Dietrich of Bern', the Ladin hero associated with the Laurin/Rosengarten legend (see page 163 in Book 1).

568-773: Lombards invade from the south, the alpine Romans are cut off from direct contact with other Roman groups south of the river Po. This results in a series of Raeto-Roman languages (for example Ladin in the Dolomites).

8th C: Expansion of the Bavarian influence south of the Brenner Pass; in 769 Duke Tassilo founds Innichen Monastery to promote the Germanisation of the Pustertal/Val Pusteria, which has been inhabited by Slavs since the 6th century. The Ladinised inhabitants retreat into the deeper valleys, preserving their language and culture.

773: Charlemagne conquers the area; the whole Dolomites are under Frankish control.

814: Charlemagne dies, precipitating the end of the Carolingian Empire.

843: Under the Treaty of Verdun the area of the Dolomites is split between the Italian and German kingdoms.

1004/1027: Trient/Trento and Brixen/Bressanone (bishoprics since 381/571) become Episcopal principalities, thus independent territories.

1282: The County of Tyrol also becomes sovereign territory, following which the Counts of Tyrol extend their holdings in the south and bring the principalities of Brixen and Trient under their influence. Gradually the three-language culture spreads throughout Tyrol.

1363: On the death of the last remaining member of the Tyrol family, the county falls to the House of Habsburg (up until 1918!).

1511: Kaiser Maximilian I, the Habsburg Emperor, releases the Tyroleans from war duty outside Tyrol, but obliges them to defend the land. This obligation builds the foundations for conscription in 1915, to defend the borders of the Dolomites until 1918.

1525/1526: The German Peasants' Revolt, Neustift Monastery plundered, Brixen's High Commander murdered (1532).

From about 1600: Agreements between landowners and farmers

Short historical summary

Fresco at Rodeneck Castle dating from the Middle Ages: horseman from King Arthur's Round Table

put use of alpine pastures on a sound footing.

16th/17th C: Due to cheap exports from America, metal prices fall back sharply; mining in the Dolomites (Primiero) and the northern side-valleys of the Pustertal comes to a standstill.

1784: Kaiser Joseph II decrees German to be the official language of the Habsburg Empire.

1788/1789: French geologist Deodat de Dolomieu discovers an unusual calcium magnesium carbonate rock in the Eisacktal/Valle Isarco; the new mineral is named after him and later is applied to the entire mountain range.

1796/1797: First war of the French/Bavarian coalition.

1803: The principalities of the German Holy Roman Empire are shattered and pull back to Brixen and Trient.

1805-1806: After the defeat by Napoleon at Austerlitz, Austria cedes Tyrol to Bavaria; other temporary boundary changes ensue.

1809/1810: Tyrolean Revolt against Bavaria and France, led by Andreas Hofer, fails.

1815: Following Napoleon's defeat, the Congress of Vienna gives all of the Dolomites to Austria, which already holds Venice and Lombardy.

1864-1867: A railroad is built over the Brenner Pass.

1866: Austria loses Venice to the Italians. The Dolomites south and southeast of Cortina (the Cadore) join the new Kingdom of Italy. Cortina and the northern and western valleys remain with Austria.

1912: The Great Dolomite Road crosses the Austrian Dolomites from Bolzano to Cortina.

1914-1918: First World War. In 1915 Italy joins the Allies; bloody fighting in the mountains between Italy and Austria, with emplacements as high as 3000m (almost 10,000ft) across the range, from the Lagorai group to the Sexten Dolomites. Areas at the Front (like Arabba) are evacuated and eventually destroyed by shelling (for example Toblach/Dobbiaco). In the Italian enclaves there is resistance, with many from the province of Trentino fighting on the Italian side. Heroes of the Italian resistance (the 'Irridentisti'), such as Cesare Battisti from Trient/Trento, are executed by the Austrians and become martyrs; many Italian streets and squares are still named in their memory.

1918: Tyrol south of the Brenner Pass falls to the Italians.

1919: The Treaty of St Germain establishes the present border between Austria and Italy. All the Dolomites become part of Italy. New borders divide the area into three new provinces: Bolzano/Bozen, Trentino and Belluno.

1922: The Fascists take over government offices in South Tyrol by force.

1923: Edict forbidding the use of the German language in schools in South Tyrol. Illegal schools spring up throughout the area. All public offices, notices, etc must be exclusively in Italian. In the same year the Fascists forbid the name 'Tyrol' and substitute a made-up word: Alto Adige (translation from the German 'Upper Etsch Valley'). They try to break the cultural identity of the German- and Ladin-speaking people and Italianise the population.

1935: With the building of an industrial zone in south Bolzano and the massive influx of workers from southern Italy the Italianisation is accelerated.

1938: After Austria is annexed by the German Reich, South Tyrol expects to be annexed as well. But Hitler promises his ally Mussolini that the Brenner Pass border will be inviolate.

1939-1945: Second World War; even before the opening of hostilities, Italians and Germans unite in a settlement in the German-speaking part of South Tyrol. Up until the end of 1939 the option remains open for Italians to stay in their homeland or for people of German origin to emigrate to the German Reich: 86% of South Tyroleans opt for emigration but, because of the war, only 30% actually do so.

1946: The Paris Peace Conference reconfirms for Italy the borders that existed before the war.

1948: The provinces of Bozen/Bolzano and Trient/Trento are given administrative autonomy. This means that German can again be taught in schools. But the administration remains in Trient/Trento, where German-speaking people are in the minority. In the following years the provinces' autonomy is constantly undermined: for instance, in 1955 a law is passed forbidding children to be christened with non-Italian names — a reminder of the Fascist era.

1956: Winter Olympics in Cortina d'Ampezzo, greatly promoting the appeal of the Dolomites as a tourist destination.

1959-1967: Austria brings the question of South Tyrolean autonomy before the full congress of the UN, which offers to help negotiations. Terrorist attacks against Italian establishments. By 1967 all parties in negotiations.

1972: Autonomy for South Tyrol grows in strength; the administration in Bozen/Bolzano receives much more authority. Equality between the Italian and German languages.

2002: Italy passes a bill allowing provincial borders to change, even when it's a matter of an autonomous province (something not previously allowed). The way is open for Ladin areas (Ampezzo, Buchenstein and the Fassatal) to become part of South Tyrol, with its political and cultural guarantees for German and Ladin people.

2008: The SVP (South Tyrolean People's Party), the main representative of the German and Ladin electorate, loses its majority for the first time. People appear to be voting less on ethnic criteria.

2018-to date: Elections in 2018 lead to a massive loss in support for German-speaking secessionist parties in South Tyrol. The SVP is also at a low ebb, forced to form a coalition with the populist/conservative LN party. There are more Italian-speaking MPs. In Trentino there is a centre-right government.

Walking in the Dolomites

You may think of bare crags, steep ridges, the alpine glow and King Laurin's kingdom in the rose garden. The fact that the famous legends, which have been handed down for centuries in the Ladin-speaking area, have survived to this day are proof that the Dolomites are a deeply mysterious, mystical region. This is not limited to the rocky summits, but extends to the dark pine forests, the flaming larch groves, flower-strewn alpine meadows down to steep valley gorges, on the slopes of which ancient farmhouses cling like eagle's nests. And you can hike in all these altitude zones!

The walks in this book range from simple strolls across alm meadows with 'inn crawls' for culinary delights to high alpine hut-hopping — and everything in between. And the best part of it is that as long as you keep off the main trails, start out early in the morning, and don't pick August for your walking break, you are often on your own. And then there is sure to be a hut somewhere to take a break… with a hearty meal of dumplings or a spicy ham platter, maybe with a glass of red wine to go with it.

Walking areas

The walks in this guide cover the Grödnertal/Val Gardena, Gadertal/Val Badia and the eastern and southeastern parts of the range — including the Fassa Valley, the Agordino, Cortina… Book 1 explores the areas closest to the main valley roads: the Pustertal/Val Pusteria embracing the S49 (the main west-east road in the northern part of the range) and the A22 motorway/S12 in the Eisacktal/Valle Isarco. Between them, the walks cover many of the UNESCO World Heritage regions (see panel on page 8).

In the wide **Grödnertal/Val Gardena** (with Sella and Puez) there are numerous lifts and tourist resorts (St Ulrich/Ortisei, Santa Cristina, Wolkenstein/Selva) with tens of thousands of hotel beds and a lot of through traffic. The real focus here is winter sports, but at the head of the valley Langkofel/Sassolungo and the mighty Sella group rise and invite you to go on high alpine walks.

The **Gadertal/Val Badia** is known for its late medieval hamlets called 'viles'. They are particularly beautiful in Wengen (La Val), but there are also

The Col Raiser high plateau (Walk 3)

beautiful specimens to marvel at near the Seres mills. The mighty Fanes group rises at the southern end of the valley — a place of ancient legends and myths. Alpine warfare in the First World War can be experienced in a spectacular way for hikers on Lagazuoi — it's good to know that you are in a more peaceful European era.

The Ladin-speaking **Fassatal/ Val di Fassa** is one of the most visited of all the valleys, and places like Vigo di Fassa, Pozza di Fassa, Moèna, Campitello and Canazei (Ladin: Cianacèl) make good bases for exploring around the Pordoi and Fedaia passes (one of the most famous walks in the range, the Bindelweg/Viel dal Pan, an easy walk on good trails, runs from one pass to the other). This valley is also a good base for walks in the Rosengarten area — if you have a good map or Book 1.

The **Agordino** offers stunning scenery of mountains and lakes without being overly crowded — here you'll find Civetta and the 'Wall of Walls', together with hikes from the Falzàrego Pass; the Pale di San Martino and Marmolada are within easy reach.

Ampezzo is best known for chic Cortina and as a winter sports centre, and prices are exceedingly high. But do not miss the easy approach to the Drei Zinnen/Tre Cime di Lavaredo via Lake Misurina!

Weather and best times to walk

In the Dolomites it is basically warmer and milder than north of the Alps — and usually drier, since the main Alpine ridge protects the range from cold winds and storms. It's not for nothing that the South Tyrol tourist board has been promoting the slogan guaranteeing '300 days of sunshine a year'.

When bad weather builds up in the south, it sometimes leads to the notorious 'Föhn' north of the Alps. The so-called 'Northföhn' is less well known. It can be caused by bad weather on the northern side of the Alps or a cold front coming in from the west. In the first case, it ensures sunny, mild weather in the valleys, in the second case the weather is nice, but there is a stormy, icy wind.

You can go through all five climatic zones in the Dolomites if you travel from the Etschtal/Adige Valley west of Bolzano into the

Walking in the Dolomites

Winter walking is increasingly popular

mountains. You would start out in an **insubric climate**, in a region where the average annual temperature is above 10°C/50°F. The winter is mild, there's seldom any frost, precipitation is about 700-900mm/27-30in, there are not many long dry periods. The southern slopes are usually snow-free in winter. But a little bit higher, the **submontane central European climate** begins, with changeable precipitation patterns. It's dry in the Eisacktal/Valle Isarco, but in other places precipitation can reach 1400mm/55in. Downy oak, hop beech and cultivated sweet chestnut characterise this climate zone. The average yearly temperature is between 9° and 10°C, and winter frosts are quite common. When you get to the **montane central European climate** zone, the annual mean temperature sinks to under 7°C/45°F, with precipitation between 900-1400mm/30-55in. Once in the mountains, up to 2200m/7200ft, there's a **subalpine climate**. The annual mean temperatures are around 4°C/39°F, with most precipitation in winter and staying on the ground as snow for quite some time. The **alpine climate** is limited to the high alpine peaks. With a yearly average temperature of about 0°C/32°F the subsoil is frozen year-round and snow lies at least half of the year — usually for eight months.

So basically it depends on the height of where you want to walk in the Dolomites. You can hike here all year round. One of the trends in recent years is **winter walking**. Many trails are cleared in winter, and huts are generally open from December to March. And there's also snowshoeing — very popular now — as it's possible at all heights and doesn't depend on how thick the snow is. But of course, like skiing, there's always a certain danger from avalanches and abruptly changing weather. Winter walking is certainly possible on the Seiser Alm/Alpe di Siusi, in the Villnösstal/Val di Funes or in the Tschamintal/Valle di Ciamin.

But the classic walking seasons in the Dolomites are **early summer** (on lower ground from May, in higher reaches and northern slopes from mid-June to the end of the month) with its endless floral carpets, **high summer** (July and August), when it's guaranteed that the lifts and huts will all be open (disadvantage: heat and afternoon thunderstorms) and **autumn** (September/October) — when the weather is usually stable, the yellowing larch foliage is magnificent, and the air is clear. In many years autumnal walks are possible well into November... but lifts and huts are closed, to get ready for the influx of winter visitors.

Flora

Even attempting to sketch out the abundance of flora in a guidebook like this is impossible: if you hike in the Dolomites, you will encounter subalpine and alpine vegetation.

The reason for the diversity is the different altitude zones. In addition, there are the various rocks and their effects on the plant world. All of this is influenced again by the climate, the dryness of some valleys and the high precipitation on some north-western flanks, the moisture of the soil in the valleys and in high alpine cirques, in swamps and moors and at the edge of lakes — as well as the surface heating on steep sunny slopes.

The dry **pine forests** on the southern slopes of the large valleys are still extensive. There are natural **spruce forests** in all areas of the region between 900m/3000ft and 2000m/6500ft; on the higher elevations these are widely interspersed with **larch**. There are, literally, light forests of larch — all other trees having been cut down for grazing land. Humans have been very hard on the **stone pine** forests. They were cleared to make way for alpine pastures, and the wood was much in demand (a stone pine is still the pride of every farmer today, and few new hotels being built today can do without this wood). But stone pines can still be found on the higher elevations and in inaccessible areas.

The **dwarf shrub** belt with dwarf pines, rhododendrons and junipers has also been heavily

Alpine anemones growing high up on a slope; above: star-like edelweiss

shaped by man and cleared for grazing. The high-alpine communities and plants growing in the highest mountain areas in which they can survive (over 2500m/8200ft and up to the summits) are mostly in their original state.

Among the 1500 species of flowering plants to be found in the Dolomites, there are many endemic flora — plants that only occur in this zone and have adapted to the lime. This is how new species and subspecies emerged. This can be clearly observed in the **stemless gentian**: *Gentiana kochiana* grows on crystalline rocks, *Gentiana clusii* grows on limestone. To the layperson, these two species of the classical gentian look identical; it would take a botanist to know the difference. But the Dolomites also have real endemics that can only be found here: a saxifrage species and the **Dolomite columbine**, the **Dolomite yarrow**, **Séguier's buttercup** and the beautiful, but rarely seen **crested devil's claw** that grows on steep rock faces.

Fauna

In the Dolomites humans have changed the environment according to their needs and so restricted, destroyed, but also expanded the habitat of many animals. While roe deer and red deer get enough space, the black grouse has become rare because Tyrolean hats sport its feathers…

You are most likely to encounter wild animals on high pastures and mountain meadows. On alpine grass, especially in the cirque hollows, you can often see marmot burrows and the males who give piercing whistles to warn others when you approach.

Above: a curious marmot

Below: the protected martagon lily

Chamois are not uncommon, and if you are lucky you can watch the **Alpine hare**, but also **hazel grouse** and **snow grouse**. The **golden eagle** circles over the Fanes and Puez groups. As soon as you reach a summit or hut, you are flown around by curious **alpine choughs**, and for a bite the birds come daringly close to hikers.

Capercaillie and **black grouse** are among the European grouse which used to be found in many areas and are now limited to a few areas of the Alps and northern Europe. They have been greatly decimated by the love of black grouse, mainly because of the cock's decorative tail feathers, which are popular on Tyrolean hats. Today their habitat is so reduced that only small remnants remain. The total number doesn't sound too bad: in the Alps and Carpathians there are supposedly around 43,000 black grouse, but in the north of the British Isles alone there are some 25,000! But the stocks are isolated and their numbers are getting smaller and smaller due to the destruction of nature and the environment. The annual courting ritual of the grouse is famous; the adult males fight with each other in clearings for the females, who look on nonchalantly.

Marmots belong to the squirrel family, but they are larger; they can grow up to 66cm long (over 2ft) and weigh 7kg/15lb. They are typical rodents with strong yellow teeth that they use to eat leaves, shoots, flowers and seeds. They are real winter sleepers, they spend five to seven months a year sleeping in their burrows, during which the normal 70 pulse beats per minute are reduced to five. A side cave is used as a toilet: if you wake up twice a month, you go to this part of the 'building' to urinate. In the past, the marmot had more enemies than today (the population is estimated at 50,000 animals); the extermination of lynx and wolf in the alpine habitat has only left eagles and foxes as enemies. Marmots live in large family groups. If the animals are outside the burrow, a few older males always watch to whistle in case of danger, whereupon everything disappears into the nearest hole.

Equipment and food

Many trails run over stony and loose, sometimes skiddy ground, so that for most hikes **ankle-high hiking boots with good grip** are necessary. A few simple hikes can be done with trainers, for all other walks we strongly advise you to wear suitable footwear!

A pair of eagles circle above the Langental/Vallunga

You should also take **sun protection**, sunglasses, a **first aid kit**, and appropriate **hat**, a **rain jacket** and (in spring/autumn or for high-altitude walks) a **thick jersey** or **multi-layer clothing**. In the winter months, **hats** and **gloves** will be required. **Hiking poles** are particularly advantageous on long, steep ascents and descents, but on some walks they are *indispensable* due to the great height difference, which could cause you to damage your knee and hip joints.

Don't stint on your supply of drinks: you should carry 1.5 to 2 litres of water per person — more on long hikes. Springs and fountains are only found on certain stretches and, while there may be plenty of huts, the distances between them are often considerable. The situation is similar with the provisions: better to have a couple of muesli bars or sandwiches too many with you than to struggle on the last kilometre up the mountain with a growling stomach or even to sink at the side of the path with low blood sugar.

One of the reasons we recommend hiking boots on many walks is that you may be walking over tree roots like these!

Emergencies and emergency phone numbers

You should always have a fully charged mobile with you so that you can dial the following number in an emergency: **112, the pan-European emergency number**. An emergency doctor and ambulance, as well as the **Italian mountain rescue** service can be reached at **118**.

If you don't have a mobile with you or you're in a dead zone with no signal, use these internationally recognised rescue signals: optical (eg, wave a handkerchief) or acoustic (eg, shout) **six times** in a row, leaving a space of **10 seconds** between each, then wait **one minute** and **repeat the emergency call** (six signals every 10 seconds). Smartphone owners have the advantage that they can make an emergency call directly via the emergency service app ('Emergency Service South Tyrol'). This app also lists the nearest hospitals, pharmacies and emergency doctors on a daily basis.

Planning your walks and getting to them

The walks in this book all end at the point where they started out: perhaps it's a circuit, an out-and-back walk, or a linear walk with a

Waymarking and signposting are exemplary. These signs are on Walk 26, and the trail number is also painted on a rock

bus back to the start. A lift often helps to optionally shorten the ascent or descent. You can choose from a wide range of short, easy walks through to strenuous day-long hikes. *The times quoted are pure walking times without breaks.* It can take longer if you have children or if there are some sights along the way. If you have a dog with you, please keep it on a lead. Early departures are generally recommended — to avoid the heat in summer and minimize the risk of getting caught in a thunderstorm. And outside high season, the shorter days usually force you to leave early anyway.

If you plan to be **car-free** (see 'Getting around by bus' on page 11), which is not difficult due to the good bus network and inexpensive guest cards, inquire about bus times (at www.sii.bz.it all route plans can be downloaded as PDFs), and remember that on weekends buses often only run every few hours or with a 'lunch break'. If you want to use a mountain lift, the relevant operating times are shown in the same chapter as the walk, *but double-check on the ground or in advance on the net.* (Lifts usually operate from 9am to 5pm in summer, often longer, and seasonally from mid-June to mid-September, sometimes longer.) Buses often go directly to the valley stations of the lifts.

Waymarks and signposts, grades, maps, GPS

Trails in the Dolomites are usually well cared for and maintained. **Waymarks** are clearly recognizable and mostly applied throughout. Red and white or red-white-red is the general waymarking colour found on rocks, trees, posts and signs. You will also come across some walks **signposted** using the name of a particular trail. But almost all hiking trails are numbered. The identifying name or number of all trails followed during a walk is indicated in the logistics section at the top of the page. Since some trails have multiple numbers on certain stages — or there are occasionally differences between the signs and hiking maps — please don't rely solely on numbers! There is no danger of getting lost on any of the walks in this book. And you will rarely be on your own…

There is a quick overview of each walk's **grade** in the Contents, with more information at the top of each walk. In outline:
● easy-moderate; good surfaces underfoot; ascent up to 600m
● moderate-strenuous; less good terrain, ascents often above 600m
● difficult — only suitable for very experienced hillwalkers
❗ indicates exposed sections where you must be sure-footed, with a head for heights.

The **maps in this book**, drawn by the original German publisher, **are all at different scales**. We have adapted them partially, to be more in tune with our usual style, but we were not able to change the scales without redrawing them entirely. *This can be deceptive; please check the map scale before setting off!* Opposite is a key to the map symbols:

Walkers, climbers and general enthusiasts should use the **excellent large-scale maps** (1:25,000) published by **Tabacco**, available at all bookshops and newspaper kiosks in the Dolomites. The **Kompass** and **Freytag & Berndt** maps are generally less detailed but sometimes more up-to-date, as they are reprinted more frequently. While our maps should suffice for the main walks in this book, it is assumed that you will have at least the relevant Tabacco map covering your base area. There is a wealth of detail to be gleaned from these Tabacco maps, and they may be needed if you take up any of the dozens of unmapped walking or cycling tips described or mentioned in passing.

Symbols used on the maps

- ══════ Motorway
- ────── Main road
- ────── Secondary road
- ────── Track (motorable, jeep, farm)
- ------ Footpath
- ─2→─ Main walk and direction
- ·2→· Alternative and direction
- •─•─• Lift (chair or cable car)
- ⚭ † Church.Cross or crucifix
- ♫ ⁙ Castle or palace.In ruins
- ⬟ ▽ Rock.Interesting feature
- 🏛 *i* Museum.Information
- 🚌 P Bus stop.Parking.
- ▬ ▬ Railway station.Building
- ⌗ ⊖ Gate/gateway.Closed
- ⚘)(Viewpoint.Bridge
- ⛁ ★ Cairn.Natural attraction
- ○ ⊝ Fountain.Source
- ⊘ ✺ Waterfall.Sportsground
- 🏞 ⛺ Picnic area.Hut/refuge/dairy
- 5 ★ Waypoint.Attraction

Free **GPS tracks** are available for all these walks: see the Dolomites page for Book 2 on the Sunflower website. Please bear in mind, however, that GPS readings should *never* be relied upon as your sole reference point. And those of you who cannot be bothered to use GPS on the ground *may* nevertheless enjoy opening the GPX files in Google Earth to preview the walks in advance!

1 GRÖDNER TAL/VAL GARDENA
St Ulrich • St Christina • Wolkenstein

Walks: 1-14; *walking tips:* Luis Trenker Promenade and old railway line to Wolkenstein (page 39); Mont de Sëura to Rifugio Comici (page 43); Col Raiser to the Regensburger Hut (page 43); *cycling tip:* from the Seiser Alm down into Gröden (page 41)
Website: www.valgardena.it (for all three above villages)
Opening hours: see individual attractions

The Grödner Tal/Val Gardena (Ladin: Gherdëina), usually referred to simply as 'Gröden', may appear to be peaceful farming country, but today the fast-growing villages of St Ulrich/Ortisei, St Christina and Wolkenstein/Selva virtually merge into each other, and the area is 100% touristic. So the sports possibilities are unbelievable, there are pleasant rooms in all price categories and even the night life is passable.

It's always 'the season' in this valley — and that doesn't just refer to the hotel and restaurant prices. Perhaps with the single exception of November, you *must* reserve a room in advance. Christmas, February, Easter and from the middle of July to the end of August are simply packed out. Every year Wolkenstein alone has one million overnight guests, and that says it all. Germans and Italians are the principal visitors, then Austrians, Dutch and other nationalities — most recently the Poles and Russians. 'Tradition' these days is limited to Ascension Day, when the young girls wear traditional dress.

Sports possibilities are unbeatable: there are about 80 lifts (a record for South Tyrol and the Italian Alps), hundreds of kilometres of walking paths, countless hiking trails of all grades, some of the most famous protected climbing routes in the world, and mountain bike routes that leave from the front door of your hotel and follow good little roads and tracks up to well over 2000m. The mountain huts cater for everything from snacks to overnight stays.

Transport: There are good **bus connections** into the valley (SAD bus company) all year round, linking it with Bozen/Bolzano (via Kastelruth/Castelrotto) and Brixen/Bressanone (via Lajen/Laion); departures are frequent. In summer there are also buses to the passes Grödner Joch and Sellajoch, with onward connections via Sella Ronda buses to Canazei, Arabba and Corvara running round the Sella group in both directions.

The **Gardena Card** (6 days for 98 €, 3 days for 73 €) gives you free use of 12 lift areas. This card is available from the tourist offices. The **Val Gardena Mobilcard** is given to most visitors by the accommodation providers and allows free travel with the buses in the whole valley.

For **walkers** the '**Super Summer Card**' lets you use 100 lifts, including with bike: 1 day 47 €, 3 in 4 days 110 €, 5 in 7 days 147 €; season card 350 €. More information at www.dolomiti supersummer.com.

On the Luis Trenker Promenade (walking tip) in St Ulrich/Ortisei

Events: Many events are organised by the whole valley in both summer and winter: concert weeks like the **FestiVal Gardena Musica** with classical music in the summer, walking weeks, evening shopping in high season (until 22.30) and the '**Gröden in Tracht**' festival early in August, when typical dress is worn.

St Ulrich/Ortisei

St Ulrich (Urtijëi in Ladin) is the largest village in the Grödner Tal, very touristic, with good hotels — and not cheap! In winter all age groups come here for the skiing, in summer there is a mixture of active sports enthusiasts, walkers and those just looking for fresh air.

Today in St Ulrich you will be hard-pressed to find the 'welcome intimacy of a mountain village', which was trumpeted in a Ladin book some years ago. If you stroll around the little town from the main road by the church (Streda Rezia) down to the Antoniboden, you'll pass a couple of beautiful old houses, but that's it. Nothing is left of a 'village', there are no more old farmhouses in the surrounds. Only in the (well worth seeing) museum in the Cësa di Ladins will you see the old dress of the area, the way the farmhouses were once equipped, and the old farm tools.

So: leave town as soon as possible and get out on the tracks, paths and trails! **Walking** is the classic sport in this valley; almost everywhere you can walk out the door of your hotel, step onto a lift and start out. That's the only reason to stay here. From town the slim form of Langkofel/Sassolungo stands out as a landmark; the massif catches all the last rays of the sun. What if you were up there at sundown? Well, why not?

Transport: Although there is a bypass round the village, traffic jams are common. There are large **car parks** by the valley station for the Seiser Alm and Seceda lifts; otherwise park further out, on Streda Rezia, Streda Trebinger or on the road to the railway station. The most central **bus stop** is on the Plaza S Antone (Antoniboden) at the lower end of the pedestrian precinct.

Sights and excursions: Don't forget — apart from the Museum de Gherdëina (a must; see below) there's not a lot to see in St Ulrich. The shopping area stretches along **Streda Rezia** from below the church square down to the so-called 'Antoniboden' with its little church. This bit of road is full of boutiques, cafés and inns with terraces. Somewhat above the west end of the street is the **parish church of St Ulrich**, dating from 1797 (built over older foundations). The pews, dating from the 18th century, are especially attractive.

Between the church and the street is an ugly concrete monstrosity dating from the 1970s: the '**Kongresshaus**', where you'll find the tourist office. The building also houses a permanent exhibition of **Gröden woodcarving**.

At the **Antoniboden** the simple church separates the pedestrian zone from the wide square with the bus stop and taxi rank. **St Anton in Boder** (Plaza S Antone), with its pointed roof and ridge turret, dates from 1673 and is dedicated to the desert hermit Antonius.

The **Museum de Gherdëina** in the **Cësa di Ladins** is a folk museum located in the Ladin Cultural Centre on Streda Rezia, with a number of very interesting objects on display, above all exhibitions of **Gröden lacemaking**, including some from the important Vinazer family, who were established here from 1622 until 1817. Next to the religious statues and madonnas you'll see marionettes, jumping jacks, pull-toys and other toys dating from between 1810 and 1940. There are also **minerals** from the Dolomites and other parts of the world, a very interesting **geological section** describing how the Dolomites were formed, and finally an entire

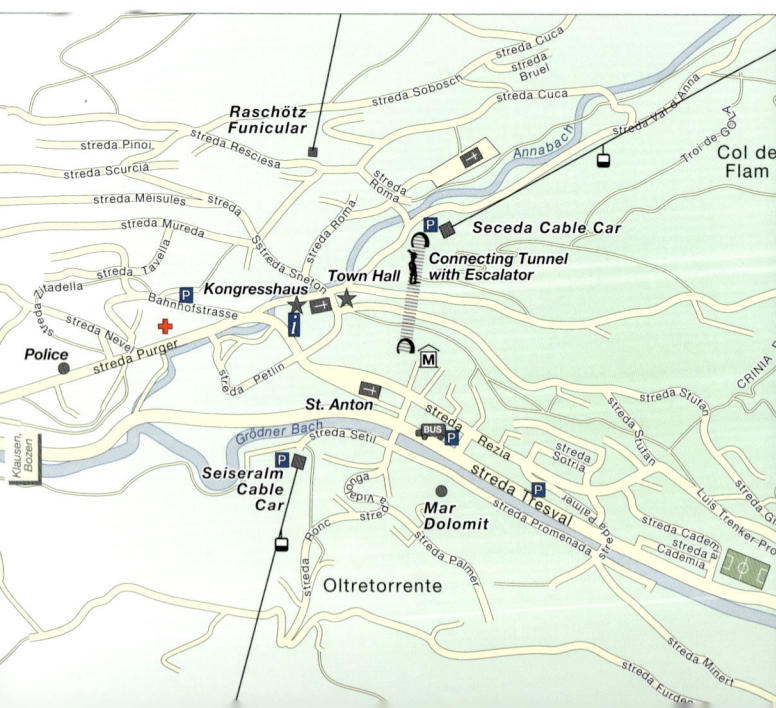

room with memorabilia of **Luis Trenker** (see the panel on page 41). In the entrance to the upper floor there is a huge **fasting cloth** from the church of St Jakob, with 20 scenes from Christ's Passion (17C). In earlier times this would have hung in the church choir during Lent. *Museum open mid-May to mid-Oct Mon-Fri from 10.00-12.30 and 14.00-18.00; Jul/Aug Mon-Sat 10.00-18.00; 6 Dec to Easter Tue-Fri 10.00-12.00 and 14.00-18.00. Entry 8 €, families 16 €. www.museum gherdeina.it.*

The village of **St Jakob/ S Giacomo** (Sacun in Ladin) is a short way east of St Ulrich. The spire of **St Jakob's church** rising above the trees gives it away before you get up to it. This Gothic church (unfortunately always closed) and its circular cemetery (always open) stand behind high walls in a clearing in the woods half an hour above the village (see Walk 1). If you come by car, park by the signposted turn-off and walk on to the church (there is no road). Part of its baroque furnishings can be seen in the folk museum (see above), like some of the altar statues and the magnificent fasting cloth. On the outside south-facing wall (best light at noon) are very beautiful, restored late Gothic frescoes, including a gigantic St Christopher carrying the Christ Child on his shoulder. *Guided visits summer and winter; see www.valgardena.it for times. Entry free.*

● **Walking tip: to Wolkenstein/ Selva on the Luis Trenker Promenade and the old railway.** How pleasant it is to be able to get to Wolkenstein and Plan via St Christina on this lovely walkway rather than the road. The promenade has been laid out over a narrow-gauge railway built during the First World War. It's now a lovely stroll, slightly descending, between the three villages. At the outset, at Streda Stufan in St Ulrich, it's called the '**Luis Trenker Promenade**'; shortly after you pass the tunnel to the Seceda lift on the left, and outside St Ulrich it's called the '**Alter Bahnweg**' (Old Railway Line). From St Ulrich to Wolkenstein takes about 1h30min; you can either walk back in about the same time or take one of the regular SAD buses. If you would like to see it on a map, use the Tabacco 1:25,000 map N° 05)

The new **Raschötz funicular** (mid-May to mid-Oct, from 08.30-17.00 (18.00 in high season); one way 15 €, up and back 21 €) runs up from Streda Resciesa in St Ulrich (1280m) via an intermediate station to the alm pastures of the **Ausserraschötz** at 2093 m. From up here the view to Schlern, the Seiser Alm and the Langkofel group is phenomenal.

An **easy walk**, with only 80m of ascent, runs from the top station to the **Raschötz Hut**; everybody can manage this. The more hardy can then go on to the **Ausserraschötz summit** (2281m) and look out over the imposing rock flanks in the Villnösstal on the other side of the mountain.

A **cable car** (in summer normally open from mid-Jun to

The Ladins

The Ladins of the Dolomites live around the massive Sella group in the Ladin valleys — the Grödner Tal, Gadertal, Fassatal, Buchenstein and Ampezzo. They make up the majority of the population in these areas. The Ladin-speaking area became part of the Roman Empire in 15 BC. The Romans introduced Latin, which evolved into Dolomites-Ladin in this area — part of the Rhaeto-romance language, also spoken in Surselva and Engadina in eastern Switzerland (Romansh) and the Comelico-Ladin spoken in the upper Cadore (for example in Auronzo) and Friulian. All speakers of Rhaeto-romance languages can understand each other. Until now there has been no Dolomites-Ladin official grammar or written rules, but this is being developed on the Swiss model.

Even Italians have problems understanding Ladin, despite having learned (over several generations) to cope with German in South Tyrol. This has political repercussions: while most German speakers in the province of South Tyrol have a great deal of autonomy, Ladin is spread over three provinces, but is still without political representation. Despite a bill allowing provincial border change (see page 26) to South Tyrol, nothing has moved — with the government adopting the strategy of 'sitting it out'.

The German-speaking South Tyroleans, the Italian-speakers in the province of Trentino and the Ladins have a long common history, having lived together since the Bavarian land acquisition in the early Middle Ages in one region — Tyrol. For 500 years the Habsburgs ruled over all three peoples. Together they developed a culture, they wore the same clothing, ate the same food, built the same style of house and practised the same life-style. Thus south of the Sella group, where the neighbours were Italian, not German, the Ladins thought of themselves — and still think of themselves — as Tyroleans. Even in Cortina d'Ampezzo, otherwise so strongly Italian in character, Ladins are members of the typical Tyrolean 'Schützen' (see page 17). And in the Fassatal, Buchenstein and Ampezzo the Ladins feel more empathy with the German Tyroleans than with their Italian neighbours. After the First World War the Ladins, who all previously belonged to the Austrian Tyrol, were divided up between the provinces of Bolzano/South Tyrol, Trentino and Belluno. But this has not changed their feeling of being one people.

---

mid-Oct, 08.30-17.30; one way 25.50 €, up and back 35 €) runs up to **Seceda**. The valley station indicates how important this lift is: from the pedestrian area (Plaza S Antone) there is a series of covered escalators up to the Luis Trenker Promenade, from where another escalator (in a tunnel) runs straight to the cable car! In winter the top of the mountain is well served by all kinds of lifts, but at the start and end of the skiing season one can only go as far as the intermediate station.

In summer Seceda is a real **walkers' paradise**. Those just out for a stroll stay on the slopes of the **Aschgleralm** and visit the Troier and Daniel huts. But if your knees can take it, you can walk 1200m down to St Ulrich or Wolkenstein (see Walk 9).

From St Ulrich it's also easy to reach the **Seiser Alm**: take the **cable car from Oltretorrente** on Streda Setil. This runs from the end of May to All Saints 08.30-17.00 (18.00 in high season); one way 14 €, up and back down 20 €. The upper station is at the **Col de Mesdi** on the Seiser Alm (2005m; see Book 1). The views from here to Langkofel are so fantastic that you might be tempted not to go any further. But there are plenty of **walking trails** through the flower-filled meadows of this alm — and dairy farms and inns all within a stone's throw of each other. The mountain restaurant Mont Sëuc with 'panorama windows' has both snacks and warm meals daily; on Wednesday evenings there are 'candle-light dinners' (when the lift runs till 23.30 and costs only 6 € up and back).

Cycling tip: from the Seiser Alm down into Gröden by mountain bike. Since mountain bikes are allowed on the Seiser Alm cable car to the Col de Mesdi, this makes a delightful day out (see Tabacco 1:25,000 map N° 05). A little road begins at the upper lift station: take this down to the **Schgaguler Schwaige** (dairy hut) and a small pass, where another road joins from the right. Follow this new road in a big bend to the left over the high expanses of the alm — first to the **Ritsch Schwaige** (keep left at the fork just before this inn), to the **Radauer Schwaige** (where you go left again). Now a forestry road is followed through the **Val de Iender** almost all the way down to the floor of the Grödner Tal. At this point keep left at a fork, and lightly-trafficked roads will take you back to **Oltretorrente** and **St Ulrich**.

> **Luis Trenker** (1892–1990) *came from St Ulrich — the very heart of the Dolomites. Although he studied as an architect, he built a career as mountain climber, author, actor and director — all based on a characteristic mix of adventure, mountaineering, nerves of steel, 'schmalz' and sex appeal. The silent film 'Kampf ums Matterhorn' (in English called 'The Challenge') catapulted him to fame in 1928. This film — and later films like 'Berge in Flammen' (Mountains in Flames) — idealised living close to nature, in contrast to 'spoiled' town life. This romantic approach appealed to the Fascist powers in Berlin and Rome as much as to the public.*
>
> *Since Trenker didn't protest against the dictatorships, after 1945 he was persona non grata in Germany. But because of the way he projected himself — the attractive, if eccentric, mountaineering enthusiast with a pipe — his films have become icons in German-speaking mass culture. Many of his films are available in English — just look on the web!*

St Christina/S Cristina
Of the three large places in Gröden, St Christina (S Crestina in Ladin) is the most unspoilt, even though it's geared for tourists and full of businesses. It's an ideal starting point for **walks in the Puez group**, to the Seiser Alm and to Langkofel. A whole array of good hotels, pleasant restaurants and other facilities cater for leisurely or very active holidays.

In the cemetery of St Christina's parish church, beautiful wrought iron is used instead of the more usual Gröden wood carving.

Transport: There are a few **parking places** on the main road below the town hall (Rathaus) and large **car parks** by the Iman Sports Centre. There are **bus stops** below the Rathaus (town hall), at the entrance to the village and at the exit (by Maciaconi Shopping).

The Gröden is narrower here than at St Ulrich, so St Christina is a long strung-out village, built to avoid the steep slopes. Only on the sunny terrace between Plesdinaz and Ulëta are there houses again — and the inhabitants enjoy fantastic views to the Langkofel group, Sella, the Seiser Alm and Schlern. To the south the cool steep shaded slopes constrain settlement. No one wants to live there, only skiers find these slopes interesting, since their pistes go right down into the valley. Sights?

Just the parish church and the Fischburg; all the rest is nature. *Note:* Strictly speaking, the left side of the stream, in the Cislestal, belongs to Wolkenstein (for example the Maciaconi supermarket), but in daily life it's considered part of St Christina and so described here.

Sights and excursions: The only 'sight' is the original Romanesque **parish church**, of which the tower still remains. It was rebuilt in Gothic style in the 15th century (the choir dates from this time). Around 1730 the church was enlarged and modernised in the baroque style; from 1840-45 historicism also played a role. The main altar, in gold, amber and white still remains from the baroque era (by Dominik

> **Largest Nativity in the world?**
> Don't miss a visit to the **Nativity** by the Iman Centre, reputed to be the world's largest. It's open all year round. All the life-sized figures in this 72 sqm stall are of hand-carved wood; they stand, sit or kneel before Mary with Child, Joseph, the Three Kings and a shepherd — to say nothing of the animals... Children love it!

Vinazer, around 1690). The reliquaries below the side altars are also baroque, the bones of several saints lie behind glass. The cemetery in front of the door is most inviting for a little circuit, as most of the graves have beautiful wrought-iron crosses. Don't miss the massive stone houses below the church, several stories high, now the elementary school. They are the only remains of the time before tourism invaded the village.

On the other, shady side of the

valley is the beautifully-kept **Fischburg**. Two arcaded courtyards, two living areas, a chapel, two four-cornered main towers and three minor towers combine to create a very eye-catching ensemble. The castle was initially built between 1622 and 1641 by a man from Wolkenstein, at a time when no one built this kind of residence. Unfortunately it's private property and can't be visited.

From not far above St Christina's parish church the old Calvary (**Via Crucis Col da Mëssa**) runs up to the strung-out hamlet of **Plesdinaz** on a sunny terrace. It's a trail lower down, but a road near the top. The 14 Stations of the Cross have been restored by Gröden artists (bronze on porphyry).

● **Walking tip: Mont de Sëura to the Rifugio Comici.** From **Monte Pana** south of St Christina (reached by **chair lift**: one way 9 €, up and back 16 €) there's **another chair lift** up to **Mont de Sëura** (2025 m; one way 12 €, up and back 18 €. Both lifts operate mid-Jun to mid-Sep, from 08.30-12.15 and 13.15-17.30. In winter skiers tackle a quite difficult run down from here to Monte Pana, but in summer this top station is the starting point for magnificent **walks and mountain treks**.

The easy walk to the **Rifugio Comici** is especially popular (1h30min return), because you can always get a meal there. Or you could start the circuit of Langkofel from there if you're really fit (Walk 8; map on pages 70-1). There are fantastic views to the Seiser Alm and Schlern on one side and the Sella group on the other.

● **Walking tip: Col Raiser to the Regensburger Hut/Rifugio Firenze. Col Raiser** (2107m; see map on page 48) is quickly reached by lift, and the **Fermeda Hut** a pleasant place to take a break. The **lift to Col Raiser** operates Jun to mid-Oct 08.30-17.00; one-way 15 €, up and back down 20 €. But even less energetic visitors like to take a little stroll, and for that the short walk to the **Regensburger Hut** in the **Cislestal** is ideal (only 60m descent/ascent; 30 minutes each way). This 'classic' mountain hut serves authentic Tyrolean dishes.

Or one can take the very beautiful little walk through the flowering meadows of the **Aschgleralm** to the **Troier** Snack Bar with the old and new alm huts. If you have more energy, you can climb Seceda (Walk 9, in the reverse direction).

Wolkenstein/Selva

Wolkenstein is the most active of the three large villages in Gröden — just a hamlet a few decades ago, now an internationally known holiday centre.

Most of the accommodation is in quite expensive hotels and apartments, but there are a few economical private rooms; 'cheap' does not exist. People don't come here, however, because of the good hotels or food; they come for the action. Winter sports dominate, with skiing, ice-skating (large covered rink) and tobogganing.

Three lift areas give access to the surrounding mountains — Langkofel, Sella and the Puez group, all of them around or above 3000m. Summer sports are also catered for: walking, mountain climbing, mountain biking and

44 Dolomites, Book 2: Centre and East

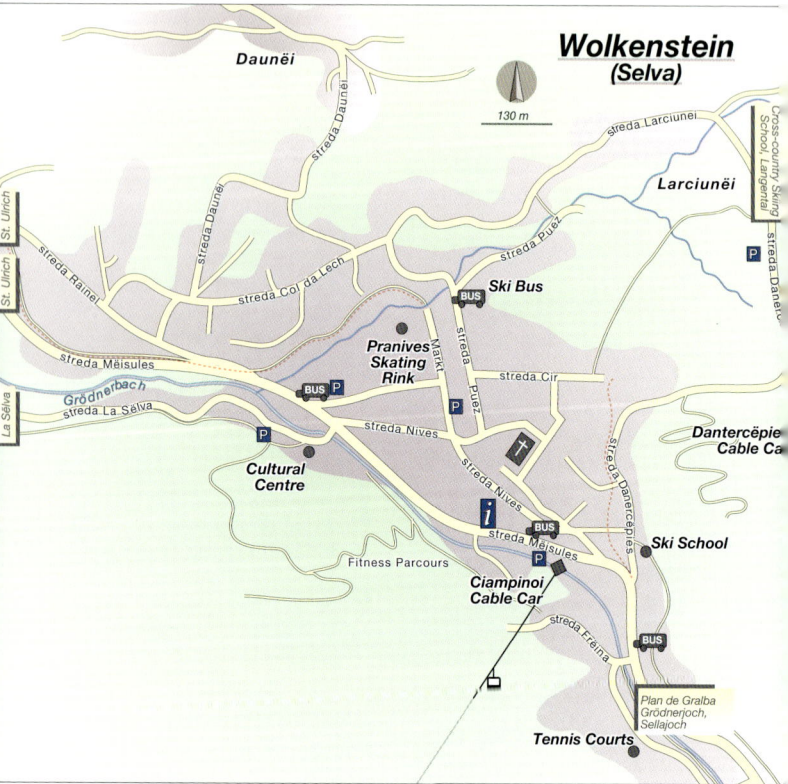

paragliding. Or you can just go out mushroom-hunting in the beautiful spruce woods on the north slopes of the Langkofel group.

Transport: Parking on the main road is not allowed; there are covered **car parks** near the pharmacy and the Hotel Gran Baita. There are **bus connections** to Bozen/Bolzano, Brixen/Bressanone and Plan de Gralba; in summer there are also buses over the Sella Pass to Corvara in the Hochabteital/Alta Badia and Canazei in the Fassa Valley, with several bus stops along the main road.

Sights and excursions: The remains of **Wolkenstein Castle** are unspectacular, but the setting is most impressive. The castle was built below a rock overhang and in some places into the rock itself, so it's hard to tell where the rock ends and the ruins begin. The castle was destroyed during the German Peasants' Revolt of 1525.

Even the least energetic walker can get deep into the heart of the **Puez-Geisler Nature Park** on the easy trail in the **Langental/ Vallunga** — the route to a cross and spring at the end of the valley is really easy and it's even cleared in winter (Walk 6 on page 62; allow about 1h).

Beyond there the trails are narrower and more demanding; walkers must have climbing gear

Grödner Tal/Val Gardena

for some trails. Well equipped walkers can head on over the top of the valley with its bubbling karst springs up to the modern Puez Hut on Route 14 or take Route 14a to the Somafurcia Pass and continue on Dolomites High Route 2 through the corrie above Lake Crespëina to the Forcella Danter les Pizes and down to the top station of the Dantercepies lift. Walk 13 tackles this route in the reverse direction, beginning at the Dantercepies lift.

The **Dantercepies cable car** (operates from end Jun to end Sep, 08.30-17.30; one way 13.50 €, up and back 19 €) is particularly popular because there's also a cable car on the Hochabteital/Alta Badia side, and people love walking the flower-filled meadows between the two mountain stations, visiting the Jimmi Hut and then descending to Kolfuschg with the Frara lift.

Ciampinoi (Ciampinëi in Ladin) is reached from Wolkenstein by **cable car** (mid-Jun to end Sep, from 08.30-17.30; one way 14.50 €, up and back 20 €). Not only is there a world-famous ski route from this peak down into the valley, but also **walks** in the area north of Langkofel and around the mountain. Even if you just stay at the lift station, your day is made: the panorama — south to Langkofel, east to Sella, north to the Puez group and west to the Seiser Alm and Schlern — is breathtaking. But for the energetic, the walk *par excellence* is the Langkofel circuit (Walk 8), which you could join at waypoint 10 after just short walk from the Ciampinoi lift.

The **Grödner Joch/Passo Gardena** links Gröden with the Ladin Hochabteital and Gadertal and is the shortest route to Bruneck/Brunico. The **Sellajoch**

> **Sella Ronda**
> Whatever drivers and motorcyclists can do, a skier can do: that must have been the basic idea behind the Sella Ronda. There are so many lifts on the mountain, and the network of pistes is so tightly woven, that it's possible to ski round the Sella group in just one day. But of course to do this is extremely strenuous and has the added disadvantage that the last lifts go down at 17.00 (or even 16.30). So what do you do when you're stuck in Corvara but your room is in Wolkenstein (of course it's no problem if you have a mobile and someone willing to play taxi). The organisers describe the 'ronda' as 'not difficult', but with 26km of pistes (40km total distance) and a height difference of 4500m, it's unlikely you'll have much energy for après-ski.

links Gröden with the Fassatal in Trentino; this is also Ladin country between Canazei (which you reach on the other side) and Moèna. The Grödner Joch is full of inns, while there is hardly a building on the Sellajoch; the **Sella Dolomiti Resort** (former 'Sellajochhaus', named for the pass) is 1km further north and downhill. That's where you'll find **parking places** and a **2-person, 'telephone box' cable car** (mid-Jun to early Oct, from 08.15-17.00; one way 14 €, up and back 18 €) to the **Langkofelscharte** with the **Toni Demetz Hut**, where a couple of walking routes begin. Walk 8 starts at the Dolomiti Resort and takes an hour less than starting at the Ciampinoi lift. Only climbers tackle Sella's mighty walls from this pass (via the protected Pössnecker climbing route).

Walk 1: FROM ST CHRISTINA/SANTA CRISTINA TO ST JAKOB/SAN GIACOMO CHURCH

Distance/time: about 5.2km/ 3.2mi; 1h35min (55min out, 40min back)
Grade: ● easy, with an ascent/ descent of 195m/640ft. A short family walk on mainly shady woodland and meadow paths with no problems; the last stretch is on road. St Jacob's church can only be visited in summer, as a guided tour (Saturdays at 15.15).
Waymarking: red/white Trail 32A waymarking and signposted as 'Legendenweg'
Equipment: walking shoes
Refreshments: nothing en route except for a spring at **4**, but plenty of opportunities in St Christina — for instance at the centrally located restaurant La Posta on Streda Dursan (www.laposta.eu)
Walking map: Tabacco 05, Val Gardena-Alpe di Siusi/Gröden-Seiseralm, 1:25,000
Transport: 🚗 park near the parish church in St Christina — for instance on Via Paul (46° 33.523'N, 11° 42.931'E). 🚌 350, which links Bolzano with Wolkenstein/Selva and usually runs about every half hour, stops in the centre of St Christina at the town hall (Rathaus). From here it's just 15 minutes to the church — you can see its spire from far off. The last bus back leaves at 19.19 (with a change of buses).

This short out-and-back walk on the 'Legends Trail' first rises through sweet-smelling conifers. It then climbs steadily uphill through alm meadows dotted with bright blooms and past old farms to the attractively sited church of St Jacob/San Giacomo.

The walk begins in **St Christina**, at the small square in front of the parish church. On the cemetery wall there's a 'Legendenweg' sign (**1**); see the panel opposite. Follow the signposting into Streda Paul and walk uphill with a view down to the valley. Some five minutes from the start you leave Streda Paul at the **apartment block Hetty** (**2**) and head left, following more 'Legendenweg' signs (in Ladin 'Troi dla Lijenda'). You pass the Residence Sovara and continue on a gravel track.

After a few metres cross a small stream on a wooden bridge and come to the first of many info boards. Then you rise steadily up a wide path through a light conifer wood. A good 10 minutes past Hetty apartments, there's a bench (**3**) below a high rock wall on the right-hand side of the path. At this point the woods open up, affording a fine view to mighty Langkofel/Sassolungo.

Further on you pass a carving of St Jacob and several more benches. Some 10 minutes past the rock wall follow Trail 32A straight ahead at a fork (**4**; **25min**), heading for 'St Jakob'. Soon after a **spring** the woods open out to a meadow with impressive larch trees. You pass two old inns, **Festil** and **Pedracia**, while the slender spire of St Jacob pierces the trees and is always in sight.

Shortly after, your meadow path merges with a tarred road. Turn left uphill here and soon, at a fork (**5**), go left again on Trail 32A, a farm track. This runs through alm meadows and light woods straight towards the church. For the last metres you are on a steep gravel track, then you reach

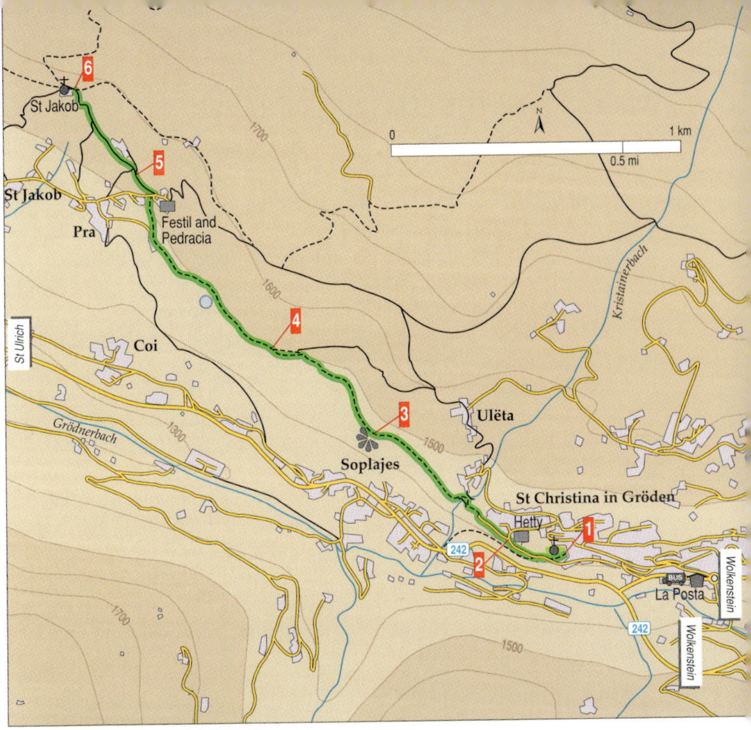

Info board on the Legends Trail

How the 'Legendenweg' (Legends Trail) got its name

The name 'Legends Trail' has to do with the ruins of Stetteneck Castle near St Jakob's Church. A Gebhard von Stetteneck was once its owner. A legend grew up about his son Jakob, a pilgrimage to Santiago de Compostela, and the subsequent building of the church. All is explained in pictorial info boards along the way.

the **church of St Jakob/San Giacomo** (**6**; **55min**). There are more benches in front of its large wooden door, inviting you to take a rest and admire the views of Langkofel to the south. The church, only open in the summer, was founded in the 13th century. The St Christopher on the south wall is by a painter from the Brixen school.

Allow 40 minutes to retrace your steps to **St Christina** (**1**; **1h35min**).

Walk 2: OVER THE ALMS OF COL RAISER

Distance/time: about 9.1km/ 5.6mi; 3h
Grade: ● easy-moderate, with an ascent of 280m/915ft and descent of 830m/2720ft. The trails are good, with gentle ups and downs, but there is no shade before the Regensburger Hut. The descent to St Christina can be a bit hard on the knees — walking poles help.
Waymarking: red/white waymarks; Trail 7 from **2** to **4**; then 2B to **5**; Trail 13 to the Regensburger Hut (**5**) and N° 1 to the end of the walk
Equipment: walking shoes or boots, sun protection, walking pole(s)
Refreshments: quite a few places at huts en route, for instance the Odles Hut (**1**), Troier Hut (**3**) or Regensburger Hut/Rifugio Firenze (**7**), where there's also a tap
Walking map: Tabacco 05, Val Gardena-Alpe di Siusi/Gröden-Seiseralm, 1:25,000
Transport: 🚗 free car parking at the Col Raiser cable car in St Christina (46° 33.880'N, 11° 44.176'E). 🚌 350 links Bolzano with Wolkenstein/Selva and usually runs about every half hour, stopping in St Christina: alight at 'Dosses'. The last bus back, via Waidbruck, is at 19.16. From there take 🚌 357 or walk 10 minutes back to the cable car. The Col Raiser cable car runs from the beginning of June to mid-October.

This alm walk runs at the foot of the Geisler/Odle group, past several huts offering good refreshments and through flower-saturated meadows — to the popular Regensburger Hut/Rifugio Firenze. Then there's a long descent through the Ciaulonch Valley back to St Christina.

The walk begins from the panorama terrace of the **Almhotel Col Raiser**, at a waymarking sign (**1**) pointing north to the 'Odles-Hütte'. An you reach the Odles Hut in a few metres — a little paradise with calves, rabbits and a children's play area. Follow the wide motor track for some 10 minutes towards the rock walls of the Geisler peaks. Past a little hollow, keep right at a fork (**2**) for 'Trojerhütte'. Follow Trail 7, climbing gently over endless rolling meadows — in early summer a sea of gentians, globe

The idyllic Pieralongia Hut

Walk 2: Over the alms of Col Raiser 49

flowers and mountain anemones. About 20 minutes past the fork dreamy **Lake Iman** reveals itself on your right in a hollow.

Soon after you reach — via wooden steps and then gravel — the **Troier Hut** (3) with its fluttering flag — a first good place for a break.

Continue north for about five minutes, then keep right at a fork (4; **45min**) on Trail 2B ('Regensburger Hütte'). Now you follow a narrow mountain path at the foot of the Geisler/Odle range. In the south are Langkofel/Sassolungo and Plattkofel/Sassopiatto. In the west is Pic, and in front of you the Puez group with the Gardenaccia high plateau. With a bit of luck you'll see some marmots playing on the steep slopes.

Some 20 minutes past the Troier Hut, after another hollow, you come to the cosy little **Malga Pieralongia Alm** with its beautiful sunbathing lawn. Again, head for the 'Regensburger Hütte', going through a cattle gate about 15 minutes past the alm. Behind it you reach a fork (5; **1h20min**) and keep right on Trail 13A. Head downhill on gravel, straight towards the fractured Col de la Pieres in the Puez group.

About 10 minutes past the fork, at another split in the trail (6), go right (Trail 13, also signed 'Regensburger Hütte'). Walk for about 20 minutes through light pines, larch, juniper and tree heath. Soon you see the stone-built **Regensburger Hut/Rifugio Firenze** (7; **1h50min**) ahead of you. (Whoever doesn't want to take the long descent from here can use Trails 2 and 4 to get back to the cable car station in about 30 minutes.) The hut, built in 1888, has a tap on its west side where you can fill water bottles. There are all kinds of places to sit, and there's rustic cooking to be enjoyed — try the Austrian pancakes (*Kaiserschmarrn*).

From the hut follow the wide motor track (Trail 1) downhill towards 'Cason'. To your left is the Stevia high plateau, which drops steeply — and rockily — to the west. A good five minutes later some springs come up in the middle of a meadow. From now on the Cisles Stream accompanies you, splashing in the valley.

Walk 20 minutes through light conifer woods, to a **fish pond** (8) from where you follow signposting for 'N° 1, Cason/St Christina' further downhill. After crossing a stream and another 10 minutes of

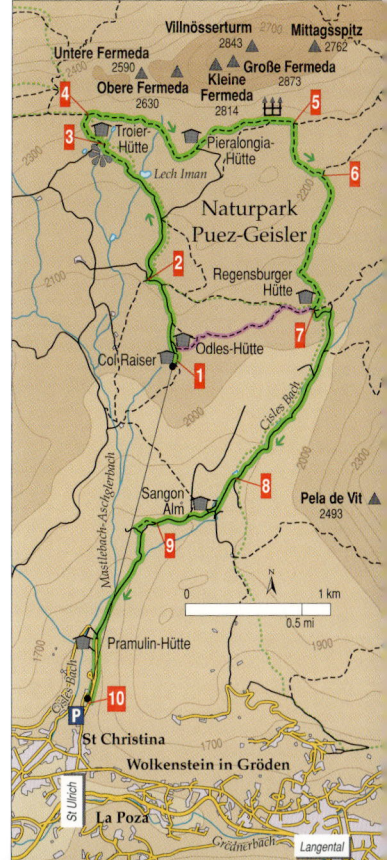

climbing, you see the Sangon Alm on the right, between the trees.

Shortly after this alm Trail N° 1 leaves the motor track (**9**) for about five minutes. Continuing on, you walk in the traces of the Col Raiser cable car. After about 20 minutes downhill through alm meadows and wooded sections you spot the **Pramulin Hut** on the right — a last change for something to eat or drink. Then its tar underfoot and in a few minutes you're back at the **car park** (**10**; **3h**) for the Col Raiser cable car, where the walk ends.

Alm huts below Langkofel/Sassolungo

Walk 3: FROM COL RAISER TO PIC AND THEN TO ST CHRISTINA VIA THE SEURASAS ALMS

Distance/time: about 9.1km/ 5.6mi; 3h10min
Grade: ●! moderate-strenuous, with an ascent of 370m/1210ft and descent of 915m/3000ft. A varied mountain hike that begins on alm meadows and runs over a steep ridge to the summit of Pic (**9**). *You must be sure-footed and have a head for heights.* Around the summit the path is narrow and stony, otherwise the trails (including some on roads) are good. Sunny throughout.
Waymarking: red/white; Trail N° 2 to **4**; then N° 6 to **6**; Trail 20 to Strada Plesdinaz; Trail 32 to **10**; finally N° 18 to the hamlet of Insom
Equipment: walking boots, sun protection, walking pole(s)
Refreshments: take your own food and drink. There is a spring at **9**; otherwise only at the start and at the Seurasas Alm (**7**).
Walking map: Tabacco 05, Val Gardena-Alpe di Siusi/Gröden-Seiseralm, 1:25,000
Transport: 🚗 free car parking at the Col Raiser cable car in St Christina (46° 33.880'N, 11° 44.176'E). 🚌 350 links Bolzano with Wolkenstein/Selva and usually runs about every half hour, stopping in St Christina: alight at 'Dosses'. The last bus back, via Waidbruck, is at 19.16. From there take 🚌 357 or walk 10 minutes back to the cable car. The Col Raiser cable car runs from the beginning of June to mid-October.

This very varied mountain hike takes you over alm meadows, a steep ridge, along a rock fall and up to the panoramic summit of Pic. At the end you can take a break at an idyllic alm run by a wood carver.

The first 10 minutes of this hike are identical to Walk 9: **you start out** from the panorama terrace of the **Almhotel Col Raiser**, at a waymarking sign (**1**) pointing north to the 'Odles-Hütte'. And you reach the Odles Hut in a few metres — a little paradise with calves, rabbits and a children's play area.

Follow the wide motor track for some 10 minutes towards the rock walls of the Geisler/Odle peaks. Past a little hollow, at a fork (**2**), go straight ahead — continuing on Trail N° 2 towards 'Fermeda-Hütte' over gently rolling alm meadows. A few minutes later you come to the old **Fermeda Hut**, clad in dark wood.

Continuing on, keep to Trail 2 for 'St Ulrich', heading west.

Climb over two little streams on wooden boards and, 10 minutes past the Fermeda Hut, come to a **knoll** (**3**; **25min**) with signposts. Keep left here on Trail 2 for 'St Ulrich' and N° 6 for 'Seurasas' — walking through meadows towards the steep ridge leading to the Pic summit.

On the left **Lake Sant**, with its shimmering green water, snuggles into the meadows. It's one of several prehistoric locations along the ancient Troj Pajan Trail (see the panel on page 53: Engravings at Lake Sant').

The trail moves steadily uphill to a weathered **wooden cross** dating from 1888. Past this, there is a depression, where, at a fork (**4**), you keep left for 'Pic' on Trail N° 6.

52 Dolomites, Book 2: Centre and East

Now you carefully follow a stony mountain path between larch and juniper uphill along a crest. As you rise, the views become more spectacular: Raschötz/Rasciesa, Seceda, the Geisler/Odle group, the Puez high plateau — a veritable feast for the eyes!

Some 10 minutes along the crest it narrows, with steep drops on both sides. Rhododendrons and weathered mountain pines accompany you on the climb. On the left, Lake Sant glistens below you. Soon it's really alpine: on the right the steep northern flank of Pic falls steeply away — you need a head for heights! It's another 10 minutes up this ridge, where you need to be sure-footed and vertigo-free.

Then you see the rocky knoll of **Pic** (**5**; **1h05min**) rising before

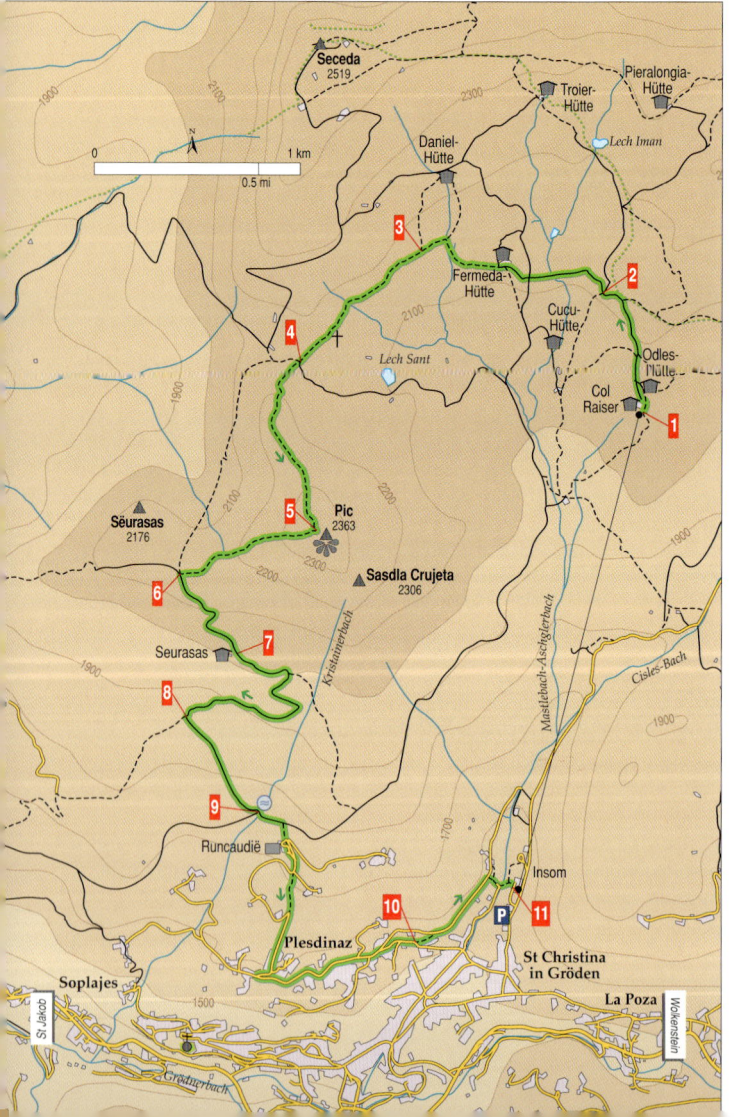

Walk 3: From Col Raiser to Pic and St Christina 53

you on its high plateau, and can sink down onto its summit bench. The panorama is not to be beaten: ahead of you in the south are Sella, Lang- and Plattkofel (Sassolungo and Sassopiatto), the Seiser Alm/Alpe di Siusi with Schlern/Sciliar — as well as the Rosengarten/Catinaccio group. It's like a necklace — all the pearls of the Dolomites surround you!

After a long break, carefully

> **Excavations at Lake Sant**
>
> In 1984 excavations at Lake Sant ('Holy Lake') uncovered a bronze needle and ceramics from the Bronze Age as well as pottery shards and animal bones from the Iron Age. Archaeologists think that there was a burnt offering place here — not far from the prehistoric Troj Pajan Way. This ancient route ran from the Eisacktal/Valle Isarco through the Gröden/Gardena Valley to the Grödner Joch/Passo Gardena.
>
> Also linked with the Troj Pajan are a burial place found at the Col de Flam west of St Jakob church and a spectacular bronze dagger dating from about 1300 BC, found on Balest west of Pic in about 1830. Finally, below the Grödner Joch, on the Plan de Frea, under a huge boulder, they unearthed a prehistoric habitation with many pottery shards in 1978.
>
> Traces of the Troj Pajan can be found as far as the Grödner Joch, but they then disappear. It is thought, however, that it could have run to Venice.

follow Trail 6 downhill towards 'Seurasas'. The path is steep, narrow and skiddy as it descends the karstic northern flanks of the mountain. Far below are the alms and meadows of Seurasas.

After about 20 minutes the ridge gives way to gentle meadows and you come to a signpost (**6**). Keep left here on Trail 20 ('Seurasas/St Ulrich'); soon you're walking steeply downhill on a motor track between mountain pines for about 15 minutes.

Then you come to the beautifully sited **Seurasas Alm** (**7**; **1h40min**) with its panorama terrace, children's play area, especially fluffy Austrian pancakes *(Kaiserschmarrn)* and a tenant who sells his wood carvings (a small edelweiss or wooden sheep sells for about 15-20 €).

From the alm follow the motor track towards 'St Christina', heading downhill in wide curves through mixed conifers. Some 25 minutes from the alm keep left at a fork (**8**) on Trail 20 for 'St Ulrich'. For the next 15 minutes you continue down a wide motor track. Where this merges with another motorable track, you will find a **spring** (**9**; **2h20min**) where you can quench your thirst. Then go left and after just a few metres right on a path stabilised with wooden logs (Trail 20). When you get to the Runcaudië Inn the trail changes briefly to tarred road, then it's cross-country again on steep ground.

Further downhill follow the tarmac road left downhill between larch and houses for a good five minutes before turning left on the road to Plesdinaz (signed 'St Christina', Trail 32).

Now you walk just gently downhill, passing several very attractive estates in the old style of the valley. Because of the high cost of the 2008 financial crisis it's unfortunately not possible in all cases to restore them. So they have been replaced by new-builds. But, still, keep a lookout: especially on the south-facing side of the valley there are many examples in good condition clinging to the upper slopes.

After about 15 minutes on Streda Plesdinaz, follow Streda Insom left uphill (Trail 1B). I can hear you groan … but you're almost there; it's just another 100m up the steep bit. You walk under a barn that has been built over the road, and approach the really spectacular **hamlet of Insom**.

Just after the hamlet, take the wooden steps down into the meadows. The car park for the **Col Raiser cable car** (**1**; **3h10min**) is just ahead.

Colourful summer meadows backed by the teeth of Lang- and Plattkofel/ Sasso -lungo and -piato

Walk 4: TO SECEDA VIA RASCHÖTZ/RASCIESA AND THE PANASCHARTE/FORCELLA PANA

Distance/time: about 8km/5mi; 3h35min
Grade: ●❕ difficult, with an ascent of 635m/2080ft and descent of 270m/885ft. Good trails up to the Broglesalm (**3**) and mostly sunny. From there the walk is pure alpine and only for experienced hill walkers who are sure-footed and have a head for heights. When the sun is high, this walk is hot!
Waymarking: red/white; Trail N° 35 to the Broglesalm (**3**); then N° 6 to **5**; Trail 1 to **7**
Equipment: walking boots, sun protection, walking pole(s)
Refreshments: available at the Cason Hut (**1**), Broglesalm (**3**; there's a tap here too), the Sofie Hut (shortly after **9**) and at the upper Seceda station (**7**). For the stiff climb up to the Panascharte be sure to take enough to drink!

Walking map: Tabacco 05, Val Gardena-Alpe di Siusi/Gröden-Seiseralm, 1:25,000
Transport: 🚗 free car parking near the main through road in St Ulrich or at the valley station of the Seceda cable car (46° 34.681'N, 11° 40.336'E) and then on foot to the valley station of the Raschötz funicular. 🚐 350 from Bolzano runs about every half hour to St Ulrich, from where there's a local 🚐 356 direct to the Raschötz valley station. The last 🚐 356 back leaves at 18.34, the last 🚐 350 (via Waidbruck) leaves at 19.31. The Raschötz funicular (15 € one way, 21 € return) runs from the middle of May till the beginning of October, the Seceda cable car (25.50 € on way, 35 € return) from mid-June to early October.

This spectacular mountain hike for vertigo-free walkers begins deceivingly as a pleasant ramble through extensive alm meadows. It's only when you come to the foot of the mighty Geisler/Odle range that its true character comes to the fore — when you climb steeply up to the impressive Panascharte/Forcella Pana. From the mountain station of the funicular it's only 10 minutes to the summit of Seceda with its outstanding panoramic view of the Geisler peaks, the Puez group, Sella group, Langkofel and Plattkofel/Sasso -lungo and -piatto … and the main Alpine ridge in the north!

The walk starts at the **mountain station of the Raschötz funicular** (**1**). Follow Trail 35A for a few metres, then turn right on Trail 35B for 'Brogles Hütte'. After a stroll though mixed conifers you'll reach the idyllic **Cason Hut**. From here head uphill towards 'Flitzerscharte/ Brogles Hütte' on Trail 35 — as far as a wayside cross with seating.

Before you are the wide grassy southern slopes of Innerraschötz/ Resciesa Dedite. A motor track, wide at the outset, takes you steeply downhill through mixed conifers. Soon the woods thin out, and you have a great view of your goal — Seceda, as well as the Geislers, Langkofel, Plattkofel and Pic in the east.

Continuing on, walk downhill, then up again — through thin mountain pines and between juniper and rhododendrons. Ahead, the sharp-looking meadow ridge of Innerraschötz (on whose northern flanks you'll often spot black-eyed 'brillen'sheep (see Walk

Seceda's panoramic summit

12 in Book 1) jump about, marks the boundary with Heaven.

After about 15 minutes' uphill ignore a turning to the left (**2**) and keep straight ahead on Trail 35 for 'Brogleshütte', with the Flitzer Scharte on your left. Now the trail crosses Innerraschötz. There are meadows on either side, bright with blooms. Seceda and the Geislers rise ahead.

Keep to Trail 35 through lovely meadows all the way to the **Broglesalm** (**3**; **1h20min**). This alm, at the foot of the mighty Geisler range, is spectacularly sited — a perfect place for a meal or a snooze on the grass. On the

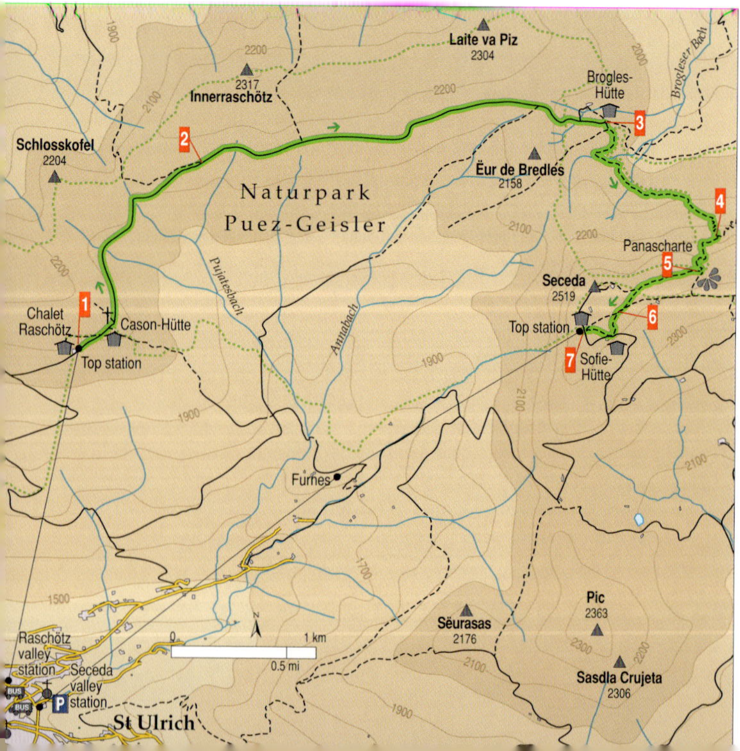

Walk 4: To Seceda via Raschötz and the Panascharte

northwest side of the hut there's a tap where you can fill your water bottles.

From the hut follow signposting for 'Panascharte' on Trail 6, heading south. After about five minutes steeply downhill you cross the Brogleser Stream, by finding stepping stones where the water is low.

After a scree slope the trail goes steeply uphill in tight zigzags. That will get you sweating! Rocks tower above you, and the narrow groove of the path up to the Panascharte looks vertical.

After about 30 minutes' uphill the path forks (**4**). Head right on Trail 6; you reach the entrance to the groove some 10 minutes later. Take time here to catch your breath and enjoy the great view back to the Broglesalm and Raschötz!

Then you start on the steepest part of the hike. The climb circumvents huge boulders, sometimes on wooden log steps and with protective cables. Here you really have to be *sure-footed, with a head for heights!*

Some 30 minutes from the entrance the groove widens out a bit. In a good 15 minutes more, after another short stretch of protective cabling, you're at the **Panascharte/Forcella Pana** (**5**; **2h10min**).

The view from here to the extensive alm plateaus around Col Raiser appears unreal — many huts and several little lakes are sprinkled on the slopes. On the horizon Langkofel and Plattkofel reach skyward.

Follow the signposting right to the 'Sofie-Hütte'. A short while later you reach the ridge again at a fork ('Seceda-Bergbahn') and look down on dreadfully steep rock faces. At the next fork (**6**) go steeply downhill through meadows. In five minutes you come to the **Sofie Hut** with its large panorama terrace, ancient wood-panelled steps and giant — if not very cheap! — Austrian Pancakes *(Kaiserschmarrn)*.

From the hut take the cobbled trail direct to the **mountain station of the Seceda cable car** (**7**; **3h35min**).

Walk 5: FROM WOLKENSTEIN/SELVA TO THE STEVIA HUT

Distance/time: about 7.4km/ 4.6mi; 3h25
Grade: ●! moderate-strenuous, with an ascent/descent of 700m/ 2300ft. A grand panoramic circuit with steep ups and downs, mostly on narrow skiddy paths. You must be sure-footed and have a head for heights. Most of the walk is shady.
Waymarking: red/white; Trail N° 3 to **4**; then N° 17 to **6** ; the descent is on Trail 17A
Equipment: walking shoes or boots, sun protection, walking pole(s)
Refreshments: available at the Juac Hut (**4**) and Stevia Hut (**6**), but, unfortunately, *both of these huts are closed in autumn!* So take food with you then, and plenty of water!
Walking map: Tabacco 05, Val Gardena-Alpe di Siusi/Gröden-Seiseralm, 1:25,000
Transport: 🚗 drive from Wolkenstein/Selva to Daunei and take the road to Tublà from there; after about 200m you come to the car park for this walk (46° 33.823'N, 11° 45.207'E). 🚌 350 runs from Bolzano to Wolkenstein about every half hour: get off at the 'Nives Platz' stop. The last bus back out of the valley is at 19.07. From the bus stop it's about 45 minutes on foot to the start — so the public transport option adds a good 1h30min to the walk!

After a steep climb this mountain walk really delivers: there are spectacular views all round the clock from the lonely Stevia high plateau. The walk is especially colourful at the end of October, when the larch woods wear their flaming autumnal dress.

The hike begins at the **parking place** (**1**) outside Daunei. Follow the tarred motor road uphill and, shortly, fork right (**2**) for the 'Juac-Hütte'. You walk amidst larches on a stony mountain path.

At the next fork (**3**) keep straight ahead on Trail N° 3 for 'Juac-Hütte'. (The trail to the right goes to the Stevia Hut and is your return route.) Walk uphill through more larch trees. Several small huts lie dotted around this rolling landscape. Your trail continues through the meadows on boardwalks.

Shortly past a wooden fence you come to a fork (**4**; **30min**). The Geisler peaks reach for the heavens ahead of you here. If it's open, you may like to walk the few metres to the Juac Hut, but the main walk keeps right on Trail N° 17 for 'Stevia', at first climbing a meadow ridge and then heading through mixed conifers. The view keeps opening up to the steep Stevia wall just above you.

After a good 15 minutes' climbing the trees open out, giving a view to Sella in the southwest, Langkofel/Sassolungo in the south, and the Geisler group in the north. A fantastic panorama!

You pass a scree channel and then climb a scree in tight bends. Wooden fencing helps again and again at the exposed points. Some 25 minutes from the scree channel you come to two benches — a welcome place for a panoramic pause!

After another 10 minutes of steep climbing you go through a wooden fence and come abruptly to a small pass. A breathtaking view opens up to the southeast — to vertical channels and rock

Late autumnal gold

chasms reaching all the way down into the Langental/Vallunga.

From the pass you go steeply downhill for about five minutes, to a junction (**5**; **1h30min**). Keep left here on Trail 17 ('Stevia Alm') and follow a steep strip of meadow northeast. The path crosses a rock channel and after a scant 20 minutes comes to the **Stevia Hut** (**6**; **1h50min**). This is a wonderful place for a break with hungry

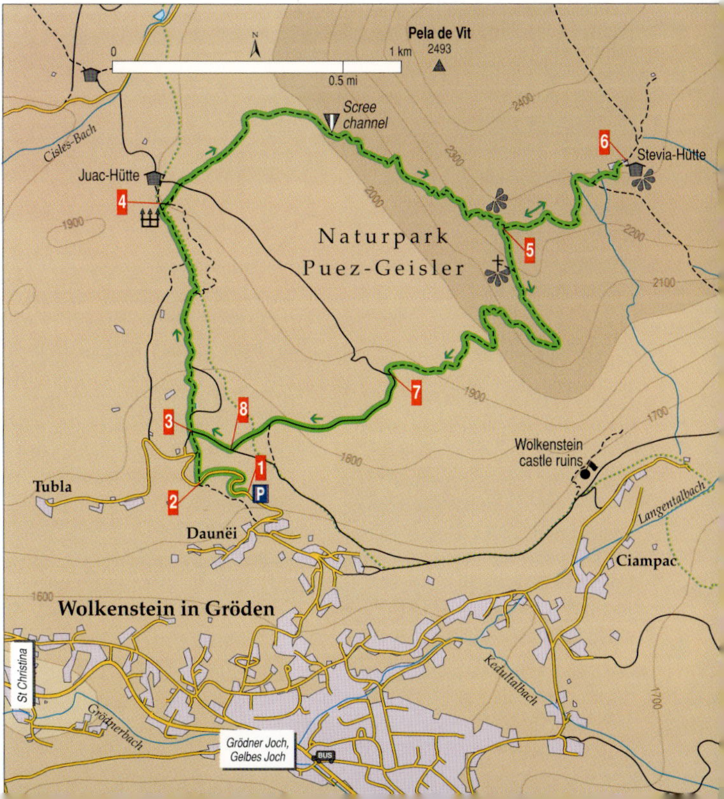

Terrific view into the Langental/Vallunga

jackdaws, splendid views to Sella, Langkofel and the Langental … and — at least outside high season — heavenly silence!

Just below the hut is the end of the spectacular climbing trail Sandro Pertini, which comes up from the Langental. It's officially closed and it's not expected that climbers will want to disturb the nesting eagles (see 'Eagles in the Langental' in the panel opposite. But some walkers don't pay attention to the rules and presumably don't even know that eagles live there …

After a good long rest, head back in 20 minutes to the turn-off (**5**). Then follow Trail 17A left towards 'Wolkenstein'. About five minutes later a narrow path forks right to a weathered crucifix, standing at the western edge of the Stevia high plateau. From here you have a terrific view to the Grödner/Gardena Valley almost vertically below!

Back on Trail 17A, you are shortly going downhill through meadows, then you reach the end of the small plateau. Here log steps take you steeply down through

Walk 5: From Wolkenstein/Selva to the Stevia Hut

Climbing to the Stevia high plateau

Eagles in the Langental/Vallunga
A loud rustling, a black shadow — we're surprised; we stand and stare and keep still ... Two to three golden eagle pairs live in the Puez-Geisler Nature Park. Again and again they cross the steep walls of the Stevia high plateau and let themselves be be taken to vertiginous heights by the updrafts. In the Langental alone seven eyries are known which have already served as homes for them. The magnificent birds can live up to 35 years old. Many have a wingspan of 230cm/8ft and weigh almost 7kg/15lb.

mixed conifers for about 15 minutes, then you're following broad serpentines. Somewhere here you may meet eagles flying majestically over the treetops ...

At a fork (**7**; **2h55min**) go left with Trail 17A, descending a wide forestry track which merges with another forestry track (**8**) about 10 minutes later. Turning right, you reach the fork (**3**) from your outward route and 10 minutes later you're back at the car park (**1**; **3h25min**).

Walk 6: FROM WOLKENSTEIN/SELVA INTO THE LANGENTAL/VALLUNGA

Distance/time: about 6.4km/4mi; 1h40 (out 55min; back 45min)
Grade: ● easy, with an ascent/descent of 175m/575ft. Wide trails and plenty of shade
Waymarking: red/white Trail 14 waymarks throughout
Equipment: stout shoes, sun protection
Refreshments: available at La Ciajota snack bar (**1**; see 'Food with Ladin Flair' in the panel on page 64); several springs en route
Walking map: Tabacco 05, Val Gardena-Alpe di Siusi/Gröden-Seiseralm, 1:25,000
Transport: 🚗 following signs to 'Langental', drive from Wolkenstein/Selva to the parking area about 2km from the centre (46° 33.838'N, 11° 46.400'E). 🚌 350 runs from Bozen/Bolzano to Wolkenstein about every half hour: get off at the 'Nives Platz' stop. The last bus back out of the valley is at 19.07. From Nives Platz take 🚌 357 towards the Dantercepies cable car and alight at the Langental bus stop (summer only; last bus back at 18.04). From the bus stop you can follow Trail 14 to the car park via the Ciampàc snack bar in 10 minutes. If you walk from the centre of Wolkenstein (also Trail 14), reckon on a good 35 minutes.

This walk for all the family runs without any big climbs or descents past a chapel dating from the Middle Ages into the impressive Langental/Vallunga with its steep rock walls reaching up to the sky.

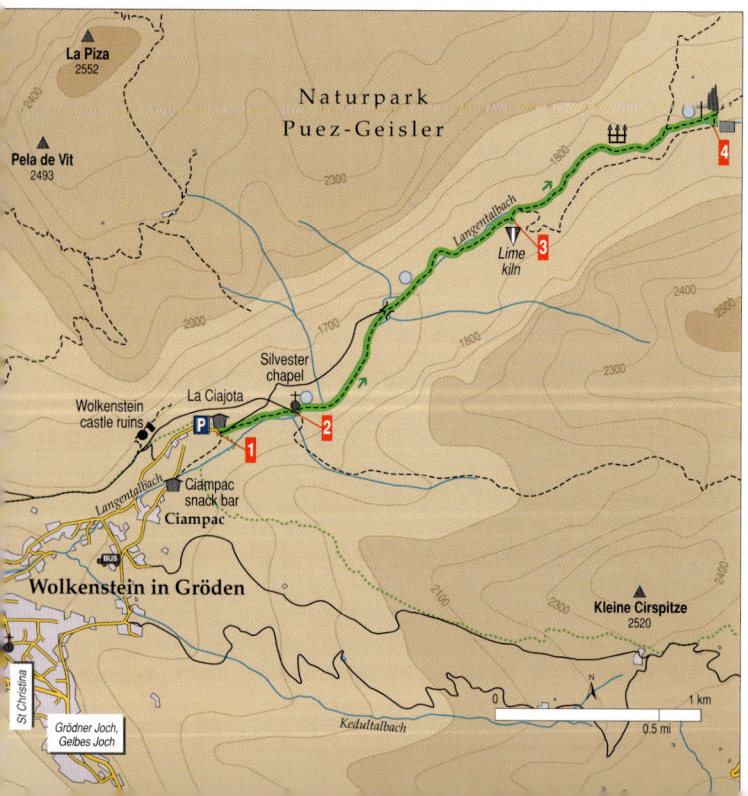

Walk 6: From Wolkenstein/Selva into the Langental/Vallunga

Going into the Langental/Vallunga

The walk begins at the large car park (**1**) at the entrance to the Langental/Vallunga. From the eastern end of the car park, go through a wooden gate and follow a wide and level gravel path to a chapel dedicated to St Silvester. It lies nicely ensconced in alm meadows, surrounded by larch and pine trees. On both sides of the valley vertical rock reaches skyward; the horizon is closed off by attractive black walls, of which the highest is Puezkofel/Pitla Piza de Puez.

For years a pair of eagles have been nesting in this valley. If you're lucky, you will see one of these majestic birds gliding high above you (see 'Eagles in the Langental' in the panel on page 61). Lynx have also been spotted here — they have probably come from Slovenia.

A good five minutes from the start you reach the **chapel** (**2**). The door is usually unlocked, so you have a chance to take a peek at the impressive 17th century frescoes inside. Exactly when this little church was built is unknown — also unknown is who built it. It is assumed that it was the work of local farmers and shepherds.

Just past the chapel there's a bubbling spring with drinking water. You're walking on a wide path through conifers, and soon you cross a narrow stream on a boardwalk. Then you climb on a gravelly surface.

Not far past the boardwalk there's a lovely place to take a break — in a clearing with several boulders and another **spring**.

Historic lime kiln en route

minutes later you reach a huge scree field full of larch trees. At the end of it, you go through a cattle gate and keep heading up the valley.

Views open out and an extensive alm plateau lies ahead of you. A few metres further on, another spring splashes its water beside a wayside cross. Some metres to the right of it is a huge boulder in the middle of the meadow. On the right-hand valley wall there's an unmanned hut hiding under trees (**4**; **55min**). Here's where your walk turns back, but first take a rest on the benches. Or find a place on the flat meadow for a picnic! Your view sweeps all the way to the end of the valley with its black rock walls, to the mighty Col Turont in the east and to Puezkofel and the Puez needles in the north.

After a long rest, and after filling your water bottles from the spring next to the cross, it will take about 45 minutes to retrace steps to the car park (**1**; **1h40min**).

Keep climbing gently through open woodland and over rolling meadows. Some 10 minutes from the spring a depression opens up on the left with a little wooden shelter. In the summer you'll often find cows grazing here. The tinkling of their bells echoes off the walls on both sides of the valley.

A few metres from the shelter a path forks off to the right, to the **remains of a lime kiln** (**3**; **35min**). It was in operation up until 1960. The lime burnt here was used in the building of the 19th century parish church in Wolkenstein.

Further along, about five

> **Food with Ladin Flair**
> *The long-established snack bar La Ciajota is in the car park at the start of the walk. The Mussner family, who run it, will set you up with apple strudel and a glass of wine after your walk. This alm is a popular meeting point for locals, especially in the evenings. If you were to sit here quietly for a while and listen carefully, you'll hear Ladins talking — a sound no doubt completely foreign to your ears. But it's how most of the people living in Gröden/Gardena speak amongst themselves ... not in German or Italian. The snack bar is open every day from 10.00-18.00 in the season.*

Walk 7: FROM THE CIAMPINOI LIFT TO THE SELLAJOCH/PASSO SELLA

Distance/time: about 4.4km/ 2.7mi; 1h15min
Grade: ● easy-moderate, with an ascent of 155m/510ft and descent of 210m/700ft. A high-altitude walk in the heart of the Dolomites with spectacular all-round views. After a steep descent at the start, it's mostly even-going on wide trails. *No shade!*
Waymarking: red/white; Trail N° 21 to **2**; 21A to **3**; 526 to **4**; then signposting for 'Steinerne Stadt'
Equipment: stout shoes, sun protection
Refreshments: available at the Ciampinoi cable car station (**1**), the Comici Hut (**3**) and at the Sellajoch
Walking map: Tabacco 05, Val Gardena-Alpe di Siusi/Gröden-Seiseralm, 1:25,000
Transport: 🚗 free parking at the valley station of the Ciampinoi cable car (open from the beginning of June to mid-October; 14.50 € one way; 46° 33.200'N, 11° 45.685'E). 🚌 350 runs from Bolzano to Wolkenstein about every half hour: get off at the 'Ciampinoi' stop. The last bus back out of the valley is at 19.07. Return from the Sellajoch with 🚌 471 from the end of June to mid-September generally every half hour till 17.30.

This panoramic high-altitude walk runs through the heart of the Dolomites, along the walls of Langkofel/Sassolungo. After a steep descent at the start, the way is mostly even, through scree fields and larch over to the Sellajoch/Passo Sella. The Sella group is in sight throughout.

The walk begins in front of the mountain station of the Ciampinoi cable car at the large **panorama info board** (**1**). The Sella group, all the peaks and high places in the Grödner/Gardena Valley — and even Schlern/Sciliar and the wide slopes of the Seiser Alm/Alpe di

---

Modern mountain huts
The Sella Mountain Resort and the Comici Hut (shown here) are two examples of controversial building in South Tyrol that get people heated. More and more mountain huts are being renovated and modernised — or even destroyed and completely rebuilt, like the Sellajochhaus. There are often architectural competitions and sometimes very modern, even futuristic buildings are the result. Traditionalists bemoan the fact that the original spirit of the 'alpine hut' has been thrown by the wayside: everything is about marketing and winning prizes. The modernisers say that expectations and demands have changed, that the number of users is ever-increasing, and that builders must balance ecological considerations with cost efficiencies. In addition to the Sella Mountain Resort there are other examples of spectacular new buildings in the Dolomites, for example the Boè Alpine Lodge in the Hochabteital/Alta Badia. Another successful example of complete modernisation is the Tierser-Alpl Hut above the Seiser Alm (see Book 1).

66 Dolomites, Book 2: Centre and East

Siusi are spread out before you on this large canvas.

Follow wide Trail N° 21 signposted to 'Sellajoch/Comici Hütte'), heading west below a lift. After a fence the trail bends straight towards mighty Langkofel. You walk downhill at the edge of a piste: the wounds that the winter sport season inflicts on the grass sward are all too evident.

About 15 minutes from starting out you come to a depression and a fork (**2**). Keep right for 'Comici Hütte', at first walking through meadows. The the terrain becomes more and more stony. Rhododendron, larch, pine and boulders line the trail.

Soon the trail forks again. Turn left and after a few metres you'll be in front of the spectacular **Comici Hut** (**3**; **30min**), described in the panel 'Modern Mountain Huts' on page 65). With its inviting wooden terrace, large play area, E-bike rental station and ultra cool bright blue toilets. The cuisine includes fish dishes — perhaps a reminder

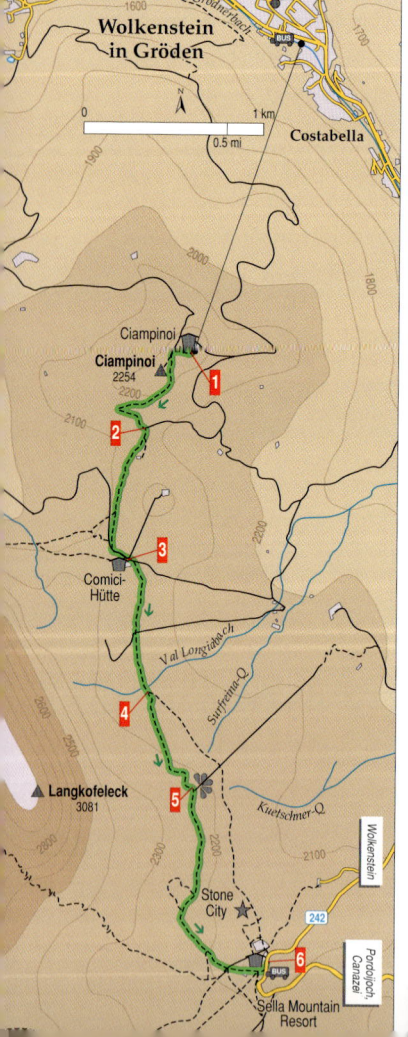

Walk 7: From the Ciampinoi lift to the Sellajoch/Passo Sella 67

of the damp primeval days of the Dolomites, when prehistoric fish swam on top of the sediment … But today's taste is more attuned to their powerful apple strudel, which is worth calling by for if nothing else!

A few metres before the hut, near the valley station of a small ski lift, follow signposting to Trail N° 526, heading south. After two lift routes and a scree corrie you come to a fork (4). Classic Trail 526 goes downhill here, but choose instead the more recent **Panoramaweg Naturonda** downhill to the Steinerne Stadt.

Giant boulders lie scattered all around. The whistling calls of marmots echo off the walls of Langkofel. If you are patient — and providing there's no dog off the lead running around — you ought to be able to watch them from here!

Crossing a wide lift route, after

The Steinerne Stadt ('Stone City') and the Langkofel/Sassolungo 'telephone box' lift

68 Dolomites, Book 2: Centre and East

a short climb you reach a knoll with a bench and **panoramic platform** (5; **50min**). Then the trail goes downhill. There are frequent info boards about the fauna and flora of the Grödnertal/Val Gardena. After a final lift route, you come to the **Steinerne Stadt** ('Stone City'). The labyrinthine confusion of boulders here, taller than a man and thickly overgrown with dwarf pines, rhododendrons and moss, is the result of a prehistoric rockfall. It's a brilliant place for kids to play hide and seek or just to clamber around.

Leave the Steinerne Stadt and head directly towards the old Sellajochhaus, now the ultra-modern **Sella Mountain Resort** (6; **1h15min**), full of wood and glass. It's worth just having a look at the architecture. The bus back to Wolkenstein stops in front.

On the high-altitude trail to the Sellajoch/Passo Sella

Walk 8: CIRCUIT ROUND LANGKOFEL/SASSOLUNGO

Distance/time: about 15.5km/ 9.6mi; 4h55min
Grade: ●! moderate-strenuous, with an ascent/descent of 825m/ 2705ft. A very long mountain walk, demanding stamina. You must be sure-footed and have a head for heights — especially between (**10**) and (**11**). The walk ranges from wide motor tracks to narrow exposed paths and everything in between. There is also little shade, but that depends on the time of day and the season too.
Waymarking: red/white; Trail N° 557 from **2**; 527 from **6**; 526 and 526A from **8**
Equipment: walking boots, sun protection, hiking pole(s)
Refreshments: there are plenty of places to take a break — take your pick from the Sella Mountain Resort (**1**), Friedrich August Hut after **3**; Rifugio Sandro Pertini (**4**), Plattkofel Hut/Rifugio Sassopiatto (**5**) or the Comici Hut (**10**).

You can take on drinking water between **3** and **4**. But because the walk is so long, you should also take along food and drink.
Walking map: Tabacco 05, Val Gardena-Alpe di Siusi/Gröden-Seiseralm, 1:25,000
Transport: 🚗 free parking at the Sella Mountain Resort (46° 30.555'N, 11° 45.458'E). If you come early enough in the morning, however, your will find a free place among the many lay-bys on the pass road between the resort and the Sella Pass. 🚌 350 runs from Bolzano to Wolkenstein/Selva about every half hour: get off at the 'Ciampinoi' stop. The last bus back out of the valley (via Waidbruck) is at 19.07. Then change buses to 🚌471 which calls at the Sellajoch (runs generally every half hour from the end of June to mid-September; last bus back is at 17.30).

T his long high-altitude walk rounds the mighty rock massif of Langkofel/Sassolungo and Plattkofel/Sassopiatto. Peppered with spectacular views, the hike follows a well-trampled route — partly along the Friedrich August Weg, named for the last king of Saxony, an expert mountaineer who loved the Dolomites. There are numerous huts where you can take a break for light or more sustaining meals.

The walk starts at the **Sella Mountain Resort** (**1**). Follow the signposting to 'Rifugio Salei/Col Rodella' to walk by the chapel at the pass and come to a motor track (**2**) five minutes from setting out. Follow Trail N° 557 here; in just under 10 minutes of steady uphill walking you come to the **Rifugio Salei** with its panorama terrace, play area and small animal enclosure. To the east are the Boè needles and Sella, in the southeast is the northern flank of Marmolada, with its shining glaciers. Shortly past the refuge you pass the Chalet Margherita on the right.
    Turn right on a broad knoll at signposting (**3**; **30min**) for the 'Rifugio Sandro Pertini'/'Friedrich August Weg', still on Trail 557. In the south the rocky massif of Rosengarten/Catinaccio is spread out before you. Walk downhill and in about five minutes you come to the **Friedrich August Hut** (meals served), beyond which you cross a stream.
    Eventually you're walking

Right: view to Langkofel not far from the upper Ciampinoi lift station

through meadows, passing several barns, always below Langkofel's southern walls. Then you cross another stream and walk gently uphill until, about 20 minutes later, you come to the **Rifugio Sandro Pertini** (**4**). This is a very popular place, and especially full during the Italian holidays.

From the hut continue on Trail 557 — with fewer people around now. You cross meadows frequently broken by scree streams. About 15 minutes from the refuge you begin a steep climb on a path supported by wooden logs. Then you see Schlern/Sciliar and Plattkofel in the west for the first time ... and walk between sharp rocks straight towards the hut.

Further along Trail 557 you first pass the **Malga Sasso Piatto** and then come to the beautifully sited **Plattkofel Hut/Rifugio Sassopiatto** (**5**; **1h45min**). This is a great place for a meal — for instance the home-made *Schlutzkrapfen/mezzelune* (ravioli filled with alm cheese, in thyme butter) — mmmmmhhhhh!

From this hut you keep north on Trail 527 towards 'Langkofel-hütte'. With Puflatsch/Bullaccia and the Seiser Alm/Alpe di Siusi in view, follow the wide motor track very steeply downhill. About five minutes past the hut keep on Trail 527 as it turns right (**6**).

The trail snakes gently downhill. On your left lie the attractive Murmeltierhütte in the middle of lush alm meadows. To the right, above you, are the jagged eastern flanks of Plattkofel. Soon you cross a mountain stream and, 10 minutes later, keep on Trail N° 527 (where a left fork leads down to the Murmeltier-hütte.)

More and more mountain pine line the edge of the trail, and healthy junipers grow on both sides. At the next junction (**7**) keep to the upper trail (N° 527), to arrive at a knoll, **Piz da Uridl**, with benches offering a great lookout to Raschötz/Rasciesa, the Geisler/Odle group and the Puez massif.

Carrying on, the trail runs downhill in two steep curves, increasingly through open mixed conifers. About 20 minutes from the knoll you come to a grassy hollow, where cows graze in the summer.

Then you head uphill again,

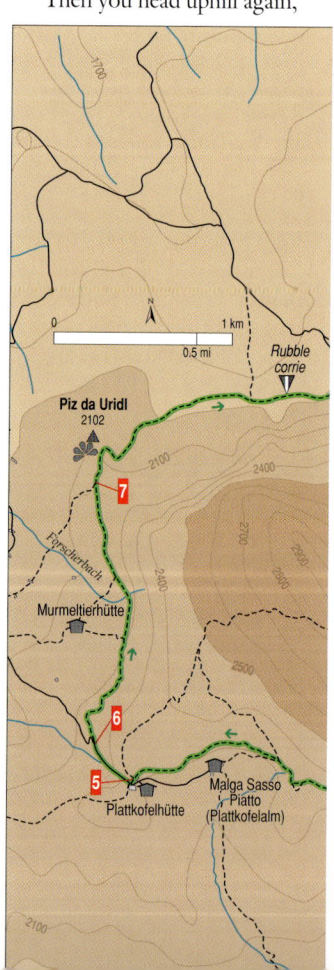

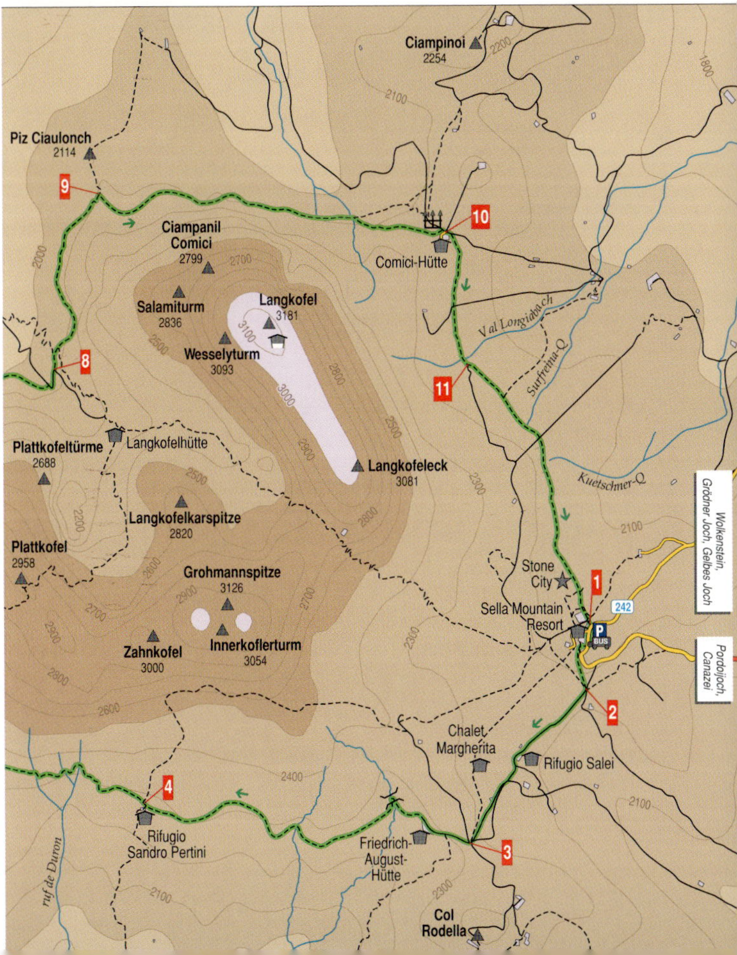

Map labels

- Ciampinoi 2254
- Piz Ciaulonch 2114
- Ciampanil Comici 2799
- Salamiturm 2836
- Langkofel 3181
- Wesselyturm 3093
- Comici-Hütte
- Val Lonziàch
- Surfreuta-Q.
- Plattkofeltürme 2688
- Langkofelhütte
- Langkofeleck 3081
- Kuetschmer-Q.
- Plattkofel 2958
- Langkofelkarspitze 2820
- Grohmannspitze 3126
- Stone City
- Sella Mountain Resort
- Zahnkofel 3000
- Innerkoflerturm 3054
- 242
- Wolkenstein, Grödner Joch, Gelbes Joch
- Pordoijoch, Canazei
- Chalet Margherita
- Rifugio Salei
- Ruf de Duron
- Rifugio Sandro Pertini
- Friedrich-August-Hütte
- Col Rodella

Waypoints: 1, 2, 3, 4, 8, 9, 10, 11

towards the Langkofel cirque. Crossing a wide rubble corrie you head for the entrance to the Langkofel cirque. After about 15 minutes, after a curve in the trail, you spot the Langkofel Hut for the first time, clinging daringly to the rock.

At the next junction take the scree-filled track (N° 527) uphill towards 'Langkofelhütte'. Shortly after, you come to another junction (**8**; **3h**). Now follow Trail N° 526 for 'Toni-Demetz-Hütte'. A few metres further on, a signpost showing the way to 'Sellajoch/Trail 526' shows you you're on the right route.

You traverse under a black-red rock wall and then walk through open larch woods and stands of dwarf pine. Soon you begin a 10-minute steep climb through karstic terrain, sometimes on steps. At the end of this, there's a cable-protected stretch of path. For those ***prone to vertigo***, this is a very tricky section demanding the utmost ***attention!***

At the end of the cable section there's a junction (**9**) with a signpost, benches, and a view to Plattkofel's northern wall and the Seiser Alm.

Following this, walk along Trail 526A towards 'Comici-Hütte' —

Walk 8: Circuit round Langkofel/Sassolungo

first through a wide-spread scree field and then uphill via several passages with huge boulders. Again and again you're forced to scramble over the smaller boulders. About 15 minutes from the junction the highest point is reached, then you go downhill for several metres on a cable-aided stretch.

At the foot of a black rock wall — you're now on the shady north side — you have to cross permanent snow — even in July! *Take care!* The path is narrow and skiddy. Again and again there are passages with overhanging rock, with water either dripping or streaming down on you. This really unpleasant section lasts for about 10 minutes.

When it finally ends, you go steeply uphill for about 15 minutes, through karstic grassy slopes and then through a field of debris, where cairns show you the way. It's a right old scramble and at this point in the hike really tough.

Right after a cattle gate the silhouette of the **Comici Hut** (**10**; **4h10min**) is in front of you. With its large wooden panorama terrace and the blue and white façade it looks fresh and modern. It's known for its Mediterranean cooking (!), but there's also delicious apple strudel.

A few metres north of the hut, follow signposting on Trail 526, heading south through a cattle gate and under two lifts. After a scree stream keep left at a fork (**11**) — where a right turn uphill is the more recent Panoramaweg Naturonda to the Steinerne Stadt followed in Walk 7). About 20 minutes later you come to the **Steinerne Stadt** ('Stone City'), a real fairyland of boulders and split rock with rhododendron and juniper, distorted mountain pines and dwarf pines. It's the result of a prehistoric rock fall from Langkofel.

The path snakes for about 10 minutes through the Steinerne Stadt, and then abruptly meets the large car park for the 2-person 'telephone box' cable cars to the Toni Demetz Hut (shown on pages 66-67) at the **Sella Mountain Resort** (**1**; **4h55min**).

Photo: the Plattkofel Hut/Rifugio di Sasso Piatto — a very popular goal for walkers

Walk 9: FROM SECEDA TO THE REGENSBURGER HUT/ RIFUGIO FIRENZE AND WOLKENSTEIN/SELVA

Distance/time: about 8.8km/ 5.5mi; 3h
Grade: ● straightforward mountain walk on mostly good tracks across alms; ascent of only 100m; descent 1000m
Waymarking: red/white; Trail N° 1 to **2**; N° 6 to **3**; Trail 1 again to **7**, then motor track to **8**, followed by Trail 3
Equipment: sturdy shoes, sun protection
Refreshments: Troier Hut (**4**), Regensburger Hut/Rifugio Firenze (**7**), Juac Hut (**9**)

Walking map: Tabacco 05, Val Gardena-Alpe di Siusi/Gröden-Seiseralm, 1:25,000
Transport: 🚗 free car parking near the main through road in St. Ulrich or at the valley station of the Seceda cable car (46° 34.681'N, 11° 40.336'E). 🚐 350 from Bolzano runs about every half hour to St Ulrich. The last 🚐 350 (via Waidbruck) leaves at 19.31. The Seceda cable car (25.50 € one way, 35 € return) operates from mid-June to early October.

Up on Seceda your heart beats faster — if only from the sight of the massive scree-slopes ahead, falling from the mountain down to the west. Fantastic views await you up here — the Geisler/Odle peaks, Puez group and across alms to Sella and Langkofel/Sassolungo.

Start out at the **top lift station on Seceda** (**1**): walk straight ahead on a path (Trail 1); then, at a fork (**2**), go left on Trail 6, a slightly descending route signed to the 'Panascharte'. You head towards Sass Rigais and the Geisler/Odle peaks. At the narrow pass, the **Panascharte/Forcella Pana** (**3**) there is a vertiginous view down to the north side of the Geisler/Odle peaks, but almost nothing to be seen of the Villnösstal/Val di Funes.

From here go right and down the slope, ignoring any turn-offs to the right or left. Back on Trail 1, you pass the **Troier Hut** (**4**) and go more or less straight ahead (still on Trail 1), keeping straight ahead at a crossroads (**5**). Drop gently and then — beyond a **fence** (**6**) more steeply to the much-loved **Regensburger Hut/ Rifugio Firenze** (**7**; 1h15min).

Follow the access track (Trails 1 and 3) downhill for about 20

Walk 9: From Seceda to the Regensburger Hut and Wolkenstein   75

minutes, then go left on Trail 3 (**8**). From the shoulder near the **Juac Hut** (**9**) you can see Wolkenstein/Selva below. Keep on Trail 3, crossing an asphalt road.

Meeting the road again in the hamlet of **Daunei**, go right for just 30m, then turn left downhill towards Wolkenstein (**10**). Follow the road to a lane on the left with Trail 3 signs (**11**). Head down the lane, to a crossroads: turn left for 80m, then follow the sign 'Puez' to the right. Once in **Wolkenstein/Selva** (**3h**), use the plan on page 44 to get to the **bus stop** (**12**) on the main SS242 in the centre.

Starting out from Seceda, with a view to the Geisler/Odle peaks

Walk 10: FROM THE GRÖDNER JOCH/PASSO DI GARDENA TO THE PORDOIJOCH/PASSO PORDOI VIA THE SELLA MASSIF

Distance/time: about 10.6km/ 6.6mi; 5h20min
Grade: ●❗ strenuous, with an ascent of 1160m/3805ft and descent of 1040m/3410ft. A high alpine tour par excellence; you must be sure-footed and have a head for heights. Good physical condition and mountain experience are required; reliably good weather is an absolute prerequisite! If you want to shorten the hike from **11**, keep an eye on the operating times of the Sass Pordoi cable car (end May to Oct 09.00-17.00, 12 € one way, 20 € up and back).
Waymarking: red/white; Trail 666 to **9**; then Trail 627 to the end
Equipment: hiking boots, sun protection, walking pole(s)
Refreshments: At the start is the Rifugio Frara (**1**; see 'Tip' below). En route you pass the Pisciadù Hut (**4**; with spring), the Boè Hut (Bamberger hut; **9**) and the Rifugio Forcella del Pordoi (**11**). So you don't need to carry a lot of food, but do take enough water with you!
Walking map: Tabacco 05, Val Gardena-Alpe di Siusi/Gröden-Seiseralm, 1:25,000
Transport: 🚗 free car parking at the Grödner Joch at Rifugio Frara (**1**; 46° 32.981'N, 11° 48.553'E), where 🚐 471 also stops (see 'Dolomitenpässe' on page 93 under 'Transport'). From the Pordoi Joch (**13**) 🚐 471 goes to Arabba and Corvara. The journey takes about 70 minutes and costs 12 € (last bus at 17.30). The 471 bus only runs between Jun and mid-Sep!

This grandiose high-alpine tour leads from the Grödner/Gardena Pass to the Pordoi Pass. It crosses a stone desert over 2800m high on narrow slopes with incomparable views of the surrounding mountain ranges. There are some cable-secured passages ... and a steep, knee-crunching final descent. This hike calls for extensive mountain experience and a head for heights!

The hike begins at the small **car park** (**1**) at the Rifugio Frara (below the hut there is a larger car park for hikers, from which a cross-

Tip: *In order to save the morning bus trip on this long hike and catch the bus at the Pordoi Joch in good time, it is worth spending the night at the Rifugio Frara on the Grödner Joch; see www.rifugiofrara.it*

path leads to the ascent path). Follow the signpost towards the 'Boèhütte/Pisciadù-Hütte', taking Trail N° 666 (also Dolomites High Route 2) uphill towards the peaks of Sas dla Luesa and Camp Campidel, towering over you. A little later the trail climbs very steeply via several hairpin bends up a grassy ridge, then across a scree field. In the north are the Cir peaks and the Sass da Ciampàc.

You hike towards a wide rubble cirque that streams down from the rock walls. At its edge you reach a fork (**2**; **35min**) and now see a narrow gorge opening between the rock faces. Continue uphill on Trail 666; almost five minutes later, at another fork, again keep uphill and follow the path in sharp bends through loose scree.

Walk 10: From the Grödner Joch to the Pordoi Joch 77

To help with orientation, there's a stone marked in red and white every few metres at the edge of the path. You feel really tiny between these vertical rock walls. After about 30 minutes of steep ascent, you reach a ledge on the right edge of the cirque and the start of the first **protective cables** (**3**).

For a few metres the trail rises steeply on the right-hand edge of the narrowing cirque. Then the path leads into the cirque and zigzags towards a black rock face dripping with water.

After the wall and a good 10 minutes after the first protective cable, a longer passage begins with cable protection and iron steps: these lead upwards almost vertically, but they are not technically difficult. After that there's a section zigzagging over jagged plates. Five minutes later, you're standing abruptly at the edge of a high plateau!

The view behind you is just as breathtaking as the one ahead — to the rock face of the Pisciadù peak in the south and the surrounding mountain ranges. A good five minutes later, having crossed a scree desert, you reach the **Pisciadù Hut** (**4**; 1h35min). It's picturesquely sited in the middle of the stony landscape and is an impressive first stop for refreshments. At the **spring** a few metres to the west, you can fill up your water bottles.

Following a wide scree path a little below the hut, you come to the (protected) lake shown on page 81, **Lech de Pisciadù**. It's a picturesque body of water in early summer, but quite a sad, shallow puddle in autumn. You cross its northern drain on a boardwalk. Continuing on, your trail leads south through scree below the mighty west face of Pisciadù.

Another cable-protected section begins about 15 minutes past the hut. It leads through rugged rock for about 10 minutes. Then it's back on a narrow path through scree.

You come across a signpost (**5**)

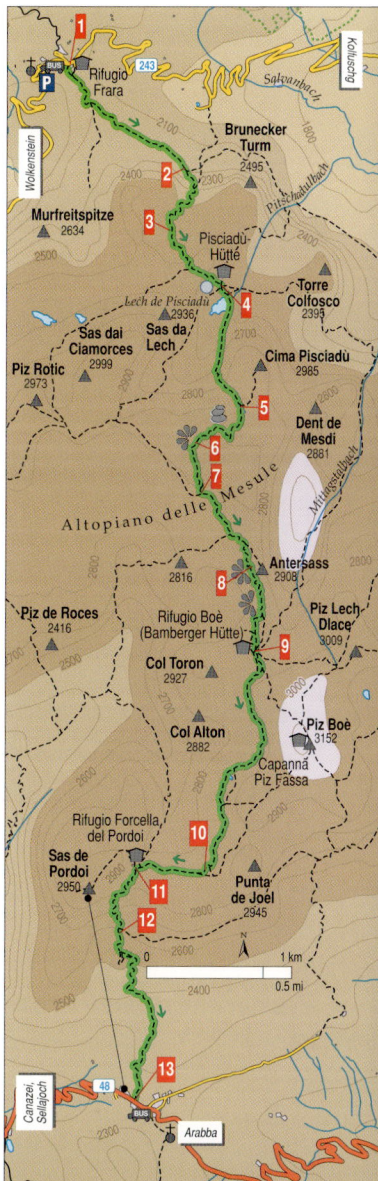

Above: the steep descent to the Pordoi Pass; left: good waymarking helps in the 'rock desert'

on a small plateau. Here your path N° 666 continues uphill towards the 'Boè-Hütte' (to the north there is another path to the Pisciadù peak). About 10 minutes after the signpost, the trail squeezes through a narrow crevice, and soon afterwards you reach a small **plateau with cairns**. After another 10 minutes ascent in hairpin bends, you come to another plateau, which represents the highest point (**6**; **2h30min**) of the surrounding landscape. There's pile of stones here, and a marker pole.

What a panorama! The karst plateau, Altopiano delle Mesules, spreads out in the west and south-west, endlessly barren (the reason why Sella is often characterised as a 'lunar landscape'. In the south, the massive Boè peak towers up, with its ugly reflector sign and hut glued to the rock; the mountain station of the cable car from the Pordoi Joch is clearly visible on Sass Pordoi.

Here you are at 2955m and, even in summer, there is usually a

Walk 10: From the Grödner Joch to the Pordoi Joch 79

cool wind blowing. Trail N° 649 now leads you downhill in a south-easterly direction through loose scree. About 10 minutes later, at a junction (**7**), keep on Trail 649 to the Mesules plateau. A few metres further on, the path is also marked N° 666! Both are correct, so don't be confused and just keep going downhill.

After a short descent you reach a signpost with cairns on a plateau. This is the narrow pass, the **Forcella d'Antersass**. For about 100m follow Trail 647 (which is also Trail 666) towards 'Antersass/ Boèhütte' and come to another junction. Here, stay on Trail 666 in the direction of 'Antersass' and do *not* take the path leading south below Antersass.

Climb in steep hairpins for about 15 minutes to the 2908m-high **Antersass** (**8**), where you reach a summit plateau with a Tibetan prayer flag. It's a good idea to walk a few metres northeast from the summit. Suddenly you stand at the abyss of the magnificent Val de Mesdi, which stretches for several kilometres to the edge of the Sella massif.

After a 10-minute descent from Antersass, follow Trail 647 towards the 'Boèhütte' at a fork. It first leads you briefly to the eastern edge of the upper Val Lasties and then over some rocky steps in about 10 minutes to the **Boè Hut** (**9**; also called **Bamberger Hut**), which is sheltered on a plateau. Another spectacular resting place!

From the hut keep on Trail 627/638 for about five minutes in the direction of 'Passo Pordoi/Piz Boè' until you come to the fork left to the Boè peak. Keep right here, on Trail 627. About 30 minutes past the fork there is another passage with cable protection, and shortly afterwards you reach a fork on a high plateau (**10**). From here Trail 627 leads you to the right, towards Sass Pordoi. On your right is a valley, the Valon de Fos, which flows north into the mighty Val Lasties.

A good 10 minutes after the fork, you suddenly reach the saddle with the **Forcella del Pordoi Hut** (**11**; **4h15min**). (If you want to call it a day here, you could climb Trail 627a to the mountain station of the cable car in about 15 minutes.)

The main walk keeps to Trail 627 at the hut, which looks as if it drops vertically between steep rock faces to the Pordoi Joch. It actually descends for about 20 minutes via extremely steep zigzags through a rubble field — **you should never dare this descent without walking poles!** At a fork (**12**) stay on Trail 627 to 'Passo Pordoi', soon descending poorly marked tracks covered with scree and stones. Below you can already see the large car park and houses on the Pordoi Joch. The impressively glaciated northern flank of the Marmolada glistens above it.

Some 20 minutes past the fork you're on a small high plateau littered with rocks. Your trail, now stabilised, leads through meadows towards the Pordoi Joch. About 15 minutes after the plateau, you finally reach the Pordoi Joch road (SS48; **13**; **5h20min**) via wooden steps — precisely at the bronze memorial to the legendary racing cyclist Fausto Coppi and only a few metres from the valley station of the cable car.

Walk 11: PISCIADÙ HUT AND LAKE

Distance/time: about 5.6 km/ 3.5mi; 3h10min
Grade: ●❗ strenuous, with an ascent/descent of 500m/1640ft. You must be sure-footed and have a head for heights. There are protective cables on some steep sections, where inexperienced walkers may cause hold-ups.
Waymarking: red/white; Trail 666 throughout
Equipment: hiking boots, sun protection, walking pole(s)
Refreshments: available at the Rifugio Frara (**1**; overnight stays are also possible here; see 'Tip' on page 76) and the Pisciadù Hut (**4**; with spring).
Walking map: Tabacco 05, Val Gardena-Alpe di Siusi/Gröden-Seiseralm, 1:25,000
Transport: 🚗 free car parking at the Grödner Joch at Rifugio Frara (**1**; 46° 32.981'N, 11° 48.553'E), where 🚐 471 also stops (see 'Dolomitenpässe' under 'Transport' on page 93). The 471 bus only runs between Jun and mid-Sep!

This hike covers the same ground as the start of Walks 10 and 12, but I've increased the timings by about 30 per cent for less experienced walkers. Anyone steady on their feet and well shod should enjoy this hike.

The hike begins at the small **car park** (**1**) at the Rifugio Frara (below the hut there is a larger car park for hikers, from which a crosspath leads to the ascent path). Follow the signpost towards the 'Boèhütte/Pisciadù-Hütte', taking Trail N° 666 (also Dolomites High Route 2) uphill towards the peaks of Sas dla Luesa and Camp Campidel, towering over you. A little later the trail climbs very steeply via several hairpin bends up a grassy ridge, then across a scree stream. In the north are the Cir peaks and the Sass da Ciampàc.

You hike towards a wide rubble cirque that streams down from the rock walls. At its edge you reach a fork (**2**; **45min**) and now see a narrow gorge opening between the rock faces. Continue uphill on Trail 666; almost five minutes later, at another fork, again keep uphill and follow the path in sharp bends through loose scree.

To help with orientation, there's a stone marked in red and white every few metres at the edge of the path. You feel really tiny between these vertical rock walls. After about 30 minutes of steep ascent, you reach a ledge on the right edge of the cirque and the start of the first **protective cables** (**3**). Inexperienced walkers are likely to cause hold-ups here.

For a few metres the trail rises steeply on the right-hand edge of the narrowing cirque. Then the path leads into the cirque and zigzags towards a black rock face dripping with water.

After this wall, and a good 10

Walk 11: Pisciadù Hut and Lake

Lake Pisciadù and Cima Pisciadù. Snow stays on these heights into summer.

minutes after the first protective cable, a longer passage begins with cable protection and iron steps: these lead upwards almost vertically, but they are not technically difficult. After that there's a section zigzagging over jagged plates. Five minutes later, you're standing abruptly at the edge of a high plateau!

The view behind you is just as breathtaking as the one ahead — to the rock face of the Pisciadù peak in the south and the surrounding mountain ranges. A good five minutes later, having crossed a scree desert, you reach the **Pisciadù Hut** (**4**; **2h**). It's picturesquely sited in the middle of the stony landscape and is an impressive stop for refreshments. At the **spring** a few metres to the west, you can fill up your water bottles.

After taking a closer look at the lake, return the same way. For beginning walkers, the descent may be more difficult than the climb, so have patience on the return to the car park at the **Rifugio Frara** (**1**; **4h**).

Walk 12: TWO-DAY HIKE FROM THE GRÖDNER JOCH/ PASSO DI GARDENA TO PIZ BOÈ AND THE BOÈ LIFT

Distance/time: about 11.7km/ 7.3mi; 6h30min-8h
Grade: ●❗ strenuous, with an ascent of 1200m/3935ft and descent of 1150m/3770ft. Like Walk 10, this is another high alpine tour *par excellence*; you must be sure-footed and have a head for heights. Good physical condition and mountain experience are required; reliably good weather is an absolute prerequisite!
Waymarking: red/white; Trail 666 to **8**; Trail 672 to **10**; Trail 638 to the Boè lift at the end
Equipment: hiking boots, sun protection, walking pole(s)
Refreshments/overnight stay: Pisciadù Hut/Rifugio Cavazza (**3**), Rifugio Boè (**6**; www.rifugioboe.it), Capanna Piz Fassa (**7**; www.rifugiocapannafassa.it), Rifugio Franz Kostner (**10**; www.rifugiokostner.it), Piz Boè Alpine Lounge, by the upper lift station, very modern, with lots of glass and wood — ideal for après-ski (**11**; www.boealpinelounge.it)
Walking map: Tabacco 05, Val Gardena-Alpe di Siusi/Gröden-Seiseralm, 1:25,000
Transport: 🚗 free car parking at the Grödner Joch at Rifugio Frara (**1**; 46° 32.981'N, 11° 48.553'E), where 🚌471 also stops (see 'Dolomitenpässe' on page 93 under 'Transport'). 🚌471 goes back from Corvara to the Grödner Joch (last bus at 17.30). The 471 bus only runs Jun to mid-Sep!

This walk is even more strenuous than Walk 10, which is why I recommend an overnight stay — in fact *two* overnight stays, if you take up the 'Tip' on page 76 and spend

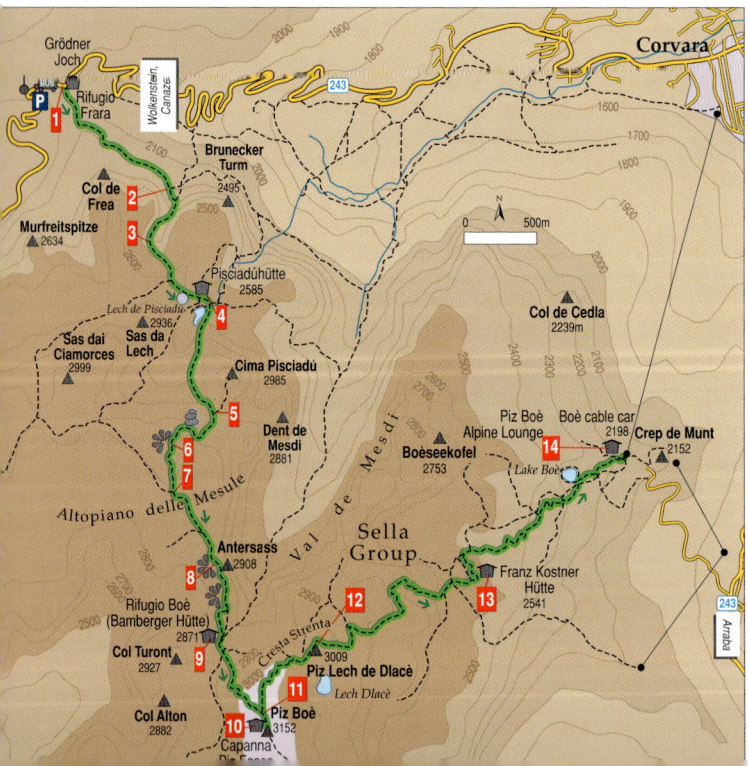

Walk 12: Two-day hike from the Grödner Joch to Piz Boè

the night before the hike at the Rifugio Frara. Although the walk is fairly tough and requires cable protection in several sections, it does not involve any *via ferrata* routes.

Start out by following **Walk 10** on page 76 to the **Boè Hut** (**9**; **3h30min-4h**). Behind it there is another steep ascent, scree, a rock ledge with cable protection; finally a fairly easy clamber over boulders and you're on **Piz Boè** with its hut, **Capanna Piz Fassa** (**10**; **4h45min-5h**).

The ongoing route runs a short way back over the ridge, until you can head right on Trail 672 (**11**) via the **Cresta Strenta**, another exposed path again protected with cables.

This takes you to the Eisseespitze (**Piz Lech Dlacè** in Ladin; **12**), below which you can see the glimmering ice lake, Eissee (**Lech Dlacè**). The way continues over easy slopes down to a large terrace before entering a narrow rock valley (more protective cables). Turn left at the bottom of the valley and you'll come to the **Franz Kostner Hut** on a low hill (**13**; **5h45min-6h**).

Signposts at the hut point the way to the end of the walk — **Crep de Munt** and the Boè cable car. En route you pass pretty **Lake Boè** before skirting the Vallon lift station and coming to the **upper station** of the **Boè cable car** and the swish **Piz Boè Alpine Lounge** (**14**; **6h30min-8h**).

Near the Boè Hut: view from the secured trail down into the Val de Mesdi (Walks 10 and 12)

Walk 13: FROM THE GRÖDNER JOCH/PASSO GARDENA THROUGH THE LANGENTAL/VALLUNGA

Distance/time: about 14.8km/ 9.2mi; 5h30min
Grade: ●● strenuous and long, with an ascent of 930m/3050ft and descent of 1175m/3850ft; some steep passages; mainly on narrow paths. You must be sure-footed and fit, with a head for heights. Full sun, except for the very final stretch in the Langental/Vallunga
Waymarking: red/white; Trail N° 2 to **9**; N° 16 to **10**; then Trail 14 to the end
Equipment: hiking boots, sun protection, walking pole(s)
Refreshments: available at the Dantercepies Mountain Lounge (**1**), Jimmi Hut (**2**), Puez Hut (**8**, where there is also a tap) and at the Bar La Ciajota (**11**). There is a spring at **6** and several in the Langental. But for the long stretch to the Puez Hut, you definitely need provisions and enough to drink!
Walking map: Tabacco 05, Val Gardena-Alpe di Siusi/Gröden-Seiseralm, 1:25,000
Transport: 🚗 From Selva, follow signs for the Dantercepies cable car, where there is a paid car park (46° 33.354'N, 11° 46.034'E). 🚌 350 connects Bolzano with Wolkenstein/Selva approximately every half an hour (alight at the 'Nivesplatz' stop). From Nives Platz take 🚌 357 to the Dantercepies cable car (or walk there in a good 25 minutes on Trail 14). Last 🚌 357 back to the centre at 18.04, and from there last 🚌 350 at 19.07 (with a change). The Dantercepies cable car runs from mid-Jun to the end of Sep (one way 13.50 €).

This high alpine hike leads past the rugged Cir peaks and over the rocky Gardenaccia plateau to the Puez Hut, with spectacular panoramic views all along. From the hut you descend steeply into a textbook example of a trough valley, the U-shaped Langental/Vallunga.

The hike starts at **Dantercepies Mountain Lounge** (**1**): follow the sign for 'Puez Hütte', heading northwest. What a panorama right at the start! The steep Cir peaks to the left above you, mighty Langkofel/Sassolungo in the south, and the Sella massif in front of you. A good 10 minutes after

View to the Seiser Alm/Alpe di Siusi from the Puez high plateau: Schlern/Sciliar and the Santner peaks are prominent in the distance.

Walk 13: From the Grödner Joch through the Langental 85

starting out, the scree-strewn path brings you up to the **Jimmi Hut** (**2**), with its panoramic terrace, children's playground and a large trampoline.

About 50m east of the hut, a steep path leads you up to a sign (Trail N° 2, 'Puez Hütte'). First you climb through dwarf mountain pines; you cross a wide rubble cirque and then hike through karstic terrain. After that a section begins with steep log-supported hairpins, for which you need about 10 minutes. At the top you reach a lunar landscape strewn with rock debris, which you can cross like a latter-day Neil Armstrong.

At a narrow pass (**3**) a wide depression stretches out in front of you, littered with boulders of every size and shape; some imposing rock needles protrude into the sky. About 15 minutes later, at the far end of the basin, you come to the **Cirjoch** (**4**). Your view opens onto the spectacular Chedul Valley. Littered with rubble, it is bordered in the north by vertical cliffs with Mont de Sëura as the highest point.

Continue on Trail 2 towards the Puez Hut. After climbing for 15 minutes over wide scree slopes, you reach the upper end of the Chedul Valley, the **Crespëina Pass** (**5**; **1h30min**). A fence and a cross mark the point. In front of you, the rugged karst of the Puez plateau extends to the horizon, with the summit of Sass da Ciampàc in the southeast and the striking cone of Col dala Sonè — a panorama reminiscent of Iceland. The trail then takes you via wide bends across a scree field. The ongoing route to the Puez Hut is easy to see. Deep green **Lech de Crespëina** shimmers below you.

Several small tributaries combine to form a stream that meanders into the lake. About 20 minutes after the pass you reach one of these tributaries, which takes its source just above your path at a boulder (**6**).

About 30 minutes after the boulder you come to the wind-blown **Ciampëi Pass** (**7**; **2h20min**). West from here leads into the Langental/Vallunga, east down to the Gadertal/Val Badia. But you head north, following the trail further in the direction of the Puez Hut: first via a steep ascent through a scree cirque, then through karst and rock at the edge edge of the slope down into the Langental.

About 25 minutes from the pass, at a fork, follow a final sign to the **Puez Hut** (**8**). On its sun terrace, you can enjoy a hearty lunch with a view of the Gardenaccia plateau, Sass da Ciampàc, Sass Songher, the Sella group and, in the north, the mighty upthrusts of Col de Puez and the east and west Puez peaks.

Fill up your water containers at the tap on the west side of the hut. Then, at the sign, follow Trail 2 ('Langental, Wolkenstein') in a southwesterly direction. With breathtaking views of the meadows of **Prà da Ri** below, follow the trail along the edge of the Langental. Towards the valley exit, the trough-shaped bulge between the rock faces is easy to see — a typical example of a valley formed by glaciers.

Almost 20 minutes after the Puez Hut, the path swings north towards the rubble-covered southern flank of **Puez**. You're walking into a wide karstic alpine pasture where sheep graze in summer ... idyllic, but wild! Then you come to a fork (**9**; **3h30min**) and follow Trail 16 towards 'Langental', soon descending steeply in switchbacks.

After 30 minutes, the trail turns into a meadow path and soon meets a gate. From here the trail descends again on gravelly ground. The valley floor is seen over and again through the trees; the sound of cowbells rises on the wind.

About 15 minutes from the

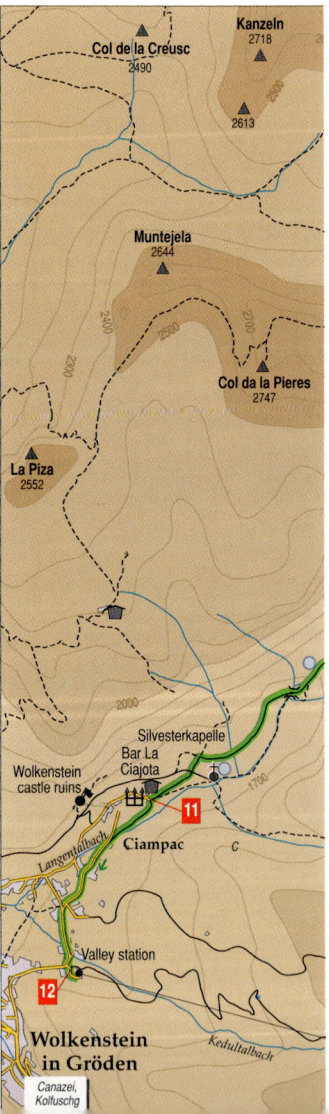

Walk 13: From the Grödner Joch through the Langental 87

gate you cross a (dry) stream bed and 10 minutes later meet a signpost (**10**; **4h30min**). Having reached the bottom of the valley, your knees are thanking you. Trail 14 now leads you right, out of the valley, on a forest track between rugged field walls, with several springs along the way. In about 45 minutes you come to a car park at the bar **La Ciajota** (**11**). (The **Silvester Chapel** a few metres before the car park is worth a short stop.)

From the car park follow the wide gravel motor track (still Trail 14) towards Wolkenstein and pass a Carabinieri station and Baita Ciampàc, then you're on asphalt. About 15 minutes past the bar, you join Streda Dantercepies. Keep left and after a few metres you're at the **valley station** of the **Dantercepies cable car** (**12**; **5h30min**).

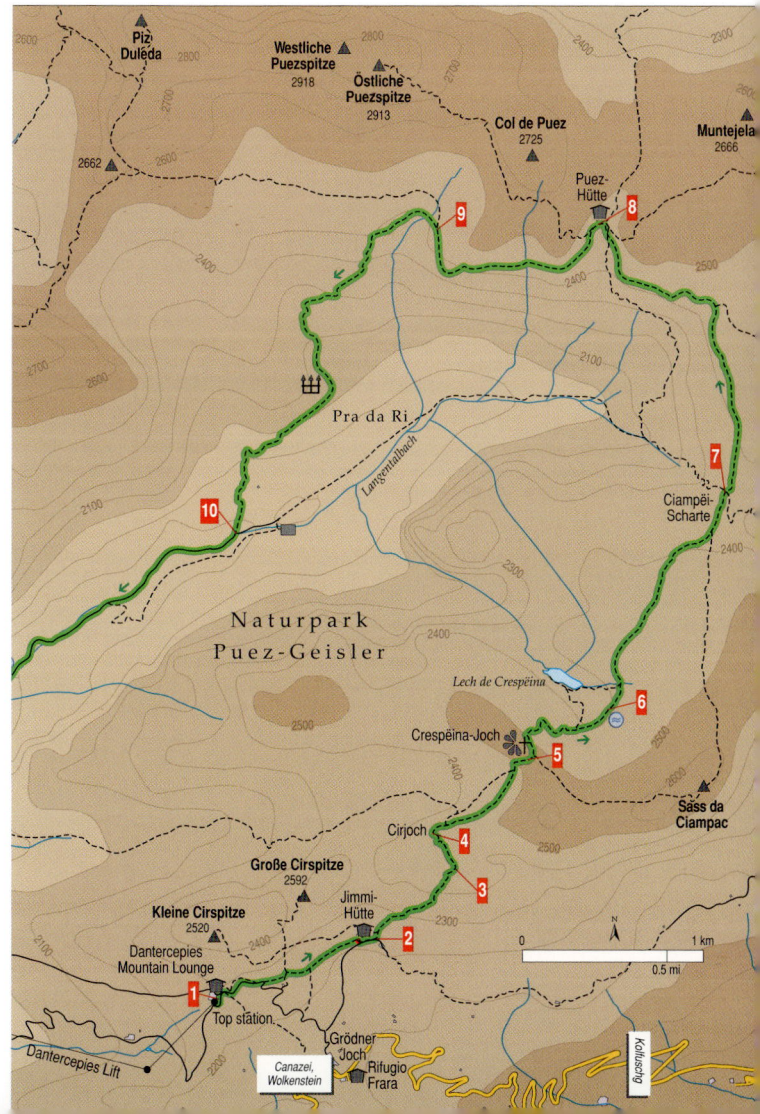

The Puez Hut in its grandiose surroundings

Puez — **treasure chest of paleontologists**

As early as the 19th century, isolated fossils were found on the Puez plateau, especially ammonites — fossilised molluscs from the cephalopod group which look a bit like fossilised snail shells and existed until the end of the Cretaceous Period (about 66 million years ago).

In 2008, a research project led by the Austrian paleontologist Alexander Lukeneder presented an incredible variety of fossils dating from different epochs of the Cretaceous Period — a wide range of species and shapes.

The wide Puez plateau is an especially good source of paleontological findings for researchers. Even hikers can come across fossil remains here — for instance, cross-sections of shells can often be found in the rock. Of course, you are not permitted to take any finds away! Selected examples of the Lukeneder's research are shown in exhibits at the South Tyrolean Museum of Nature in Bolzano and in Vienna's Natural History Museum.

Walk 14: CIRCUIT ON THE SEISER ALM/ALPE DI SIUSI FROM MONT SËUC

Distance/time: about 10.5km/ 6.5mi; 2h45min
Grade: ● moderate, with an ascent/descent of 430m/1410ft on alm paths and tracks without steep passages; mostly in sun
Waymarking: red/white; Trail N° 6A from **1** to **3**; N° 6 to **4**; N° 30 to **6**; N° 6 to **9**; then Trail 9 to the end
Equipment: hiking boots, sun protection, walking pole(s)
Refreshments: available at Mont Sëuc (**1**), at the Contrin Schwaige (**2**), Ritsch Schwaige (after **3**), Hotel Saltria (after **6**), and the Schgaguler Schwaige (**9**). This last is a small alpine dairy hut with not only a petting zoo, but also hearty South Tyrolean cuisine prepared with the farm's own products. Among other things, there is an excellent young alpine cheese. Since it is a ski area, all these alpine huts are also open in winter. If you're out to sample alm cooking, you'll be busy all day!
Walking map: Tabacco 05, Val Gardena-Alpe di Siusi/Gröden-Seiseralm, 1:25,000
Transport: 🚗 park at the valley station of the Mont Sëuc cable car in St Ulrich/Ortisei (also called the Seiser Alm/Alpe di Siusi cable car; 46° 34.381'N, 11° 40.235'E). 🚐 350 runs approximately every hour from Brixen/Bressanone to St Ulrich (alight at the 'Antoniusplatz' stop). From there it's only a five-minute walk to the valley station. Last 🚐 350 back at 19.31. The cable car runs from mid-May to early Nov (one way 14.50 €, up and back 20.50 €).

This circular hike opens up the Seiser Alm/Alpe di Siusi from the north, giving the walker a complete panorama from Schlern/Sciliar to Platt- and Langkofel/Sassopiatto and -lungo ... via the Rosszähne/Denti di Terrarossa — backed by the Rosengarten massif! From Mont Sëuc, the trail first heads down into the heart of the alpine pastures and back via Saltria on a long, leisurely final climb through lush meadows.

The hike starts at the **benches** (**1**) in front of the mountain station of the cable car. First descend the pavement, heading west in the direction of 'Contrin Schwaige', then follow the trail through light mixed conifers. After a crossing a cable car route, you hike through wide alpine pastures. In early summer, these meadows are a sea of yellow and orange blossoms. When you come to a junction (**2**; **20min**) it's worth a detour of a few metres up to the idyllic dairy hut, the **Contrin Schwaige/Malga Contrin** — just because of its panoramic location.

Before long the trail crosses another cable car route. About 10 minutes after the dairy it joins a tarred motor track (**3**). Follow this to the right in the direction of 'Ritsch Schwaige' and 'Hotel Icaro', ignoring the right turn to the hotel a little later and keeping on the trail towards 'Ritsch Schwaige'.

After about 15 minutes of gentle descent, your trail joins the **road between Compatsch and Saltria**. Turn left towards 'Saltria' and reach the **Ritsch Schwaige** about 250m further on.

Once past the dairy hut, follow Trail N° 6 for the next five minutes, going slightly uphill

The blooms of early summer on the Seiser Alm/Alpe di Siusi, where there's plenty of room for horses on the wide alm pastures

through alpine meadows. Then, before a lane, turn left on Trail 30 for 'Rauchhütte' and 'Saltria' (**4**; **55min**). Passing magnificent larches, a little later you reach a bench with a particularly beautiful view of Platt- and Langkofel/ Sassopiatto and -lungo. Shortly afterwards you come to a bend in the Compatsch–Saltria road. Keep right here on a meadow path (**5**) signposted to 'Saltria'.

The trail goes downhill through flower-filled, moist meadows. Soon you cross a small stream and then carry on downhill for a good 10 minutes, until you reach the banks of the **Jenderbach**. Here the path joins a wide motor track (**6**), which merges with the Compatsch-Saltria road after a few metres. It takes you to the **Hotel Saltria** in five minutes.

Immediately in front of the hotel terrace, turn right on a narrow path (Trail 6, signposted to the 'Schgaguler Schwaige') and head towards the Hotel Brunelle. Shortly before the sunbathing lawn of the Hotel Brunelle, at a junction (**7**; **1h35min**), turn left on the trail.

The path initially leads through meadows, past small alpine huts. After a mixed conifer wood, open alpine pastures follow. About 25 minutes after turning left, you cross a lane (**8**) and continue for about 25 minutes on Trail 6 to the **Hotel Sonne** (**9**; **2h25min**).

Some 200m past the hotel the trail meets a crossing motor track. Turn right here, to take an detour to the lovely **Schgaguler Schwaige** on the right. Then it's a 15-minute walk through light conifers up to the **Mont Sëuc mountain station** (**1**; **2h45min**).

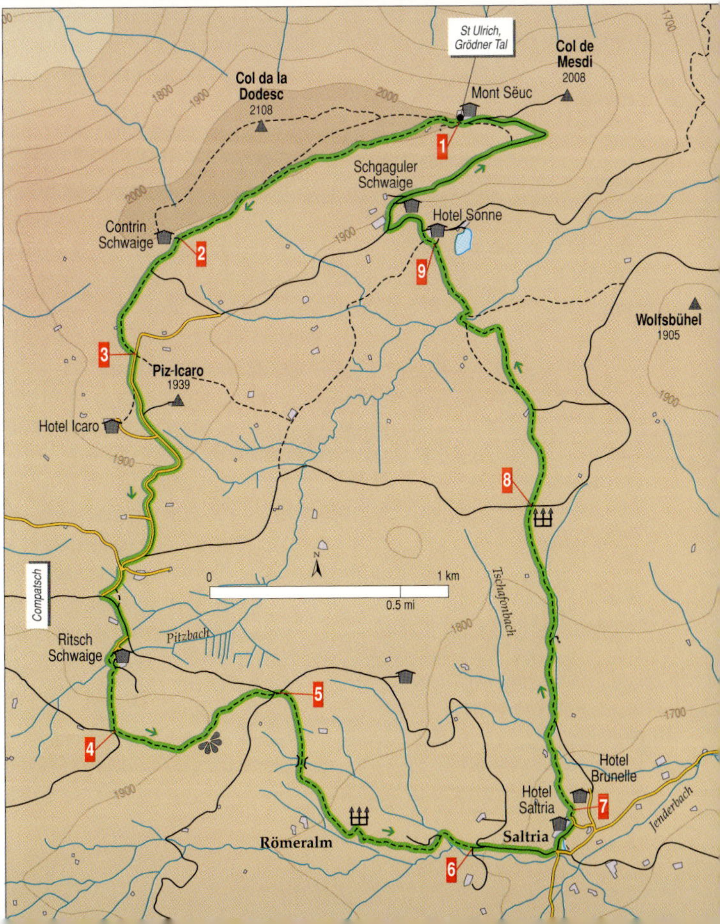

St Ulrich, Grödner Tal
Col de Mesdi
2008
Col da la Dodesc
2108
Mont Sëuc
Schgaguler Schwaige
Hotel Sonne
Contrin Schwaige
Piz-Icaro
1939
Hotel Icaro
Wolfsbühel
1905
Compatsch
Ritsch Schwaige
Pitzbach
Tschafonbach
Römeralm
Saltria
Hotel Saltria
Hotel Brunelle
Jenderbach
0
1 km
0.5 mi
1
2
3
4
5
6
7
8
9
1800
1900
2000
1700

2 GADERTAL/VAL BADIA

Hochabteital • Corvara • Kolfuschg • Sella group • Puez group • Stern • St Kassian • middle Gadertal • Abtei • Wengen • St Martin in Thurn • Campilltal and the Val di Morins • Enneberg • Fanes-Sennes-Prags Nature Park

Walks: 15-21; *cycling tips:* from St Martin towards Brixen/Bressanone (page 99); Fanes and Sennes by mountain bike (page 102)

Website
www.altabadia.org
Opening hours: see individual attractions

The Gadertal/Val Badia stretches for more than 30km from the Pustertal/Val Pusteria at Bruneck/Brunico to the foot of the massive Sella group. Although it is one of the most intensely touristic valleys in the Dolomites, it is one of the least affected by tourism.

If you're staying in the shadow of the mighty Sella massif in the upper valley (Hochabteital/Alta Badia) — for instance at Corvara, Kolfuschg/Colfosco, Stern/La Villa or St Kassian/San Cassiano — you'll notice that despite the glorious nature all around, many *viles* (as the Ladins call their narrowly built hamlets) give the impression of being locked in a time-warp. The Hochabteital attracts masses of mountain climbers and walkers with its many hotels and *pensions,* as well as dozens of alm huts. In contrast, the hamlets of Pedratsches/Pedraces, St Leonhard/S Leonardo and St Martin/San Martino in the lower valley are hardly visited. The valley is greener here, wider and more plentiful than further up. The Enneberg/Marebbe area, the third landscape of the Gadertal, borders Bruneck and Kronplatz/Plan de Corones — the German-speaking areas. St Vigil/San Vigilio, its main village, grew very quickly and is a bustling tourist centre, but the *viles* on the sunny terrace above it still live from agriculture.

The Gadertal (including all its tributary valleys) is often called the Abteital in German. The Italian (and also the Ladin) name, Val Badia, means exactly the same thing: both translate to Valley of the Abbey. In the Middle Ages and in early modern times the whole valley (except for the area of St Martin in Thurn and Kolfuschg) belonged to the Sonnenburg Nunnery in the Pustertal/Val Pusteria (described in Book 1).

Hochabteital/Alta Badia

When you descend the hairpins from the Grödner Joch/Passo Gardena, the basin of Kolfuschg/Colfosco and Corvara between the Puez group with mighty Sass Songher and the precipitous rock walls of the Sella group looks like a green paradise. But it's a paradise in which there has been a lot of building in recent years; you have to look hard to find the old farmhouses clustered around the church at Kolfuschg. The quality

Gadertal/Val Badia

of the accommodation is high, and so are the prices — Kolfuschg and Corvara advertise on quality, not on price. It's the same story in Stern/La Villa (Ladin: La Ila), a bit further down the valley, and in St Kassian/San Cassiano in its own friendly valley. Obviously there are many restaurants to cater for all the hotels and *pensions*.

There are also **walking trails** wherever you look: walks through meadows at the foot of Sella, walks on the alms of Piz la Ila and Pralongià in the east, walks in the Fanes group to the lovely Fanesalm and from there perhaps even further on Dolomites High Route 1. Then there are high-mountain routes in the Sella and Puez massifs, climbing routes like the difficult 'Pisciadù' *via ferrata*, and in winter all kinds of lifts and ski trails — including the Ski World Cup's famous Gran Risa black piste, on which the great Alberto Tomba celebrated his retirement.

Transport: When visiting the valley you can **park** by the lift stations (for instance at Corvara and Kolfuschg). **SAD buses** link the valley villages with each other and up to 14 times a day with Bruneck, but connections to the west (Gröden/Val Gardena) and south (Buchenstein/Pieve di Livinallongo) are poor. Instead there is the **'Dolomitenpässe' bus 471** service (summer only) which rounds the Sella group in both directions several times a day.

The **Alta Badia Summer Card** gives free travel on all the above buses and lifts; passes are available for 3 out of 4 days (56 €), 5 out of 7 days (72 €) and 12 out of 14 days (128 €). There is also the **Dolomiti SuperSummer Card**: see panel on page 22.

Corvara is dominated by Sass Songher

Corvara

You'll get the best overall impression of Corvara in the upper part of the village, where the **Streda Col Alt** describes a curve to gain height. You look through the whole new town and up to the slopes of Pescosta, where there are more houses every year. Above this the mighty walls of Sass Songher rear up; its tent-like peak forms the southeastern viewing point of the Puez group. The magnificent setting is Corvara's greatest asset — apart from the golf course a bit above the village, on the road to the Campolongo Pass. Otherwise Corvara is fairly uninteresting, with pseudo-Tyrolean architecture (often with false-looking decoration and a surplus of

balconies) and too much asphalt on unbuilt areas. Hotels are good, but expensive.

Sights. The new church is a typical 1950s building, but it's worth having a look at Corvara's **old church**, now just a chapel. Its altar triptych dating from 1520 has a painting ascribed to the Donau School (perhaps a pupil of Albrecht Altdorfer), depicting the decapitation of St Catherine.

Lifts: Lifts run from Corvara to **Col Alt** (cable car: one way 9.10 €, up and back 13 €), **Boè** (cable car: one way 12.10 €, up and back 18.40 €), **Vallon** (chair lift: one way 7.10 €, up and back 10.50 €), **Pralongià** (chair lift: one way 7.50 €, up and back 12 €) and **Braia Fraida** (chair lift: one way 6.10 €, up and back 9.20 €). All run usually between 08.30 and 17.30.

Kolfuschg/Colfosco

While Corvara looks north, Kolfuschg has a sunny south-facing aspect and a view to the imposing, almost vertical north wall of the Sella group, rising to 1000m. The old part of the village (at 1650m!) is almost completely hidden in the mass of new buildings.

It's hard to believe that Kolfuschg, so easily reached today, was once totally isolated. Until the late 19th century there was no road through the Gadertal and the village wasn't even a parish in its own right; it belonged to Lajen/Laion in the Eisacktal/Valle Isarco (as did all of Gröden). But there was no road there either, until one was built over the Grödner Joch (only fully completed around 1970) — just a mule track. Once Kolfuschg was joined to the

View to the flanks of the Sella massif from the Puez group — the Gadertal/Val Badia begins at its feet.

lies just in the centre of the Ladin lands, where all the Ladin valleys to Ampezzo begin.

Massive walls encircle a wild high plateau; they can only be mastered by experts using the protected climbing routes. Karst dominates the region, so there's no flowing water, mostly very dry vegetation, and bright chalk, its layers still easily seen. This is not a place for walkers; only climbers with the right equipment can approach Sella. From the north the Boè lift from Corvara is the easiest approach for most people; from the south they come on the lift from the Pordoi Pass on Sass Pordoi.

Puez group

Sass Songher (2665m) above Corvara is just one of many viewpoints on the gigantic plateau of the Puez group. This massif is shared by the Grödner Tal, Hochabteital and Villnösstal/Val di Funes: access from the Hochabteital is via the Grödner Joch, Kolfuschg (**Plans–Frara cable car**, one way 14.10 €, up and back 20.30 €) or Stern. In spite of the proximity of so many tourist centres, the wide area of the plateau is quite lonely — people are just more attracted to Sella opposite. Read more about this massif under Villnösstal, Puez-Geisler Nature Park (both in Book 1), and Gröden (starting on page 36).

Stern/La Villa

Nothing much has changed here in the old village above the road; only a few houses stand between the

Gadertal road, it came under the administration of Buchenstein on the far side of the Campolongo Pass, where there had already been a road down to Arabba since 1901.

Sights: It's worth seeing the late Gothic church of **St Vigil**, with arched windows and a small baroque onion dome.

One or two old Ladin houses (*ciasa*) with stone walls on the ground floor and some wooden cladding on the upper floors (for insulation) can still be seen in the old village, and in the surrounding hay meadows one can see a few old *majun* (the simple hay barns).

Sella group

Whether you round Sella by car, motorcycle, bicycle, on foot or on skis, it will be a memorable experience. This mighty massif, culminating in Piz Boè at 3152m, church and the Renaissance **Ansitz Ciastel Colz** (now a hotel and restaurant). The view to the Fanes group (see Walk 19 on page 116) is fantastic: from right to left you see the Conturines peaks (3064m), Lavarella (3034m) and the north-facing rock wall of Kreuzkofel (L'Ciaval in Ladin).

What attracts tourists, however, is the **cable car to Piz la Ila**; it can carry 2200 people an hour. (Open daily Jul to mid-Sep and winter, one way 11.20 €, up and back 17 €.) That's especially important in winter, when for example the Ski World Cup Race on the famous 'Gran Risa' black slope down from Piz la Ila down to Stern takes place in December. Alberto Tomba won it eight times.

In summer, however, the area between the mountain station on Piz la Ila and the **Pralongià ridge** is a **family-friendly walking area**: meadows and pastures as far as the eye can see, water to paddle in, no dangerous places. And huts with good food and play areas for kids.

St Kassian/San Cassiano

St Kassian's valley runs from Stern via the main village of St Kassian and the hamlet of **Armentarola** up to the walls of Lagazuoi in the most southerly reaches of the Fanes group. The highest point is the Passo di Valparola (2168m), only 2km from the Falzàrego Pass. There are **parking places** (and a **bus stop**) by the community building, on the main through road, and by the Piz Sorega lift.

Accommodation in St Kassian matches up well against that in the much larger villages, and it doesn't lack for walking routes either: in addition to Short Walk 19 on page 116, the Fanes, Puez and Sella groups are around the corner, and there is a lift straight up to the gorgeous meadows of Pralongià (**Piz Sorega cable car**: one way 10.10 €, up and back 17.20 €). Moreover, it's only an hour by car to Cortina.

The middle Gadertal/ Val Badia

The middle valley between Stern/ La Villa and St Martin in Thurn is, after Buchenstein/Pieve di Livinallongo, the most unspoilt of the Ladin valleys. You don't notice this so much from the valley road as you do in the little villages above and in the many *viles,* the Ladin hamlets.

The villages of Pedratsches/ Pedraces and St Leonhard/San Leonardo (together confusingly referred to as Abtei/Badia), Wengen/La Valle, and St Martin in Thurn are the centres of a widespread settlement which reaches up to the rock walls of Heiligkreuzkofel/Sasso della Croce and Peitlerkofel/Sass de Pútia. Here the old customs and skills, seldom seen elsewhere, have been preserved; the crafts are still carried on by some families. Most of the ham still comes out of a smoker.

Pilgrimages, like the one to the Säben Monastery in Klausen/ Chiusa (featured in Book 1), have been undertaken on foot for centuries. St Leonhard still puts on its 'Leonhard-Ritt' (see page 18) in honour of its patron saint. In the Valley of the Mills (Walk 15) you can see how corn was ground until quite recently. And in the farmhouse kitchens they cook it as they have done for centuries.

This is a region for the nostalgic visitor, who can explore on foot, mountain bike, or horseback (raising horses is a mainstay of the valley's economy).

The parish church of St Leonhard, with the Puez group in the background

Abtei/Badia
The Gadertal widens a bit at Abtei — enough to make room for two separate settlements, **Pedratsches/Pedraces** (on the road) and **St Leonhard/San Leonardo** (on the eastern slopes).

St Leonard lies below the mighty rock walls of Heiligkreuzkofel, at the foot of which stands an old pilgrimage church and hospice visited on Walk 16. 'Viles' lie scattered in the meadows and pastures. Some still seem to be living in the 19th century, so little have they changed since the coming of tourism.

Sights: The large **parish church in St Leonhard** above Pedratsches is very obvious; it's dedicated to St Leonard, the patron saint of cattle. The church is one of the most holy places for the farmers of southern Germany and Austria. There's rich rococo decoration by Franz Singer and Matthäus Günther, which is a must! There is also a beautiful view to the church, with the Puez group in the background, from the small play area with its artfully laid-out pond further uphill (see above).

Wengen/La Valle
The village of Wengen found itself a nice sunny slope in a tributary valley (all the Ladin *viles* get the sun, not a single one is on the shady slopes south of the village). Wengen is at the centre of a group of hamlets in the Rü de Ciampló Valley; it has a church (of which only the tower is old), inn, town hall and post office. But what is really meant by its Ladin name, 'La Val', are the *viles,* the hamlets scattered round the slopes: going up from **Pederoa** in the Gadertal you come to **Campló** and **Lunz**; higher up is **Runch**, with a stone Gothic building (once the courthouse), **Ciablun**, **Miribun**, **Tolpëi**, none with more than 10 houses of which many are old. Walking through this cultural landscape on the old farm tracks and speaking to the people is a journey into the past. Walk 21 is a beautiful little circuit.

St Martin in Thurn/ S Martino in Badia
Two valleys come into the Gadertal from the west below Wengen: the Campilltal/Val de Longiarü and the valley of Untermoi/Antermoia. Between them the prettily situated village of St Martin in Thurn (Ladin: San Martin de Tor) is spread across a green hill.

Sights and excursions: This is where the Archbishops of Brixen had their administrative seat for the Gadertal. Magnificent Schloss Thurn, which today houses the Ladin Museum, testifies to their

> **'Viles' of the Gadertal/Val Badia**
> Visitors to German-speaking Tyrol around the Pustertal are already familiar with the isolated, grouped farm buildings (you seldom see even two farms near each other) — a result of the population explosion in the 17th century, when many farms were divided up. As in the German Tyrol, the farms here consist of two buildings — the living quarters and the workplaces. But only in Ladin areas will you find hamlets with seven, eight or even 10 of these buildings so close together. The ones in the Gadertal are especially well preserved and today present the characteristic settlement of the area. Why the Ladins built their settlements like this and the German Tyroleans in a completely different way nobody knows. In all other respects the two groups are so similar culturally, that except for the different language you can hardly tell them apart.
>
> But the 'viles' are distinctive: wells and ovens in the centre, the houses narrow, with narrow passageways between them and benches for sitting on and gossiping at the end of the working day. The lower parts of the houses are built of stone, with wood above (often with lovely carvings), and steeply pitched roofs. A balcony surrounds the wooden part, where the harvest could be dried in the fresh air. Many of the plastered stone walls have frescoes depicting saints (usually Mary with Child). Window frames and walls are often decorated with geometrical 'graffiti', as was usual in farming areas during the Renaissance.
>
> The working buildings lie on the slopes or are built into the slopes, so that at the back a ramp runs up to the first floor, where hay was kept, while the stables are on the ground floor. Usually there is a little chapel nearby, and in many of these hamlets there are still huge 'scaffolds', used for drying broad beans in the autumn.

wealth. In the village and the valleys life goes on at a quiet pace. If you would like to know more about life in the scattered Ladin settlements, this is your chance.

The Ladin Museum in Schloss Thurn (Ciastel de Tor) opened in 2001 and is well worth a visit. In the heart of the landscape between Peitlerkofel and the Sennes, the historic castle with its romantic main building, large keep and the many later additions is an ideal setting. Where once the Archbishops of Brixen ruled from their seat in the Gadertal, today we can have a good look at the history and culture of the Ladins of the Dolomites. You can visit four floors of the castle and the massive keep. The most interesting exhibits are those devoted to **specialist handcrafts** (including a complete doll-maker's workshop), **geological displays** (minerals and fossils from the Dolomites), the **farmhouse room** which has been replicated in detail, and finally the presentation of the **Ladin language** through multi-media and several PCs. The Ladin **Micura de Rü** Cultural Centre is attached to the museum. *Museum open from Easter to end Oct, Tue-Sat 10.00-17.00 (Jul/Aug Mon-Sat 10.00-18.00), Sun 14.00-18.00; also end Dec to mid-Jan daily 15.00-19.00, Jan to Easter Thu-Sat 15.00-19.00. Entry 8 €, families 16 €. www.museumladin.it*

Valley of the Mills, with the hamlet of Seres (see Walk 15 on page 103)

The quiet **Campilltal (Ladin: Val de Longiarü)** is ideal for a peaceful holiday. One of the most interesting places is the stretch called **Val di Morins** (Valley of the Mills), an open-air museum. The farmers built water mills alongside the Seres Stream, where corn was ground in the past. Corn is no longer ground here, the farms have changed to raising cattle, and the fields have disappeared. But the mills still stand and thanks to EU money have been beautifully preserved; visit them on Walk 15!

The two narrowly built *viles* of **Seres** and **Misci** are amongst the most unspoilt and attractive in the Gadertal. Sometimes in summer corn is ground in one or other of the mills; ask for information in St Martin, where you can also get a leaflet about the valley. In August there is a 'Festival of the Mills' in Seres and Misci, with tasty local farm products.

Cycling tip: from St Martin towards Brixen/Bressanone. From St Martin there's a little road over to Plose and Brixen. Although you can do it in a car, it's an excellent route for mountain bikes. It first runs through little **Untermoi/ Antermoia**, where refreshments are available at the Ütia de Börz

Above: Lunz is typical of the Gadertal 'viles'; Left: poor souls in Purgatory, as depicted in the pilgrimage church at La Pli de Mareo

hut. There are two different 'baths' here at Untermoi — the Sarighela Hay Bath and the Valdander Baths. The former, described in Book 1, are a speciality of Völs/Fiè in the Seiser Alm/Alpe di Siusi area. The latter is one of the very few South Tyrolean farm baths that survived the 20th century. It's in a narrow, cool, wooded valley on the opposite side of the Untermoi valley and dates from 1820. The waters are rich in calcium, iron pyrites and fluorine. The water is soft, tastes slightly salty and rather bitter, and helps with 'women's problems' and chronic rheumatism and arthritis.

The road then rises to the **Würzjoch/Passo delle Erbe** (2006m), the pass between the Gadertal and the Eisacktal. From this pass there is a magnificent view to the northern flanks of Peitlerkofel — and a good restaurant. Continue via the top end of the **Lüsner Tal/Val di Luson** to a fork: from here you can go left to Villnöss/Funes and Afers/Eores or right to Brixen/Bressanone. Beautiful scenery throughout.

Enneberg/Marebbe

The sunny valley of Enneberg (Mareo in Ladin), another tributary valley of the Gadertal, has become a popular holiday area. In summer you can walk in the Fanes and Sennes groups, in winter you can ski on Kronplatz/Plan de Corones (reached from the south of Enneberg).

Sights and excursions: Typical Ladin *viles* cluster around the main village of **St Vigil** and especially around tiny **La Pli**, while below in the valley are row upon row of hotels and apartments. But in the background, just at the edge of the village, the Fanes-Sennes-Prags Nature Park begins — pure and solitary Dolomites nature with a couple of unforgettable alms, like the large Fanesalm below Lavarella. The tourist office offers free booklets with walk and cycle tours.

The rococo **parish church at St Vigil/San Vigilio** has not changed since it was built in around 1728; it's an historical gem and a feast for the eyes. As in St Leonhard, the painter Matthäus Günther and stucco artist Franz Singer have been at work here. The architect was Giuseppe de Costa, a local. The **statue of Caterina Lanz** in the church square is a memorial to the Ladin heroine who fought in the French Wars (see page 156).

At the end of St Vigil, on the road towards Pederü, is the **Naturparkhaus Fanes-Sennes-Prags**, an information centre. The displays are very child-friendly. *Centre open May-Oct and end Dec to Mar, Tue-Sat from 09.30-12.30 and 14.30-18.00 (also open Sun in Jul/Aug); entry free.*

Tiny **Enneberg Pfarre/Pieve di Marebbe**, north of St Vigil, is more commonly called by its Ladin name, **La Pli de Mareo**. It is the site of a pilgrimage church dedicated to Our Lady of Good Advice. This was the parish church for the whole Gadertal until about 1100; Abtei didn't get its own church until 1449. The original Gothic structure was rebuilt and decorated in the baroque style; the façade and the beautiful high altar date from this time (1638); the chancel is late baroque (1760).

Four large votive paintings are of special interest, showing pilgrimage processions which the people of Welsberg in the Pustertal make every hundred years, in thanks for being saved from the Plague in 1636 (the paintings date from 1637, 1738, 1838 and 1936).

Another interesting building in La Pli is the **Gran Ciasa** behind the church — an old mansion, now an inn with Ladin cooking.

From La Pli you can take a lightly trafficked little road (signposted to **Bruneck**), to **Maria Saalen** and **St Lorenzen**. (Since none of the following roads or hamlets are on any touring maps and they are so lightly trafficked that you can walk as well as drive them; you may like to get Tabacco map N° 031.) In the next valley you will come to an **old watermill** which, although not in use, does still work. You can also take roads up to the most beautiful *viles*: continue on the road to **Pliscia**, go back to the Ciaseles turn-off, and from there to **Ellemunt**. Return as far as **Brach**, then go to **Corterei** and **Frontü**, then back to **La Pli**.

Fanes-Sennes-Prags Nature Park

The **Rautal/Val de Mareo** (Ladin: Val dai Tamersc) leads from St Vigil deep into this nature park which comprises 25,680 hectares. You can drive there or take a bus along the public road as far as **Pederü** at 1548m, with a hut and good alpine cooking. (It's a toll road; those with guest cards are entitled to a reduction.) From Pederü there are little roads into both the Fanes and Sennes groups, but they are closed to motor traffic; see the 'Cycling tip' overleaf.

Fanes and Sennes are both huge karst plateaus with widespread

View to the Fanes group

alms. The few watercourses disappear very quickly. Tiny lakes lie in clay hollows, surrounded by steep chalk peaks giving the impression of gigantic steps. The Rautal is the only largish valley running into the park; almost all other approaches require steep climbs. There are several pleasant alms offering bed and board.

A little road leads from Pederü into the **Fanes group**, to the Kleine Fanesalm with the Lavarella and Fanes huts; half an hour's walk uphill you pass a little lake fed from a stream and a strong spring. Then the road runs higher, to the Grosse Fanesalm, where there is also a hut with refreshments (but no overnight accommodation). From here the road rounds the east side of the range and runs down into the Ampezzo, to the Toblach/Cortina road. The whole stretch (about 12 km) is quite easily done on foot or by mountain bike.

There are also magnificent **walking routes** from the Lavarella and Fanes huts across the plateau to the surrounding peaks — Heiligkreuzkofel, Lavarella, Conturinesspitze — as well as Dolomites High Route 1 to the Lagazuoi War Museum and the Falzàrego Pass or down to St Kassian (see Walk 19).

To get into the heart of the **Sennes group** you first have to climb a steep hairpin road dating from the First World War (it's almost too steep for mountain bikes, with a lot of loose gravel — although the cycling tour described below *does* come down this road, *carefully*). Once you get to the hut on Fodara Vedla at 1980m, however, you'll be glad you've made the effort. It's a lovely green, hilly alm, with old buildings and overnight accommodation. From the hut there are easy walks across the plateau to the Sennes and Seekofel huts (Walk 20), to Kreuzkofel, down to Lake Prags and Prags (see Walk 1 in Book 1) or over to Hohe Gaisl (tough) and down to the Toblach/Cortina road in Ampezzo.

Cycling tip: Fanes and Sennes by mountain bike
Time/length: 4h with ease; 34km
Grade: ascents and descents of 1250m
Map: Tabacco 1:25,000 N° 03
You don't have to be a crack mountain biker to enjoy this circuit, provided that you break it down into two days, with an overnight stop at either the Fanes or Lavarella hut.

From **Pederü** take the little private road up to the **Kleine Fanesalm** with the two above-mentioned huts and from there up to the **Grosse Fanesalm** (steep in places, but not technically difficult). From the alm carry on down the good road through **Val di Fanes** to the **Cortina–Toblach road**, which you reach on a hairpin bend with a fantastic panorama. From here head uphill through the upper **Val Boite**, to the **Sennes Hut (Ütia)**, then take the road to the **Fodara Vedla Hut** and back down to **Pederü**. *Take care* on the final steep and winding descent over loose rubble.

Walk 15: SERES AND THE VALLEY OF THE MILLS

Distance/time: about 2.5km/ 1.6mi; 1h
Grade: ● easy, with ascents/ descents of only 115m/375ft, ideal for a family outing. Mostly shady with a few sunny sections
Waymarking: signposts 'Val di Morins/Mühlental', Trail N° 4
Equipment: sturdy shoes
Refreshments: none en route; take food with you (the highest point of the walk is a good picnic spot.
Walking map: Tabacco 07, Alta Badia-Arabba-Marmolada, 1:25,000

Transport: 🚗 drive to St Martin in Thurn/San Martino in Badia and from there towards Seres/ Misci. On a right-hand bend, a gravel track signposted 'Medalges Alm' and indicating Trails 3 and 5 branches off left to the car park for hikers (46° 37.894'N, 11° 50.922'E). 🚐464 runs approximately every hour via St Martin to Campill (Lungiarü in Ladin). The last bus is at 18.05. From there it's about 30 minutes on foot along Trail N° 4 to the hikers' car park where the walk starts.

This short circular walk off the beaten track leads through a small idyllic valley at the foot of Peitlerkofel/Sass de Pútia. It passes eight mills, but only one of them can be visited today. See page 99 for more about the area.

The walk starts at the hiking car park (**1**) just off the **road to Seres**. At the far end of the car park, follow a forest path signposted 'Gasthof Lüch de Vanc' to the right through sparse larch trees.

About 100m after starting out you meet the tarred road to 'Seres/ Misci'. Follow this to the left (it's Trail N° 4a); the two hamlets with their old farms are in front of you. At the next fork, go right towards 'Seres/Mühlental'. Soon you cross the rushing Seresbach on a bridge (**2**) and turn left on the far side. Now you're on the actual **Mills' Trail** ('Mühlental/Val di Morins') — it begins here.

The first mill is still functional and can be visited (see the panel 'Mill history you can touch' overleaf). After a few metres you come to the second and third mill (the latter can be reached via a wooden bridge).

Climb up above the stream now and about 10 minutes after joining the Mills' Trail you come to

a signposted junction (**3**). Here the trail goes downhill a few metres to the left, to the next mill. You walk under a wooden mill race and continue along the right bank of the stream. Then you cross the

Left: one of the restored mills; above: the wooden mill race for channelling water to the mill wheel

Mill history you can touch
In the Valley of the Mills there are around 30 buildings in all, eight of which were built on the banks of the stream and were renovated several years ago with EU funds. Only the first of the mills can be viewed. There you can watch grain being ground and learn how flour is made. Children can also try their hands at making flour! The mill is open in summer on Mon and Thu from 09.30 to 16.30, in spring and autumn only on Thu from 12.00 to 16.00.

stream again, go up the far side and pass three more mills

After the last building, the path joins a motor track. Follow it to the right and cross the stream again on a bridge a few metres further on. On the far side take the grassy path up left to the last two mills. Above the last mill there is another mill race. At its end, the **hollowed-out tree trunk** (**4**; **35min**) shown above makes an idyllic picnic spot.

It's just a few steps back to the motor track (Trail 4). Follow this downhill towards 'Seres' for about five minutes, then take an unmarked meadow path (**5**) to the right. Stay on this for about 100m until, after a few wooden steps, you cross the stream again on a bridge (you were here on the way out). On the far side of the bridge, turn left, and a few metres further on, at a knoll, take the lower of two paths. Just after this, the trail leads steeply downhill (there is a spring below the path), and after a few metres climbs again. Below you on the left the is the attractive Valley of the Mills, with the hamlet of Seres behind it in the middle of meadows — the 'postcard' shown on page 99. About 10 minutes after crossing the stream, your trail branches off left downhill (**6**; 'Val di Morins'). After a **wooden gate** (close it after you!) and a sharp left turn, you reach the bridge (**2**) crossed earlier. Retrace your steps now to the car park (**1**; **1h**).

Walk 16: HIGH-ALTITUDE HIKE FROM THE HOLY CROSS HOSPICE TO STERN/LA VILLA

Distance/time: about 7.2km/ 4.5mi; 2h15min
Grade: ● moderate, with an initial steep ascent of 240m/785ft and a descent of 655m/2150ft. A long high-altitude hike with no particular difficulties after the initial steep climb. Many sections are in shade. Especially attractive in the afternoon or evening, when the rocks of Heiligkreuzkofel/Sasso della Croce glow red and gold.
Waymarking: red/white; Trail N° 7 to **3**; Trail 15 to **6**; Trail 12 to **9**; then Trail 11 to the end
Equipment: hiking boots, walking pole(s)
Refreshments: Take enough water with you! Good, hearty cuisine in the Holy Cross Hospice (**3**).
Otherwise none en route
Walking map: Tabacco 07, Alta Badia-Arabba-Marmolada, 1:25,000
Transport: 🚗 free car park in Abtei/Badia at the Heiligkreuz lift (46° 36.571'N, 11° 53.791'E). Or 🚌 460 from Bruneck/Brunico to Abtei/Badia. Return on the same bus from Stern (last bus back 19.57). From the valley station take the chair lift (La Crusc 1) to the middle station (**1**; 9.20 € up, 13.30 € up and back). Or go all the way to the top station (**3**) by taking the cable car (La Crusc 2) from the middle station: 15 € up for both lifts combined; 22 € up and back. The lifts run Jun to mid-Sep, from 08.30 to 17.30.

Standing at 2045m, the Holy Cross Pilgrimage Church was originally built in 1484, then later extended in the baroque style and a tower added. The original hospice, where pilgrims once spent the night, is run as a hut today. The host is both verger and cook; do try his rustic food!

Walk 16: From the Holy Cross Hospice to Stern/La Villa

After a short steep climb (which can be avoided by taking the La Crusc 2 cable car to the top station), this walk runs under the spectacular rock faces shown below before descending through extensive woodland to Stern/La Villa.

Start the hike at the **middle station of the Crusc 1 chair lift** (**1**). Take the wide gravel trail, Trail N° 7, steeply uphill. This farm track is also a *via crucis,* and you pass several large crucifixes at the stations of the cross, with well-placed benches where you can take a breather. The mighty rock face of Heiligkreuzkofel/Sasso della Croce peaks high above you through the light larch forest as you gradually ascend eastwards.

Some 20 minutes from the start, you come to a fork at station 10 (**2**). Follow signs to the hospice further uphill. Soon you'll see the mountain station of the cable car. A wide meadow opens up in front of you, in the middle of which is the dazzling white Holy Cross Hospice (**3**; **30min**) and its chapel — quite a sight!

Almost five minutes later, roughly timbered benches and tables invite you to rest. Accept this invitation happily — a long trail lies ahead, requiring some building up! Pasta, polenta, meat, strong red wine, all garnished with a magnificent view of the Sella massif and the Gardenaccia plateau. But the inside of the hospice is also worth a look: the wood-paneled room, well-trodden wooden steps and the polished stone floor bring the story to life (see panel about 'The Holy Cross Hospice' overleaf).

Thus fortified, carry on along Trail 15, a mountain scree path signed to 'St Kassian' — heading

The pilgrimage church and hospice, backed by Heiligkreuzkofel/Sasso della Croce

straight for the gleaming glacier of Marmolada. Larches and dwarf mountain pines alternate with rhododendron and junipers.

About 20 minutes from the hospice, at a junction (**4**), stay on Trail 15. Mixed conifers alternate with open areas. After about 10 minutes, at the next junction (**5**; 1h), continue towards 'St Kassian' soon through a marshy meadow landscape.

Past a hut the trail goes steeply

> **The Holy Cross Hospice**
> The Heiligkreuzhospiz was built in 1718 next to the pilgrimage church of the same name. The church dates from 1484, but has been rebuilt several times over the centuries. The hospice was intended as a home for the sacristan of the church and as a place where pilgrims could stay overnight. Under Emperor Joseph II, the church was temporarily closed in 1786 and used as a sheepfold. It has been a pilgrimage church again since 1840. Every spring, the parishes of the Gader/Badia Valley undertake a pilgrimage there. The hospice has been run by the Irsara family since 1888 and now has 22 beds (overnight stays are possible in summer, www.lacrusc.com).

downhill into dense forest. A little later it traverses a wide ridge in the middle of the forest and then goes through a cattle gate. At the end of a marshy meadow you cross a babbling brook. Then you come to a signposted fork; head right, again towards 'St Kassian', past a picture of the Madonna and another marshy meadow.

At the end of the meadow, turn right on Trail 12, a steep mountain path (**6**) signposted to 'Stern/La Villa' and head west downhill on a partly washed-out path. About 15 minutes later, your path joins a wide motor track (**7**; 1h45min). Follow this to the left but leave it again a scant five minutes later for 'Stern/La Villa', heading downhill across alpine meadows. The path is hard to see, so always look for the clear red and white waymarks.

You cross a road at a cattle gate. A wooden fence now lead you downhill. Passing two farms, you

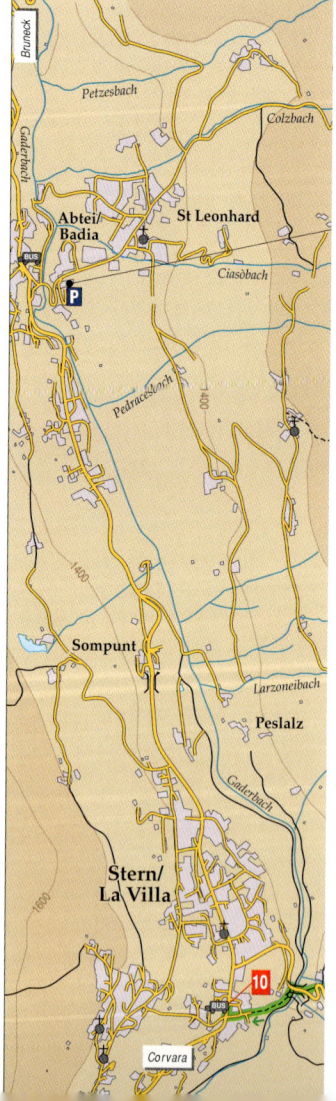

Walk 16: From the Holy Cross Hospice to Stern/La Villa 109

come to a tarred road (**8**). Follow it to the left. After a few metres, keep right and head down to the **pass road** towards Valparola and Falzàrego. Follow this briefly downhill, watching out for the traffic, then fork right at Bend N° 4 (**9**). Trail 12 signposts lead you through the first houses in **Stern/La Villa** and then (at the Hotel Rezia) to Bend N° 2 of the pass road. Follow the road, but leave it again at the next opportunity by heading right downhill.

Steps take you down past a residential building back to the pass road for the last time. Head right, cross the St Kassian Stream on a bridge, then head left (still Trail 12), and finally immediately right up a steep gravel path (Trail 11). This becomes concreted a few metres further on and takes you to the main **Corvara road**. Go right, to the **bus stop** (**10**; **2h15min**).

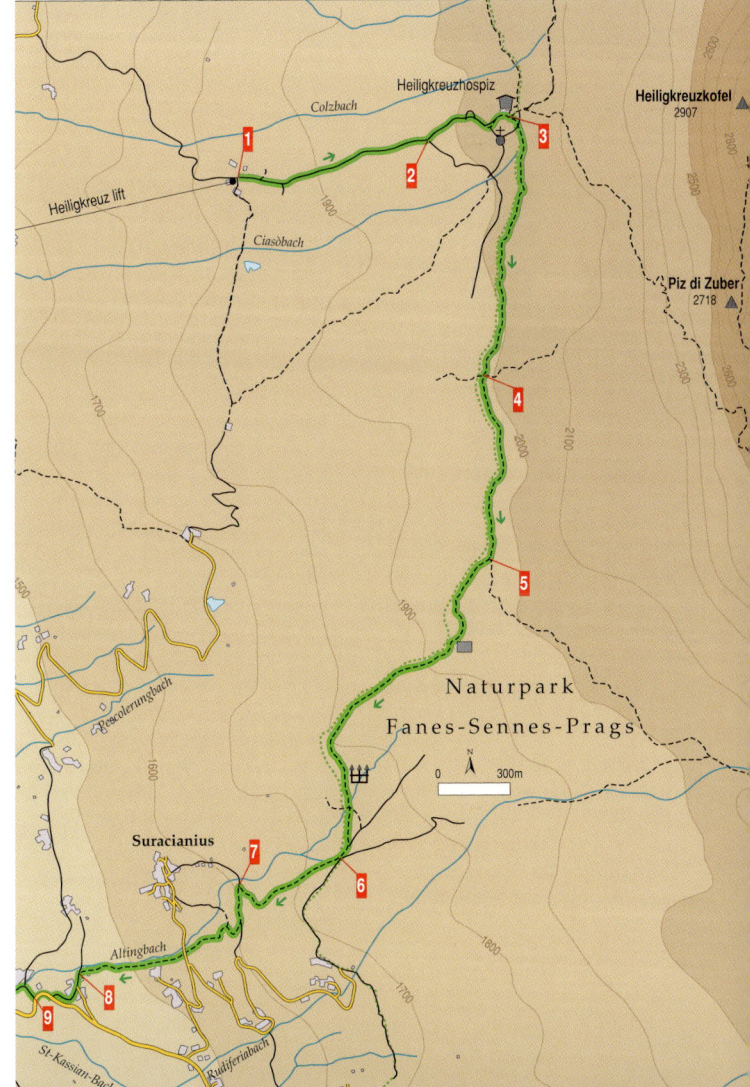

Walk 17: FROM THE CAPANNA ALPINA TO THE SCOTONI HUT AND LAKE LAGAZUOI

Distance/time: about 5.8km/ 3.6mi; 2h15min (out 1h15min, back 1h)
Grade: ● moderate, with an ascent/descent of 485m/1590ft; gravel and scree paths, little shade
Waymarking: red/white; Trail N° 11 to **2**; Trail 20 to shortly before **4**; Trail 20b for the last metres to the lake
Equipment: hiking boots, walking pole(s), sun protection
Refreshments: available at the start in the Capanna Alpina (**1**) and at the Scotoni Hut (**3**), both open summer and winter and with good, hearty cuisine
Walking map: Tabacco 07, Alta Badia-Arabba-Marmolada, 1:25,000
Transport: 🚗 Drive from St Kassian/San Cassiano towards 'Falzàregopass'. Immediately before the bridge over the Sciarè Stream, turn left to the 'Capanna Alpina', where there is a (paid) car park (46° 33.581'N, 11° 58.902'E). Or 🚐 460 from Bruneck/Brunico to Stern/La Villa, and from there with 🚐 465 approximately every hour to the 'Sciarè ' bus stop (last bus 465 back at 18.15, last bus 460 at 19.57). From the bus stop it's a good 30 minutes' walk to the Capanna Alpina.

This hike leads under high rock walls to the cozy Scotoni Hut on the edge of a picturesque alpine meadow. In the second section, it goes over a steep scree slope to idyllic Lake Lagazuoi, shimmering blue and green in the midst of mighty boulders — an ideal place for a picnic, unless you're already working off a Scotoni lunch!

The walk begins at the **Capanna Alpina** (**1**): from the barrier, follow the gravel track into the valley. After about five minutes you reach a junction (**2**) and follow the sign 'Scotoni Hut/ Lagazuoiesee'. A few metres further on, you cross the **Sciarè Stream** on a wooden bridge, then your trail leads steeply uphill through extensive pines and dwarf mountain pines.

Long hairpin bends take you several times past the ski slope which leads down from Little Lagazuoi: in summer, this ski run lights up like a green ribbon where the meadow peeks between the trees. On the right the mountain-tops of Spinarac tower up, on the left the distinctive walls of the Scotoni peaks. The further you climb, the closer they move together.

About 30 minutes after the fork, the view suddenly opens onto an idyllic plateau. The **Scotoni Hut** (**3**; **35min**) is just a few metres away on the northeastern edge of the plateau. It's a picturesque resting place, which I suggest you save for the way back!

Continue along the eastern edge of the plateau between dwarf mountain pines. About five minutes past the hut you see a small wooden **chapel**. After a further 10 minutes of moderate ascent, you reach the foot of a scree cirque. From here your path (shown opposite), supported by wooden planks, logs and some

Right: steep scree path onwards to Lake Lagazuoi

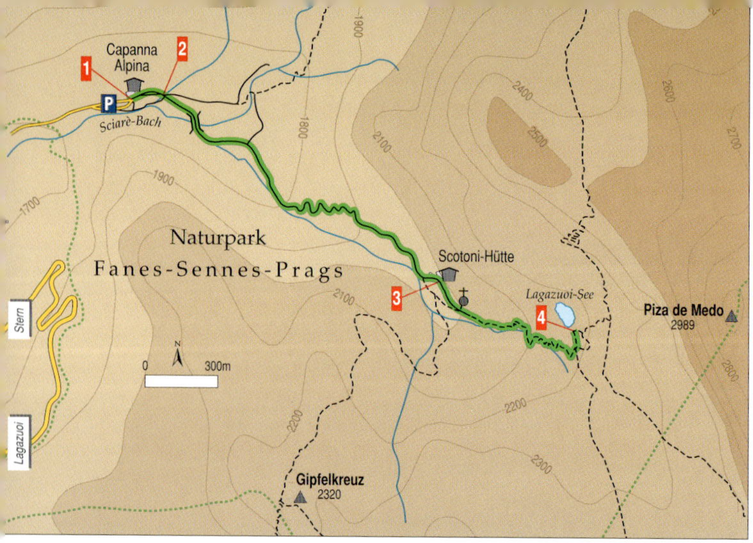

Capanna
Alpina
1
2
P
Sciarè-Bach
1900
1800
2100
2400
2500
2600
2700
1700
1900
Naturpark
Fanes-Sennes-Prags
Scotoni-Hütte
3
Lagazuoi-See
4
Piza de Medo
2989
2100
Stern
0
300m
N
2200
2200
2300
2800
Lagazuoi
Gipfelkreuz
2320

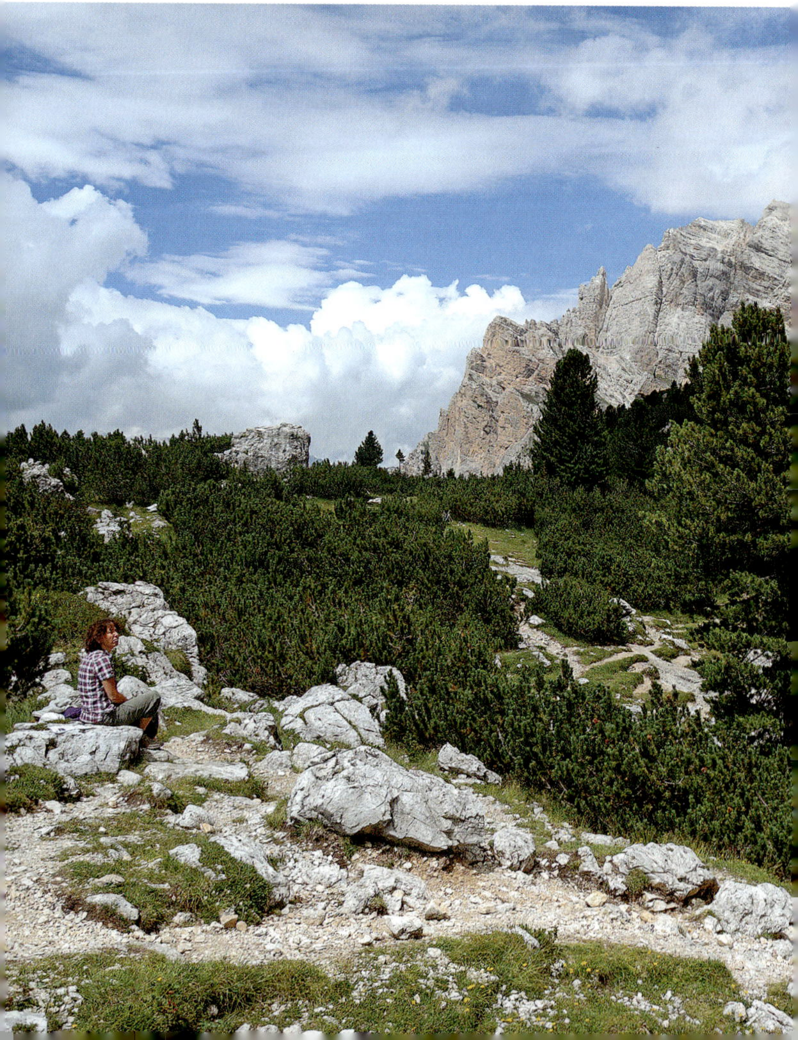

Walk 17: From the Capanna Alpina to Lake Lagazuoi 113

paving stones, zigzags steeply uphill.

After 20 minutes of sweaty ascent, the scree cirque ends. When you stop for a breather, you can look back on a fantastic view to the Conturines peaks!

Coming to a small depression, keep left to shimmering green-blue **Lake Lagazuoi** (**4**; **1h15min**), a few metres away. Sit down between boulders for a rest on its western bank. In front of you the dark rock walls of the Scotoni peaks rise skywards. Silence all around, just the twitter of birds. A wonderful place to sleep in the Dolomites! If you like, you could walk around the peaceful lake in just a few minutes.

Descending, you're back at the **Scotoni Hut** (**3**) a good 30 minutes later. It has a picnic area for hikers. After a further 30 minutes of partly steep descent, anyone who is still feeling peckish can stop for refreshment at the **Capanna Alpina** (**1**; **2h15min**).

Deep green Lake Lagazuoi — an ideal picnic spot

Walk 18: PISCIADÙ WATERFALLS

Distance/time: about 7.5km/ 4.7mi; 2h30min; 1h30min up; 1h back down
Grade: ● easy, with an ascent/ descent of 300m/985ft; good paths and tracks underfoot
Waymarking: red/white waymarks; Trail 28 to **4**; Trail 650 to **8**; Trail 645 back to **3**
Equipment: stout shoes
Refreshments: available at Corvara and Kolfuschg/Colfosco

Walking map: Tabacco 07, Alta Badia-Arabba-Marmolada, 1:25,000
Transport: 🚗 park in Corvara just by the Boè lift (46° 32.873'N, 11° 52.317'E) or at the lift itself (paid parking). 🚌 460 from Bruneck/ Brunico to Corvara (hourly); alight at the 'Col Alt Strasse' bus stop, and from there walk the short way to the Boè lift. The last bus back is at 19.48.

Here's an easy walk for all the family which takes you right up to the massive walls of Sella. You walk along shady paths and through meadows, passing picnic spots galore with seats — or you can just loll about on the grass.

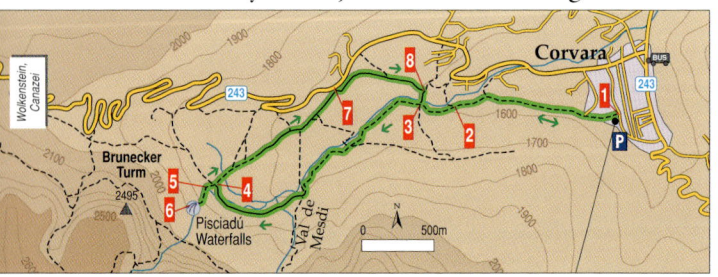

Start the walk by walking *between* the **valley stations** of the **Boè** and **Borest lifts** (**1**), to find the start of the route (Trail 28, variously signposted 'Grödnerjoch, Tru dles Cascades, Borest Trail' — or to the campsite). The lovely wide path is shady and has many places to stop — either at a bench or by a hollowed-out log with a spring.

The rise is very gentle as you pass the campsite, after which you begin to climb to the **Pisciadù Stream**. You pass two turnings to Kolfuschg/Colfosco (**2**) and (**3**) and before long have a look up the **Val de Mesdi** where Trail 651 comes down a massive scree — often at a 45° angle (look at the photo of the entrance to this gorge on page 83); this is *via ferrata* territory.

Eventually you come to a wide meadow at the foot of Sella, an ideal resting place with benches, huts and streams. Turn left at a junction here (**4**), cross a **bridge** (**5**) and rise to the **Pisciadù Falls** (**6**; **1h30min**). The view to this slender waterfall is more attractive from a short distance.

From the falls return to **4** and follow Trail 650 through flower-filled meadows, with wonderful views to Sass Songher. At the **car park** for the Sodlicia cable car (**7**) turn right on a track. Then turn right (**8**) on Trail 645 to rejoin your outgoing route at **3** and retrace steps to the **Boè cable car** (**1**; **2h30min**).

Pisciadù Waterfalls — the view is usually better from a short distance.

Walk 19: FROM STERN/LA VILLA TO THE FANES GROUP

Distance/time: about 21.8km/13.5mi; 9h30min-12h — a two-day walk
Grade: ●❗ strenuous, with an ascent of 1300m/4265ft and descent of 1050m/3445ft. Another tough high alpine hike; you must be sure-footed and have a head for heights. Good physical condition and mountain experience are required; reliably good weather is an absolute prerequisite!
Waymarking: red/white; Trail 12 to 9; then Trail 11 to the end
Equipment: hiking boots, sun protection, walking pole(s)
Refreshments/overnight stay: Rifugio Lavarella (8); Rifugio Fanes (9; recommended overnight stay); Capanna Alpina (14)
Walking map: Tabacco 05, Val Gardena-Alpe di Siusi/Gröden-Seiseralm, 1:25,000

Transport: 🚗 free car parking by the bus stop in Stern/La Villa 130m south of the roundabout where the walk begins (46° 35.013'N, 11° 54.254'E). 🚐 460 from Bruneck/Brunico to Stern/La Villa: alight at the 'Colzstrasse' bus stop. From Bar Saré at the end of the walk, take 🚐 465 approximately every hour back to the 'Colzstrasse' bus stop in Stern (last 🚐 465 back at 18.19, last 🚐 460 back at 19.57).
Short walk: Larch Trail. 6km/3.7mi; 2h; ● easy, overall ups and downs of 220m/720ft. Waymarking colours red/white. Stout shoes will suffice. Refreshments available in St Kassian. Access: 🚗 or 🚐 465 (hourly) to St Kassian (46° 34.201'N, 11° 56.001'E). Last bus back at 19.59. See description on page 118 and the map below.

A walk full of high points, literally and metaphorically. The contrast between the steep ascent through unyielding rock walls and then being able to stride out across a rolling plateau could not be more stark.

The Fanesalm, from the Limo Pass

Start out at the roundabout in **Stern/La Villa**: take the road towards **St Kassian** (**1**) and, past the bridge over the stream and the following S curve, turn left on Trail 12/13 (**2**), a road. After 200m turn right on Trail 12 (**3**), a track. It's a steady climb through meadows and pastures — at first there are even a few houses. Eventually you rise through forest, cross Trail 15 (**4**) and, 10 minutes later, come to a **damp area** with springs on the right.

As the forest makes way for buckled trees and then loose rubble, the **route forks** (**5**). Climb the slope on the right, through the **Val de Medésc**.

(Please ignore all the short cuts here, which have caused bad erosion.) Then you cross more very tiring loose rubble before eventually arriving at the **Forcella de Medésc** (**6**; **3h45min**).

The ongoing route across the plateau is mostly slightly downhill. You pass a lake (**Lé Parom**; **7**; in high summer dry as a bone), and then a view opens out to the Fanesalm, 300m below you. There follows another rather tiring descent through woods, where you pass to the left of the strong karst springs of the Vigil Stream. Descend to the **Rifugio Lavarella** (**8**), which you can see below to the right; you walk between the two ponds on the alm and beyond them rise easily to the large **Fanes Hut** (**9**; **6h**).

The next day, take the alm road to the south (Trail 11, as well as Dolomites High Route 1). Climb to the **Limo Pass** and lake (**Lé de Limo**), then go on to the large **Fanesalm** (**10**; **7h**) with dairy hut. Cross the floor of this alm to an area of fallen rock, where both the valley and your route **fork** (**11**): to the right is a route back to Lavarella (involving an easy scramble), to the left is St Kassian and the Falzàrego Pass.

Take the almost-level route to the left, still Trail 11. At the next **fork** go right (**12**; *leaving High Route 1*). Cross the **Col de Locia** (**13**; **8h15min**) and descend to the St Kassian road — perhaps first taking a break at the **Capanna Alpina** (**14**; start and end point for Walk 17). A bus stop is to the left, by the **Bar Saré** (**15**; **9h30min**).

Left: St Kassian/San Cassiano church at the junction of Trails 14 and 15. The Short walk goes uphill at left of the church, then ends by approaching the church as in this photo

Short walk

From the **bus stop/car park** in St Kassian/San Cassiano follow signs to the centre, up to the **church** (**1**). Then **start the walk**: go past the front of the church and uphill on Trail 15, a road signed to 'Rüdeferia'. Keep uphill for 1km; then, at a Y-fork, go right on Trail 15A (**2**) for 'Tru di Lersc' (Larch Trail).

You come to pretty **Rü**, where signposting leads you left, round the top of the hamlet and onto the Larch Trail proper. As it winds through woods and meadows at the edge of the nature park, information panels explain some of the key geological and cultural features of this area, where little has changed in hundreds of years.

The trail ends at a working **watermill** (**3**; **1h15min**). Follow the road for 1.2 km, past **Rüdeferia** farm, until you can turn left on Trail 14 (**4**), a track. Walk to the main road and back to the bus stop and car park in **St Kassian** (**1**; **2h**).

Walk 20: ACROSS THE SENNES TO THE SEEKOFEL HUT

Distance/time: about 18km/ 11.2mi; 6h30min
Grade: ● easy alm walking, but the ascent to/descent from the Sennes plateau is steep, skiddy and strenuous; ascent/descent of 800m/2625ft
Waymarking: red/white; Trails 7 and Dolomites High Route 1 to **8**; Trail 6 and DHR1 to **9**; Trail 26 to **12**; Trail 6 to **14**; Trail 7A back to **2**, from where you retrace steps
Equipment: hiking boots, sun protection, walking pole(s)
Refreshments: available at the Gasthaus Pederü (**1**), Ütia Fodara Vedla (**3**), Ütia de Sénes (**7**), Seekofel Hut/Rifugio Biella (**9**)
Walking map: Tabacco 031, Pragser Dolomiten/Dolomiti di Braies, 1:25,000
Transport: 🚗 or 🚐 from St Vigil to Pederü (car park/bus stop). Free car parking by the Gasthaus Pederü (46° 38.341'N, 12° 2.479'E). Bus travel involves two changes: 🚐400 from Bruneck to St Lorenzen (every 15 minutes), hourly 🚐460 from St Lorenzen to St Vigil (last bus back at 20.19); then hourly 🚐461 to Pederü (last bus back 18.08).

Short walks: Fodara Vedla or Ütia de Sénes. Three shorter walks offering refreshment are obvious goals; ● all are the same grade as the main walk: you do not escape the skiddy ascent/descent between **1** and **2**! Rise to **Fodara Vedla 3**, then either turn left with the track at **4** (6.3km/3.9mi; up/down 475m/1560ft; 2h45min) or turn left on the track at **5** (8km/5mi; up/down 550m/1800ft; 3h30min); in both cases follow Trail 7A back to **2**. Or go all the way to the **Sennes Hut 7** (10.1km/6.3mi; up/down 600m/1970ft; 4h30min).

You can get into the Sennes in half a day from Pederü (as in the Short walks above), but the long, full day's walk takes in *three* pleasant huts. We meet Walk 1 of Book 1 at our last hut, the Seekofel Hut/Rifugio Biella — it has come up from Lake Prags/Braies in the Hochpustertal/Alta Pusteria.

Start out at **Pederü** (**1**): with your back to the Gasthaus Pederü, take the track to the left that rises ahead into the **Valón de Rü**. This old military road (Trail 7; also the Dolomites High Route 1) climbs in hairpins, and the loose gravel slows you down. Keep right on Trail 7 and High Route 1 at a Y-fork (**2**; you will return on the path to the left).

Finally the climb levels out and soon you reach the pastures and meadows of **Fodara Vedla** on the far side of the (usually dry) stream. The Ütia de Fodara Vedla (**3**; **1h 30min**) is a perfect alm hut, with a sunny terrace. The alm village itself is the pretty grouping of old wooden houses shown overleaf.

Continue further north uphill. After 450m the track curves left (**4**); keep right on a path (Trail 7, Dolomites High Route 1). *(Or go left here for a shorter walk.)* You then join the track again (**5**) and follow it to the right. *(This is another chance to turn left for a shorter walk.)* You could cut a bend off the track by taking the path straight ahead at (**6**); the long version of the walk will return from the right here. Then, in a basin with a little lake (**Lé de Sénes**) you come to another hut, the **Ütia de Sénes** (**7**; **2h30min**).

Continue along the track from this alm, but after 10 minutes turn

120 Dolomites, Book 2: Centre and East

Old alm village by the Ütia de Fodara Vedla

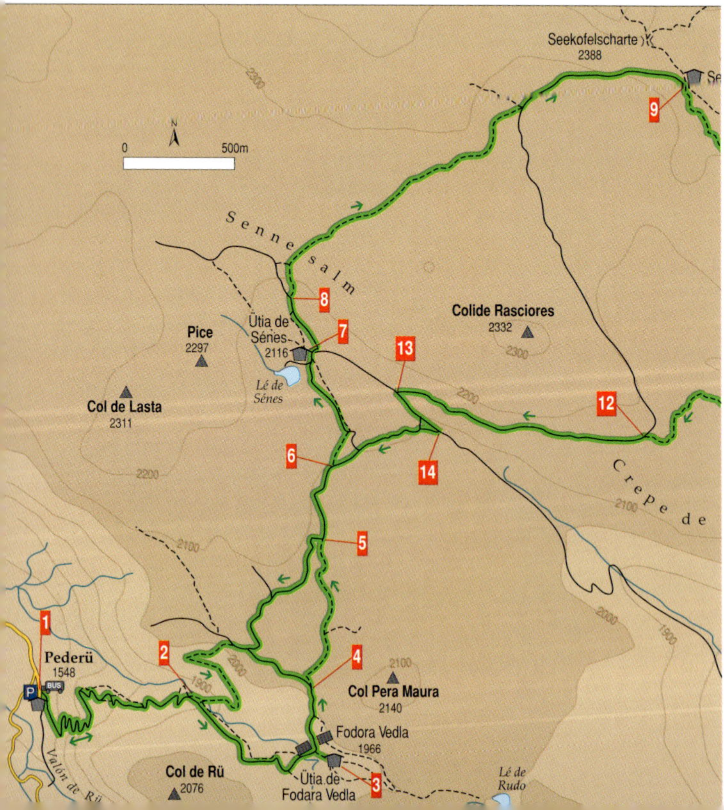

Walk 20: Across the Sennes to the Seekofel Hut 121

Chapel at Fodara Vedla

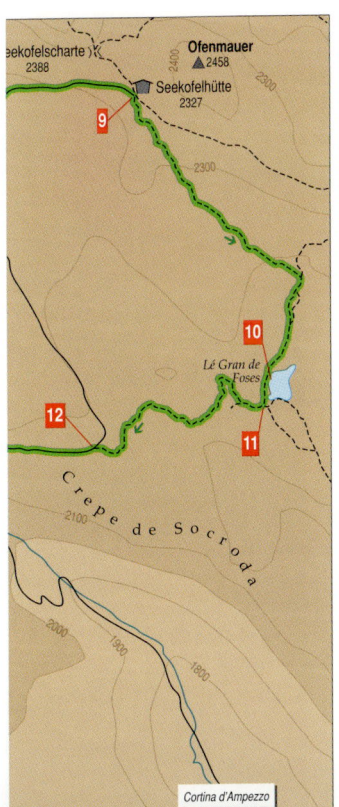

right (**8**) on Trail 6/High Route 1 towards the Seekofel Hut. You cross a stony plateau and reach the track once again, just before the hut. Take a break at the **Seekofel Hut/Rifugio Biella** (**9**; **3h30min**) and enjoy the good food! You will meet other walkers here who have tackled Dolomites High Route 1 from Lake Prags/Braies (see Book 1).

To end the walk without retracing your steps, take Trail 26: it's the right-hand fork just past the hut; you *leave* High Route 1. Follow this trail to a placid lake, **Gran de Foses** (**10**; **4h15min**), then take the first fork to the right (**11**). You rejoin a track and follow it to a T-junction (**13**) where you turn sharp left. After just 300m turn sharp right (**14**), coming back to your outgoing route at **6**. Now follow the track back to the top of your initial ascent at **2**. Unfortunately, you can *not* avoid the skiddy descent back down to **Pederü** (**1**; **6h30min**)!

Walk 21: WENGEN/LA VALLE AND THE 'VILES'

Distance/time: about 6.2km/ 3.8mi; 2h-2h30min
Grade: ● easy, with an ascent/ descent of 260m/850ft

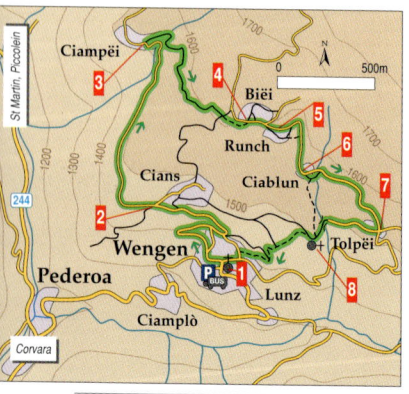

Waymarking: red/white; Trails 4/6 to start, N° 4 from **2** to **3**, N° 6 from from **5** to **6** and from **8**; also signs for 'Roda daes Viles'
Equipment: sturdy walking shoes, sun protection
Refreshments: available at Wengen (**1**) and Runch (**5**)
Walking map: Tabacco 07, Alta Badia-Arabba-Marmolada, 1:25,000
Transport: 🚗 or 🚐 to Wengen; park/alight at the church (46° 39.466'N, 11° 55.435'E). Bus travel involves a change: hourly 🚐 460 from Bruneck to the St Martin turn-off, then hourly 🚐 464 to Wengen (last bus back 18.42).

This gem of a short circular walk introduces you to several of the Ladin *viles* on their sunny slopes — it's a ramble into the cultural past. Without a breath- or thigh-sapping climb to any peak, you have tremendous views all round. The climb *is* in full sun, however, so remember to take sun protection!

Start the walk facing the **church** (**1**) in **Wengen/La Valle**: walk left uphill (Trails 4 and 6) past the **cemetery**. Then fork left towards 'Cians' (there may also be a signpost here for 'Meditationsweg'). Follow the road uphill through two big hairpin bends (with fine views to Peitlerkofel/Sass de Pútia when you head west) but, just before the second curve to the right, turn left on Trail 4 (**2**) for 'Ciampëi'. This soon runs through

The chapel of Santa Barbara at Tolpëi; this is one of the 'viles' scattered on the sunny slopes above Wengen.

woods to the isolated hamlet of **Ciampëi** (**1h**), where there's one house made entirely of wood.

Leave Route 4 as you enter the hamlet, turning right uphill through meadows on the sign-posted '**Roda daes Viles**' (**3**). Just below **Biëi** (**4**) — at the highest point in the walk — you come to **Runch** (**5**), with its Gothic building (in the lower part of the hamlet) made completely of stone, once the courthouse. You rejoin Trail 6 here.

Keeping on in the same direction, continue on the narrow road to **Ciablun** (**6**). You may spot a path with a 'Trail 6' signpost off to the right before you come into the village, but I urge you to go on all the way *into* **Tolpëi**. Once in the hamlet, approaching a T-junction, turn sharp right (**7**) on another road through the lower part of Tolpëi. The road peters out into a farm track that ends at the stream. Cross the little bridge over the stream and continue ahead on the track (no waymarks).

You will soon come to Trail 6 and the little **chapel of Santa Barbara** (**8**) shown below, with more beautiful views. From here walk back down to **Wengen** (**1**; **2h-2h30min**), which you can see diagonally below.

3 FASSATAL/VAL DI FASSA

Fassatal • Vigo di Fassa • Pozza di Fassa, Pera and Meida • Soraga • Moèna • Valle di San Pellegrino and the Monzoni group • Canazei • Ciampàc • Pordoijoch • Marmolada and the Fedaia Pass • Campitello

Walks: 22-24; *walking and cycling tip:* from Penìa to Pozza and Moèna (page 131); *walking tip:* Val Contrin (page 132)
Websites
www.fassa.com
www.visittrentino.info
www.istladin.net (for the Museo Ladin de Fascia)
Opening hours: see individual attractions

The Avisio Stream rises at the foot of Marmolada and runs into the Etsch/Adige north of Trient/Trento. Its upper reaches — between colossal Sella, Langkofel/Sassolungo, Rosengarten/Catinaccio, and Latemar on the right-hand side of the valley and the less well-known but equally spectacular mountains between Marmolada and the Monzoni group on the left — make up the Fassatal, one of the five Ladin valleys.

The Fassatal/Val di Fassa (Ladin: Fascia) is well equipped for both summer and winter sports and has even more accommodation than the Gadertal/Val Badia — so places like Vigo di Fassa, Pozza di Fassa, Moèna, Campitello and Canazei (Ladin: Cianacei) are good alternatives to the valleys north of Sella and Langkofel. Italians are the most frequent tourists here. Like all Ladin valleys in South Tyrol, the Fassa is Italian, although the valley belongs historically to the Tyrolean cultural area.

The Fassatal can be reached from South Tyrol via the Great Dolomite Road from the Karer Pass or via Predazzo and Cavalese (Fleimstal/Val di Fiemme), from Gröden/Gardena via the Sella Pass, and from Belluno via the Pordoi, Fedaia and San Pellegrino passes.

Transport: In summer all these connecting routes are covered by the Trentino Trasporti **buses** (some stretches also by the South Tyrolean service, SAD). In winter buses only cover the Penìa–Canazei–Predazzo–Trento route and the stretch via Vigo and the Karer Pass to Bolzano, but there is also a free **ski bus** Tiers–Lake Karer–Karer Pass–Vigo–Pera and another ski bus between Canazei and Pera. The nearest **railway stations** are at Bolzano and Trento (Bolzano is much quicker).

A **Fassatal and Lake Karer/Carezza Panorama Pass** is available in three versions: 60 € (3 out of 6 days), 85 € (6 out of 8 days), or 99 € (7 out of 13 days); it gives access to all the lifts in the Fassa Valley and Lake Karer area (Rosengarten!) as well as free use of all public transport. Tourists staying in the Fassa Valley get a discount on these prices using the free **Val di Fassa Card** given to all guests taking accommodation in the area. There's also the **Super Summer Card**: see page 22.

Events: In July and August there are **organised walks** to various alms (the 'Andar per Malghe'), with tastings of traditional foods. High summer also sees various music programs, like **I Suoni delle Dolomiti**: see page 21 (www.isuonidelledolomiti.it).

In mid-September the **Val di Fassa Bike**, a 45 km-long mountain bike race over all the Trentino passes (1800m) —takes place here — from Moèna to Alpe Lusia (www.valdifassabike.it).

Vigo di Fassa

In contrast to other, larger places in the Fassatal, Vigo (Ladin: Vich) is not in the valley itself but up on a sunny slope — surrounded by extensive meadows which until three generations ago were cultivated fields. The backdrop is a steep wooded slope and the rock walls of Rosengarten. From Vigo one looks out over the upper Fassatal to Langkofel and Sella; the peaks of the nearby Monzoni group on the far side of the valley glow red in the evening.

Although Vigo is a beautiful place to stay, with fine food and accommodation, it isn't packed out — even in high season. It's a good place for getting around anywhere between Bolzano and the Sella and Cavalese, but less well placed for Trento. Thousands of years ago this sunny slope attracted settlers, and from the Middle Ages until modern times the church of San Giovanni, somewhat lower down, was the *pieve* (parish church) for the whole valley. Vigo is proud to be a Ladin village. Ladin is spoken by almost everyone, and both the Ladin Cultural Institute and one of the five Ladin museums are located here.

The cabin car up to Ciampedié below the walls of Rosengarten makes Vigo a good starting point for **mountain walks**, climbing and hair-raising ski slopes. Tandem paragliding is also popular — with a guaranteed view of the Dolomites!

Transport: Good **places to park** are on the second curve of the Via Nuova below the village, in the Piazza Europa, or by the Ciampedié lift. The **SAD Bolzano–Predazzo bus** stops in the village centre, the **Canazei–Cavalese bus** only stops on the first curve of the Via Nuova below the village.

Vigo di Fassa, with Rodella (centre) and Langkofel/Sassolungo in the background

Sights and excursions: Despite tourism there are many **old stone Ladin houses** to be seen in Vigo. Some of them have beautiful old frescoes on the outside walls —

> **Wall paintings**
> It seems wherever you look in the Fassatal you see wall paintings. That was as true in olden times as it is now. The oldest preserved frescoes here date from the 14th century, but every year more are painted. Whether it was a St Christopher or a Mary with Child, a saint or an evangelist, the themes almost always had a religious content, whereas today landscapes are also in evidence. It would appear that the painters of the Brixen School were especially industrious in Campitello and Vigo in the 15th century. Some baroque painters include Giovanni Forcellini from the Agordino (17C), to whom the St Christopher in Campitello and frescoes in Moèna and Soraga were ascribed, and Valentino Rovisi (1715-1783), a student of the great Tiepolo, who painted the St Christopher at the church in Gries (Campitello) and frescoes in Moèna and Vigo.

like the houses at the beginning of Via Pontac and Via Vael. In the part of the village known as Costa and in Larcioné (both below the road to the Karer Pass) there are more beautiful old houses — take a look at N° 2 in Larcioné: it has two outside baking ovens, one on top of the other.

San Giovanni, once the parish church for the whole Fassatal, lies somewhat below Vigo; it's a beautiful late-Gothic building with three naves. The pillars, made from stone from the Monzoni group, are without capitals and so reach right up into the Gothic net vault, making the room look higher than it actually is. The baptismal font in Gothic-Renaissance style (1538) is a reminder that up until 1554 all valley baptisms took place here — as well as all weddings and burials. Frescoes in the choir depict scenes from the life of St John the Baptist (the patron saint); these date from the time the church we see today was built (dedicated in 1489).

The **Museo Mineralogico Monzoni** is a small private museum in a old log cabin-style barn *(tabià)* with beautiful minerals — above all from the volcanic Monzoni range. 8, Via Pilat (downhill, off Via Nuova). *Open mid-Jun to mid-Sep daily from 16.00-19.00 and 20.30-22.00. Free entry.*

There is another Gothic church high above Vigo, the pilgrimage church of **Santa Giuliana**. The nave was dedicated in 1519, and the church has a deeply sloping roof. The tower is older than the nave and chancel, as shown by the Romanesque windows. Its southern wall also boasts a huge fresco with a St Christopher and Christ Child, while inside are three frescoes portraying the martyrdom of St Juliana (the patron saint). The choir frescoes are especially beautiful, being examples from masters of the Brixen School (15C). The chapel of **San Maurizio** next door, first documented in 1297, is probably the oldest stone building in the whole valley. *Open Mon/Thu/Sat 16.00-18.00; guiding Wed 09.30.*

The **Museo Ladin de Fascia** is a modern museum in an old stone building. On display are a complete *stua* and *musha* (see 'Ladin houses' on page 133), beautiful panelling, carnival masks (very popular throughout the valley in olden days and still worn today, with long noses and a dangling carrot!), life-size figures with carnival dress and local costumes, farming implements and memorabilia, folk art, carvings, etc. There are also videos with historic films about life on the farm (those taken in Penìa and dating from 1982 look as if they come from the 19th century). *Museum open daily 10 Jun-10 Sep and 20 Dec-6 Jan from 10.00-12.30 and 15.00-19.00, otherwise Tue-Sat 15.00-19.00. Closed Nov and first week in Jun. Entry fee 5 €.*

The **cable car from Vigo to Ciampedié** holds 100 people and operates daily from early Jun to early Oct, 08.30-13.00 and 14.00-18.00; one way 11 €, up and back 21 €; The **chair lift from Lake Karer to the Paolina Hut** (Walk 22) runs end May to mid-Oct, 08.30-12.15 and 13.30-17.30; one way 13 €, up and back 19 €.

From the top station (1997m) you have a fantastic view to Rosengarten, Langkofel and Monzoni. In winter skiers whizz down the red Thöni Run to Vigo; two chair lifts are just nearby; the black Tomba Run goes to Pian Pecei (1900m). But in summer the mountain station is the starting point for **walks in the Rosengarten** area, above all to **Roda di Vael** with its two huts and on to the Karer Pass (see Walk 22) and the Vajolet Hut, from where there are many ascent routes up Rosengarten, the Vajolet Towers and Kesselkogel/Catinaccio d'Antermoia (Walk 23).

Pozza di Fassa (Poza), Pera and Meida

These three adjacent villages in the Fassatal are all recent except for some old barns in log cabin style that can be seen in **Meida** along the banks of the San Nicolò which runs up the eponymous side-valley.

Sights and excursions: The **Val**

Old sleigh in the Museo Ladin

di San Nicolò makes an excellent excursion; the road ends somewhat above the **Alm Ciampié**. The **Buffaure group** in the north and the **Monzoni** in the south are pretty much unknown territory for tourists. The Buffaure don't look as though they belong to the Dolomites. No wild peaks, no high plateaus, dark basaltic stone instead of bright chalk, and lots of water — these mountains are of volcanic origin. There are few waymarked walking trails; everyone makes for Rosengarten on the other side of the valley.

Isolated, pristine **Val Jumela** is unforgettable. At the top lift station there is a botanical garden; the hut, Baita Cuz at 2200m, is

By the Avisio in Moèna, with the Monzoni group in the background

manned and has a delightful view to Rosengarten. **Cabin lift Pozza–Buffaure and chair lift Buffaure–Col Valvacin** run from mid-Jun to mid-Sep 08.30-12.20, 14.00-17.50, combi-ticket 13.50 € one way; up and back 17 €.

In **Pera** there is a restored mill run by the Museum of Ladin Culture called the **Molin de Pèzol**. *Open Jun to early Sep Mon-Sat from 10.00-12.00 and 15.00-19.00, also 27 Dec to Mar; otherwise closed; entry free.*

From Pera you can get to the huts in the Rosengarten area via the **Vajolet Valley**, and from **Mazzin** just a bit further up there is access to Val de Dona, the Antermoia Hut (Walk 23) and — via the Tierser-Alpl Hut — to Schlern and the Seiser Alm.

In **Pozza** there are old frescoes on the outside walls of a handful of houses, but they are becoming ever more damaged from traffic.

Soraga

This little village (Ladin: Sorega), with its beautiful old *tabià* (wooden barns) lies somewhat above the road; the isolated church somewhat below. There are some venerable old Ladin houses to be seen in the village centre, in the higher part of the village called **Soraga Alta** and in **Palua**. Several of the houses in Soraga Alta have beautiful outdoor frescoes, for instance **Ciasa Zepelin** (Madonna with Child and two saints).

Moèna

Moèna, at the junction of the Fassatal and the San Pellegrino Valley marks the beginning of the Ladin-speaking area. The village is only built up along the main through road; on the edges you can still see the old hamlets that grew together to form the village. Back in the Middle Ages, Moèna was taken from the princes of Brixen and given to Trento, so its history is rather different from the rest of the valley. But it has kept its old language — Ladin (and a very special dialect thereof, with many Italian words).

Sights and excursions: In the lanes round Piaz de Ramon on the left side of the Avisio and Piaz de Sotegrava on the right side are a couple of dozen old houses with frescoes, among them some log cabin-style *tabià* — like Tabià Janac on Via San Pelegrino and Tabià Deville dating from 1567 in Via F Filzi (both near Piaz de Ramon).

As well as the neo-Gothic **parish church** on a hill west of the village, it's worth visiting the nearby little **Wolfgangskirche** (S Volfango). Inside is a cycle of frescoes dating from the 15th century showing several motifs, for instance a beautiful St Martin, the Annunciation, and scenes from Christ's Passion. The key to the church is with the parish priest. *On Tue free guided tours of Moèna's churches at 16.00.*

The valley of the **Rio San Pellegrino** forks off from the

Fassatal in Moèna; a road runs over the Pellegrino Pass to **Falcade** and into the Agordino of Belluno. The attractive and hardly developed **Monzoni mountains** rise on the left-hand side of the valley with their dark basaltic stone; to the right are the even lonelier ranges around **Cima Bocche** and **Cima di Laste**. There are no huts up at these heights, only bivouacs. In both summer and winter only the surroundings of **Alpe Lusia** are visited, as there are lifts and roads from the south and north.

Above the **Passo San Pellegrino** (Ladin: Pas de Sèn Pelegrin), at a height of 1918m, is the little church of **Sant'Antonio de Padova**, built in 1934. It marks the site of a pilgrims' hospice from the Middle Ages (14C) and its church, both of which were destroyed in the mountain war in 1915. Today mass is celebrated here on Sundays and holidays (even in winter), and both local people and tourists attend.

A little road goes to idyllic **Lago di Pozze**, flanked by meadows and woods (the colour of the larches in autumn is magnificent). There is just one building at the lake, the Gasthaus Miralago, with a good restaurant and rooms.

Walking Route 604 begins at the pass: this leads in about 2h to Passo Selle with its little hut (2528m); yellow Rhaetian poppies grow by the remains of Austrian emplacements from the War in the Dolomites.

Canazei

Canazei (Ladin: Cianacei), the lively centre of the Fassatal, stands at 1500 m; it's quieter in the shoulder season, when the lifts are closed.

Langkofel and Sella rise in the north, Marmolada in the east. The Sella and Pordoi passes attract motorists who enjoy pass roads and racing round Sella by car, motorcycle or bicycle. But maybe they shouldn't move on so fast, since both Canazei and nearby Campitello are as suitable as places in the Gröden/Gardena or Hochabtei/Alta Badia valleys for a holiday at the foot of the Sella group.

Lifts give access to the Sella Ronda in both summer and winter.

Transport: There are **parking places** by the Eghes Wellness Centre, opposite the Pecol lift station, and in Alba in front of the Ciampàc valley lift station. **Buses** connect with Cavalese 10-12 times a day, and an express bus runs 6 times a day to Trento. The **'Fassa Express'** (a mini-bus dressed up to look like a train) links Penìa, Alba, Canazei and Campitello.

Events: The traditional 'Skyrace' takes place here at the end of July, when runners go from Canazei to Piz Boè (9km) and return by a different route (11km) — an exhausting race, with a height difference of 1700 m. The famous **Sella Ronda** (see page 45) takes place in February.

Sights and excursions: Canazei consists of several different areas that have gradually grown together.

In the centre, the settlement around the **Piaz de Sèn Florián** with the church of **St Florian** and old stone houses still forms a recognisable nucleus. (From here, after the bridge, there is a road to the Sellajoch via Ruf de Antermont.) A little lower down, the council has treated itself to a modern world-class building by top architect Ettore Sottsass, the

Penìa, above Canazei

Neue Rathaus (town hall, with tourist information office).

The western part of the village, still quite agricultural-looking in places, is called **Gries**. At the parish church of **Madonna della Neve** (Mary of the Snow) the eye is drawn to a huge 18th-century wall fresco. It's a St Christopher by the Tiepolo School painter Valentino Rovisi. **Majón de Roces,** a beautifully kept 17th-century Ladin house (part of the museum), stands somewhat above the Strèda Dolomites; it opens for exhibitions.

Penìa is the highest year-round settlement in Trentino; the dwellings cluster around the Gothic parish church of **San**

Fassatal/Val di Fassa 131

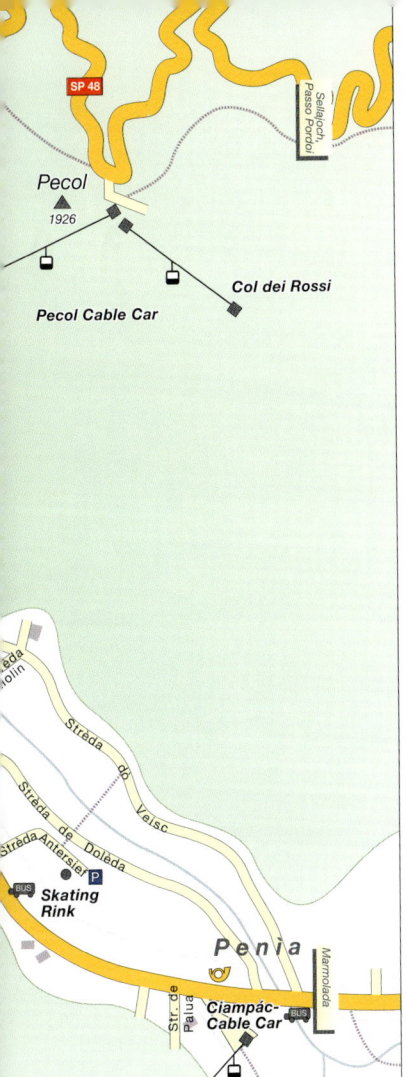

Potatoes are still farmed on the steep slope above the village, and the soil, prone to landslides because the slope is so steep, has to be carried back up to the tops of the fields.

In the lower village, on Strèda de Treve (the main road), the **Museo Colombo Dantone** is worth seeing — a private museum of Ladin farming traditions in the 19th and 20th centuries. Another important part of the display shows military objects from the First World War on the Dolomites Front. *Museum open end Jun-early Sep, daily from 17.00-19.00, entry is free, but donations are welcome.*

Penìa has a **carnival** with old masks and costumes (from 20 January).

● **Walking and cycling tip: from Penìa to Pozza and Moèna**
A beautiful track for both walkers and cyclists begins on the east side of the bridge over the Avisio in **Penìa** (the **Strèda dò Veisc**, signposted). The whole distance (see Tabacco 1:25,000 map N° 06) is about 20 km, so allow at least 5h on foot or 1h by bike. But you can break off any time, since at all villages by the river there are buses in both directions.

When you get to the next bridge, you cross to the far bank. The route then stays on that side of the river, passing the Ischia sports area of Campitello and usually keeping close to the river. You bypass Mazzin. In **Pozza** there's a short ascent and then the almost-flat, always asphalted and well marked track continues to **Someda** and **Moèna**.

In winter the track is an easy cross-country ski route down to Moèna and Predazzo — part of the Marcialonga.

Sebastiano with its large outdoor fresco of St Christopher. Despite the new buildings, it's not a wealthy place, as can be seen from the route to the two farms of Vèra (1680m) and Lorenz, the highest farm: the old village roofs are mostly patched or covered with 1950s corrugated iron. How antiquated the farming methods here were a generation ago can be seen from videos — like the ones showing hay-making in 1982.

Protected farmhouse in Gries, with the onion dome of the parish church behind it

Ciampàc

The Ciampàc **walking** and skiing area lies south of Canazei's Alba district, on the way to the Fedaia Pass. The **Ciampàc cable car** (the steep motorable track is *not* recommended) from Alba operates end Jun to mid-Sep 08.30-12.00 and 13.00-17.30. It runs up to 2160m, from where a connecting chair lift goes up to Sela Brunech at 2440m; one way 13 €, up and back 21 €.

The skiing area, with a magnificent black piste, lies between 2100 and 2440m on the snowy northern side of the mountain chain west of Marmolada, culminating in the Colac peak at 2715 m.

In summer the green alm around the cable car station is a good **walking area for families**, with several huts offering refreshments (for instance, Tobià del Ghiagher, 2200m, near the top station, a traditional hut with rustic food and a highly recommended 30-minute **botanical circuit**, open summer and winter).

But the main goal of the day out is in any case to see the view: the mighty flanks of Sella rise just opposite. From the **Sela Brunech** there's a straightforward route down to the **Ciampàc alm area** or into the **Val Jumela** towards Melda/Pozza (mostly on motorable lanes), from where you can get back by bus. The walks over the ridges to the west and east are only suitable for experienced mountain climbers (the Roseal ridge can only be attempted with climbing equipment).

● **Walking tip: Val Contrin.** Just to the south of Alba is the **Ruf** (River) **Contrin** with its two alms, the **Malga Robinson** in the middle of the valley and the **Malga Contrin** with a hut. To get there (see Tabacco 1:25,000 map N° 06) take Trail 602, a steep motorable track that begins at the Alba lift station. The climb takes 1h30min, the descent 1h15min. Once up there at 2000m, you'll be sitting just below the wild western flanks of Marmolada, rising another 1300m above you. Knowing this makes the food all the tastier! The Rifugio Contrin, at 2027m, really appeals to lovers of alpine food, with home-made butter, cheese and yoghurt.

Pordoijoch/Passo Pordoi

However they get there — on foot, by bus or car, by bicycle or on the Pecol cable car (from Strèda Roma), one of the first things every visitor to Canazei does is go to the pass below the south wall of Sass Pordoi.

Transport: You can get there by bus in summer; **buses** run from the **car park** opposite the Pecol lift. Or you can take the **Pecol cable car**, then the connecting **Col de Rossi cable car**: mid-Jun to Sep 08.30-13.00 and 14.00-17.00; one way 14 €, up and back 22 €. The **Sass Pordoi cable car** operates end May to end Oct 09.00-17.00; one way 14 €, up and back 22 €. There's are various combi-tickets available.

From the belvedere there are fantastic views to Marmolada. But if you follow the easy **Bindelweg** (Walk 24) to Lake Fedaia (from where you can take a bus back to Canazei), you'll see a lot more! The Bindelweg is one of the most beautiful walks in the Dolomites, saturated with flowers and full of gorgeous views. But of course this means that it is also saturated with walkers. It's a must on account of the dramatic views to Marmolada, even if masses of people get on your nerves.

Take the lift up to **Sass Pordoi** at 2950m, and you will be completely surrounded by high, wild mountains. The views are so astounding that you may not be tempted to go any further. But **Piz**

Ladin houses of the Fassatal

In contrast to many other places in High Tyrol, houses in the Fassatal are often plastered stone buildings, decorated on the outside with frescoes. Only the roof will be of wood. In a second building (almost always made of wood in 'log cabin' style and called the 'tabià') are the working areas with stable and barn. As in Gröden/Gardena and many parts of German Tyrol, this building stands on a hill and is partially built into the hill, so that the cattle can be easily taken in and out from below and hay can be brought to the upper floor via a wooden ramp. Up until two generations ago, there were scaffolds here (as in the Gadertal/Val Badia) for drying broad beans in autumn, but none remain.

In the house is the 'stua' (living room), panelled in wood carved with various motifs, with wooden furniture. A passageway leads to the little kitchen. There is also the 'musha', a room with a traditionally painted chimney, adjacent bench and wooden table for drying clothing. This room is usually in the southeastern part of the house and next to the elders' bedroom (which is also panelled). All rooms, including the kitchen and other bedrooms lead on to a central hallway called the 'pòrtech'. In the old days there was no running water in the house; it had to be drawn from the well. Well-kept old wells can be seen in many of the valley hamlets.

Boè, the highest peak of the Sella massif (3152m), beckons strong walkers. It's fairly easy to get there (about 2h, with a little scrambling

Marmolada as it was, before the glacial collapse of July 2022. Lake Fedaia sits below. The collapse has been a disaster for tourism in the whole Fassatal.

at the end; Tabacco 1:25,000 map N° 07) and, once there, you have the Capanna Piz Fassa with a snack bar. Trails link up with the road to the Grödner Joch/Passo Gardena and right across Sella to Kolfuschg/Colfosco, Corvara and the Grödner Joch; there are also protected climbing paths to both the Grödner Joch and Sellajoch. Take *plenty of water;* there is not a drop on this high plateau!

The Fedaia Pass and Marmolada

Approaching from Canazei, en route to the **Passo Fedaia** (in summer there are **buses** from Canazei and 7 a day direct from Trento), you first pass a once-large expanse of water, **Lake Fedaia**. There are in fact two Fedaia lakes, the natural one at 2028m, and the man-made reservoir at 2053m; both lie before the pass in Trentino.

At the pass it's worth taking a break on the south side of the lake, perhaps visiting the small but interesting **Museo della Grande Guerra** before going on to the cable car at Malga Ciapela or returning to Canazei. *Museum open end May-Sep daily (except Tue) from 10.00-12.00 and from 14.00-17.00; entry 7 €.*

There are no 'normal' routes up **Marmolada**; they are all the preserve of well-equipped, experienced climbers. But from the dam of **Lake Fedaia** there is a **chair lift to the Pian de Fiacconi Hut**; mid-May to end Sep 08.30-17.00; one way 10 €, up and back 13.50 €. Further south, there's a **cable car from Malga Ciapela** (1467m) in the Belluno region to Marmolada. The cable car up to it first lands at **Serauta** (2950m), just at the edge of the glacier; **another cable car** goes from there to a point below the eastern peak of Marmolada (3250m). These lifts run from Jul to mid-Sep and in winter from 09.00-16.00, combi-ticket up and back 35 €.

Today the highest point is measured as **Punta Penìa** at 3343m. The somewhat less steep north side of the range is covered with glaciers; the south side is a single massive wall 800m high. The glaciers, while impressive, are just small remains; glacial shrinkage is evident throughout the Alps. On July 3rd, 2022, a glacial collapse on Marmolada caused 11 deaths during a heat wave; it is thought that water below the glacier caused the avalanche.

The whole Marmolada area was a war zone during the Italo-Austrian War in the Dolomites (1915-1917); terrible fighting took place here, above 3000m. Before the offensive in autumn 1917, the Austrian emplacements lay in view of the Italians. To avoid them, they built ice tunnels through the glacier.

At the middle station, Serauta, there is an excellent new, private museum — not to be confused with the one by Lake Fedaia! This one, called **Museo Marmolada Grande Guerra 3000**, displays a wealth of everyday items from this war, as well as some interactive exhibits. One fascinating feature is the 'ice city' — a 10 km-long ice tunnel complex. *Open at the same hours as the lift; entry free.*

Campitello

Quieter than Canazei, the neighbouring village of Campitello (Ladin: Ciampedel) is more traditional and agricultural, even though it is totally dependent on tourism. If you walk from the stream along Via SS Filippo e Giacomo and then Salita alla Chiesa up to the church, you'll get a good impression of what remains of the agricultural character of the place. It's above all evident in **Pian**, the sunny part of the village on a slope 100m higher up. The stream that runs through Campitello, the Ruf Duron, has its source up on Rosengarten. The church of **SS Filippo e Giacomo** stands on a hill; it has an unusual tower which looks more like a castle tower. As so often in this area, there is a large fresco of St Christopher outside, as well as other wall paintings.

Transport: In summer there is a **shuttle service** to the huts in the area — Val Duron (Rosengarten), Val Monzoni, and the Gardeccia Hut in Rosengarten, since all the access roads are closed to traffic. Times are posted at the bus stop in the centre. A **cable car** runs up to **Rodella** (mid-Jun to early Oct, from 08.30-17.30; one way 14 €, up and back 22 €.

Excursions: Rodella is the panoramic mountain of the Fassa Valley *par excellence*. From the peak with its hut you see Rosengarten/Catinaccio, Schlern/Sciliar, the Seiser Alm/Alpe di Siusi, Langkofel, the Puez and Geisler/Odle groups, Sella's massive base, Antelao, Pelmo, Marmolada, and the Monzoni group — and above that you can even make out Cimone della Pala and the Cima d'Asta, Lagorai ... and, to the left of Latemar, the Brenta Dolomites.

You can walk to the foot of **Langkofel/Sassolungo** in half an hour, then pick up the route round the mountain at the **Friedrich August Hut** (see Walk 8). Using the map for Walk 8, you could do the beautiful walk over to the Comici Hut on the north side of Langkofel, crossing the **Steinerne Stadt** (Stone City), a magnificent landscape of fallen mountain rock. Or you can just wander around the flower-filled alm meadows at will.

The mountain hut **Rifugio Col Rodella** lies on the summit, about a 20-minute walk from the upper station; good cooking. You are likely to see **hang-gliders** at both the top lift station and the hut.

Walk 22: FROM THE UPPER STATION OF THE CIAMPEDIÉ LIFT TO THE PAOLINA HUT

Distance/time: about 5.9km/ 3.7mi; under 3h
Grade: ● easy, with an ascent of 350m/1150ft and descent of 250m/820ft; good trails underfoot
Waymarking: red/white; Trail 545 from ❸ to ❻, Trail 549 to ❼, and from there Trail 539
Equipment: sturdy walking shoes, sun protection
Refreshments: available at the Rifugio Ciampedié at the top station of the Ciampedié lift (❶), Rifugio Nigritella (❷), Baita M Pederiva (❺), Rifugio Roda di Vael/Rotwand Hut (❻), and at the Paolina Hut (❽), at the top station of the Paolina lift
Walking map: Tabacco 06, Val di Fassa e Dolomiti Fassane, 1:25,000
Transport: 🚗 to the Ciampedié cable car in Vigo (46° 25.280'N, 11° 40.297'E), or hourly 🚌180 from Bolzano; alight at the 'Funivia Catinaccio' bus stop; then see lift operating times and prices on page 127. Return on the Paolina lift and then 🚌180 running from Lake Karer/Carezza to Welschnofen/ Nova Levante and the Fassatal — back to your car or back to base.

This straightforward walk gives fine views to the Rosengarten/Catinaccio area and Latemar, but also to the Monzoni group on the far side of the Fassatal, with Lagorai in the background.

Take the large (100 persons!) cable car from Vigo up to the **Ciampedié** mountain station (❶), then **start the walk**: from the station follow the gravel tracks past the **Ciampedié** and **Nigritella** (❷) huts. Not far past the latter hut, ignore the first track off right, but turn up right on Trail 545 (❸), a lovely woodland path which takes you across the (usually dry) **Vael** Stream to **Malga Vael**, an alm where it is possible to buy some milk or cheese (❹).

You touch on the Vael Stream again (**45min**), then climb to the two huts below the walls of Rosengarten/Catinaccio, the little **Baita Pederiva** (❺; **1h45min**) and the **Roda di Vael Hut** (❻). Both of these are good places to take a break, especially at Baita Pederiva just at the pass (the Rifugio Roda di Vael is a bit higher up). As at all mountain huts, there is polenta with cheese, goulash or mushrooms, various cakes, seasonal fruit with whipped cream, and other regional delicacies.

From here follow Trail 549 southwards ('Karerpass'), along the south side of **Rosengarten**, directly under the southern ridge of **Rotwand/Roda di Vael**. The

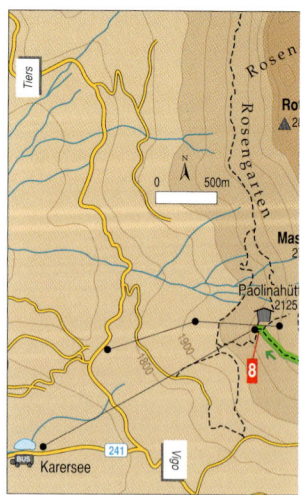

Walk 22: From the Ciampedié lift to the Paolina Hut   137

Eagle memorial dedicated to Theodor Christomannos, also shown on page 5

going is very easy underfoot, so you can enjoy the magnificent views. At a junction you pass the **memorial** (**7**) shown above, with a huge eagle, dedicated to Theodor Christomannos — whose idea it was to build the Great Dolomite Road (a bit of its history is described on page 59 in Book 1).

From here continue on Trail 539. After another short flat stretch, you descend to the **Paolina Hut** (**8**; **2h45min**) and the chair lift down to **Lake Karer/Carezza**.

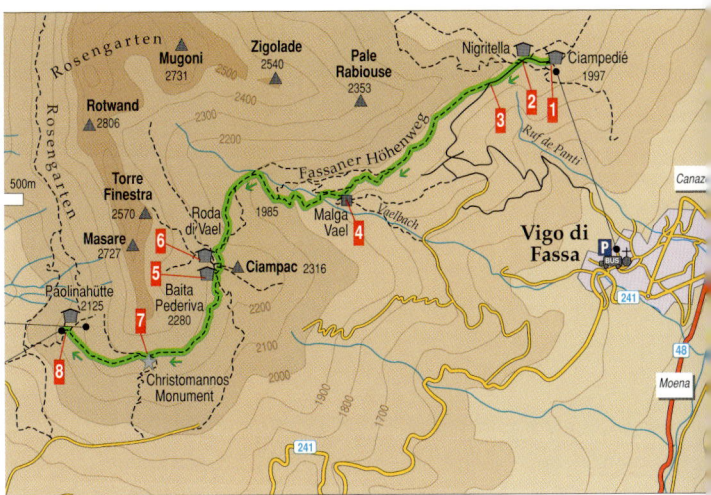

Walk 23: FROM MAZZIN TO THE VAJOLET HUT VIA THE ANTERMOIA HUT

Distance/time: about 13.3km/8.2mi; 6h15min-8h
Grade: ● very strenuous mountain hike on sometimes less than good trails; ascent 1400m/4590ft; descent 1200m/3935ft. You need a fine day; take local advice, there is a danger of hailstorms in this area.
Waymarking: red/white; Trail 580 to **8**, Trail 584 to **11**, then Trail 546 to the end
Equipment: hiking boots, sun protection, walking pole(s)
Refreshments: available at the Rifugio Antermoia (**7**), Rifugio Passo Principe/Grasleitenpass Hut (**10**), Rifugio Vaiolet/Vajolet Hut (**11**), and the Rifugio Gardeccia (**12**) at the end of the road in the Vajolet Valley
Walking map: Tabacco 06, Val di Fassa e Dolomiti Fassane, 1:25,000

Transport: 🚗 or hourly 🚌 101 from Cavalese to 'Mazzin di Fassa'. Park by the bus stop on the main SS48 (46° 27.478'N, 11° 42.073'E). Return by pre-arranged 🚐 minibus from the Gardeccia Hut.

Short walk 1: *Spina da Lèch* (5km/3mi; 3h up and back; ● ascent/descent of 425m/1395ft). Follow the main walk to **2** and return the same way.

Short walk 2: *Vajolet and Preuss huts* (3.2km/2mi; 1h55min up and back; ● ascent/descent of 235m/765ft). Park at the **Gardeccia Hut 12** (reached from the 'Giro d'Italia' roundabout on the SS48 below Ronch; 46° 26.825'N, 11° 38.423'E) and walk up the wide track (Trail 546) to the **Vajolet and Preuss huts** (**11**). Walk 30 in Book 1 comes in from the left here. Return the same way.

Most walkers deviate from our route by taking Trail 578 via Val Duron to Campitello, but I think this much longer hike via Lake Antermoia and the Vajolet Towers is far more satisfying. You meet Walk 3 from Book 1 at the Vajolet Hut; it has come up on Trail 542 from Rosengarten.

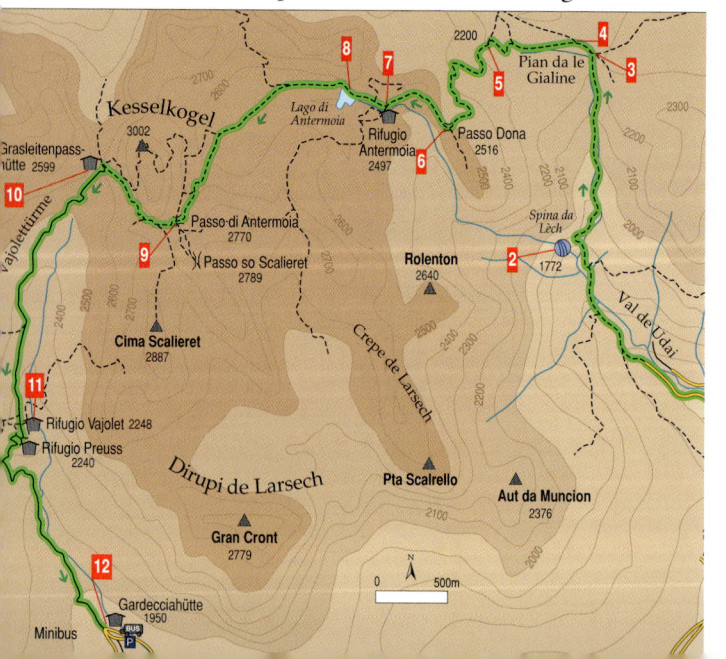

View from the Passo di Antermoia to the Vajolet Towers

Start out at the **bus stop** in **Mazzin**: walk up the road opposite the **church** (**1**). Take the first left, then the second right ('Val Udai', Trail 580). The road first runs to the right of the stream but soon crosses it on a bridge. Follow it to the end, then continue up the valley on a good but little-used track. At one point you will come close to a strong spring coming out of a rock wall, the **Spina da Lèch** (**2**). Now the trail gets steeper, but the views improve.

Finally, after turning left at a T-junction (**3**; **2h45min**), you pass a shed on the flat floor of the alm **Pian dele Gialine** (**4**). Then well-used Trail 578 comes in from the right (**5**; from Val Duron); it's well used because it's shorter, but it's not as lovely! You cross some rubble and rock ribs and come to a little hut on **Passo Dona** (**6**) — just another shed. But just around the next bend is the much longed-for **Antermoia Hut** (**7**; **3h45min**), where the view to Kesselkogel opens out.

After taking a break at the hut you pass **Lago di Antermoia** (**8**), a mountain lake embedded in rubble. It's only 5m deep — a karst lake with no surface inlet or outlet; only seasonally is there any water. No fish live in the cold clear water under Kesselkogel/Catinaccio d'Antermoia...

From the lake take Trail 584 to the **Passo di Antermoia** at the left of Kesselkogel. This ascent is really strenuous — steep and covered with loose gravel. Once at the pass (**9**; **4h45min**) you're in for a surprise: Rosengarten/Catinaccio and the Vajolet Towers are before you — magnificent!

A short way down from the pass you come to the little **Grasleitenpass Hut/Rifugio Passo Principe** (**10**), built into a rock overhang. Then you descend a wide track into the Vajolet Valley, passing just below the **Vajolet Towers**. Next come the **Vajolet** and **Preuss huts** (**11**) and the **Gardeccia Hut** (**12**; **6h15min**), where you meet your minibus.

Walk 24: THE BINDELWEG/VIEL DAL PAN

Distance/time: about 7km/4.3mi for the Lake Fedaia finish; about 6.6km/4mi for the Porta Vescovo finish; 2h45min for either route
Grade: ● easy walk on good trails (*but* sometimes shared with mountain bikers). Fedaia finish: descent of 400m/1310ft, ❗ you must be sure-footed and have a head for heights; Porto Vescovo finish: ascent of 200m/650ft
Waymarking: red/white; all Trail 601, also Dolomites High Route 2
Equipment: sturdy shoes or hiking boots, sun protection, optional walking pole(s)
Refreshments: Rifugio Viel dal Pan (**3**)
Walking map: Tabacco 06, Val di Fassa e Dolomiti Fassane, 1:25,000
Transport: 🚗 or hourly 🚌 471 from Canazei, Arabba or Gröden/Val Gardena to the large car park at Pordoi Pass (46° 29.293'N, 11° 48.643'E). Return by the same bus from Arabba or from Lake Fedaia to Canazei (connections to Gröden)

One of the most beautiful walks in the Dolomites, saturated with flowers, the Bindelweg is also known as the Viel dal Pan (Bread Path) in Ladin. It follows the high Padon Ridge between Sella and Marmolada and was a grain-smuggling route in the Middle Ages, used to avoid paying taxes to the Republic of Venice.

Start the walk at the **Pordoijoch/Passo Pordoi** (**1**): take Trail 601 (also Dolomites High-Level Route 2) south uphill to a pass (**2**; **30min**) from where you will have a fine view west along the **Padon ridge** and your first views of the mountains to the south. Marmolada is still somewhat hidden, but as you progress it will gradually reveal its full width.

The wide route easily traverses the southern flanks of the steep ridge and crosses alpine meadows with a wealth of flora. The food is good in the **Viel dal Pan Hut** (**3**; **1h15min**), so linger a while on the terrace enjoying the fantastic views — to Lake Fedaia below and up to Marmolada — with Gran Vernel, Punta Rocca, Punta Penìa (at 3343m, the highest peak in the Dolomites) ... and its ever-smaller glacier (where a collapse in July 2022 killed 11 climbers).

From the hut the path is some-

The Padon ridge, with a view west to the Col dei Rossi lift

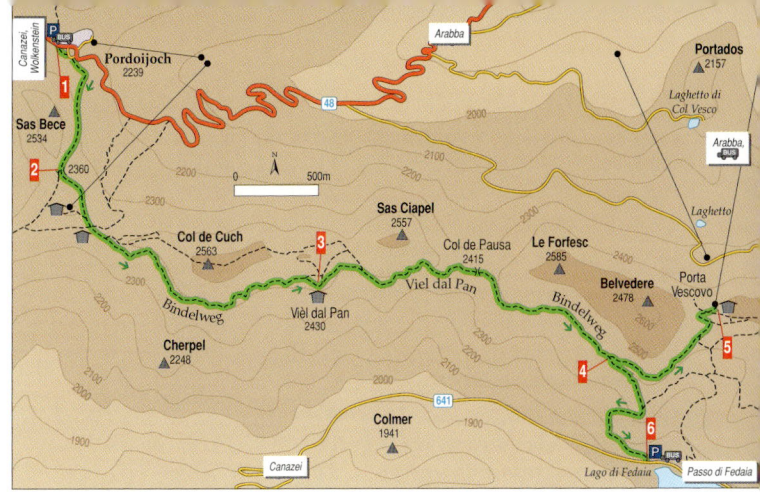

what narrower and less well used (most people having turned back from the hut). Lake Fedaia (a reservoir) draws ever closer, until you are almost above it.

At a fork (**4**; **2h**) you have a choice: go left uphill to **Porta Vescovo** (**5**; **2h45min**), from where you can take the Arabba cable car, or go right on a somewhat exposed, but well protected and not difficult path down to the dam of **Lake Fedaia** (**6**; **2h45min**).

4 VAL DI FIEMME/FLEIMSTAL

Cavalese • Predazzo • Val Travignolo and the Rolle Pass

Walk: 26
Websites
www.visitfiemme.it

Opening hours: see individual attractions

In contrast to the Fassatal, the Italian-speaking Fleimstal is less developed for tourism. The bordering mountains have no huts, and only trekkers use the bivouac shelters. So the landscape is more pristine and lonely — but hardly less imposing than that further north.

From Auer/Ota or Neumarkt/Egna in the Etsch/Adige Valley a narrow, rather exposed road with fantastic views leads via Montan/Montagna to the pass of Kaltenbrunn/Fontanefredde. Then the road drops along a sunny slope into the Fleimstal/Val di Fiemme. The view is fantastic: you look along the valley and over to Monte Agnello and the wild, jagged Lagorai range, and then to beautifully sited Cavalese.

You come to Tèsero with its large parish church with a Gothic tower, baroque decoration and a huge fresco of St Christopher. Only when you reach Ziano does the road meet the valley floor and fork: to the left is Predazzo and the Fassa Valley, to the right is a road along Val Travignolo up to the Rolle Pass, San Martino di Castrozza and on to the Pale group.

Transport: Access to this valley is via good roads to Auer, to the Fassatal and Rolle Pass; the roads in the Fleimstal are very winding. Good **bus** connections to Trento (via Auer) and the Fassatal, San Martino, Primiero and twice a day to/from Bolzano (change at Vigo). The nearest **railway station** is Auer.

The **Fiemme Mountain Pass** is valid in summer for the Fleimstal and Obereggen/San Floriano: 3 out of 7 days (47 €), 7 days (57 €) and 6 out of 13 days (72 €).

Frescoed façade of the Palazzo della Magnifica Comunità in Cavalese

Cavalese

Cavalese lies on a sunny terrace above the Fleimstal and has been the major centre for the whole valley since the Middle Ages. As you approach Cavalese from Auer, the village, with its Gothic parish church in front of the jagged profile of the Lagorai group on the south side of the valley, looks like the lid of a chocolate box.

Cavalese is a good place for both winter and summer sports: there's a cable car straight up to Alpe Cermis on Lagorai, and in Pampeago (7.5km northeast) a connection to the Fleimstal/Obereggen ski area. There was a terrible accident on the Alpe Cermis cable car in 1976, when the cable snapped and the gondola fell, killing 42 people.

Transport: Direct **bus** connections to Trento (via Auer and the Etschtal or, more slowly, via the Fleimstal), Bolzano, Canazei and, irregularly, Primiero and Feltre. There is a **bus station** with offices for Trentino Trasporti.

Events: Village events include the '**Prozesso alle Streghe**' during the first week of January, a folk festival in commemoration of the Witches' Trials, and the '**Desmontegada de le càore**', usually in the third week of September, when the goats and sheep come down from the mountains and are driven in herds through the streets.

Sights and excursions: The **Palazzo della Magnifica Comunità di Fiemme** in the middle of town was once the summer seat of the Archbishop of Trento and the seat of government in the Fleimstal; it still bears their coats of arms. The building dates from the Renaissance, when the Archbishops Bernard von Cles and Cristoforo Madruzzo ruled, but the whole building, including the façade, has been much rebuilt. The façade bears the image of St Vigil, as is usual in Trento and the whole Trentino area. In 1850 the palace was the seat of self-government in the valley, the so-called 'Magnifica Comunità di Fiemme'. The building may only be seen on a guided tour. The 'Comunità' still exists, principally to administer woodlands; profits are used for supporting animal husbandry and agriculture in the Fleimstal. *Museum open daily ex Tue 14.00-18.30; entry 6 €, concessions 2.50 €. www.palazzomagnifica.eu.*

The parish church of **Santa Maria Assunta** was dedicated in 1136 and rebuilt in late Gothic style with a tall clock tower. Nearby stands a temple-like classical building, the **Heiligtum der Sieben Schmerzen Mariä**, in which there is an old statue of St Mary, a Gothic Pietà.

Four kilometres east of Cavalese, in **Tèsero**, the Gothic church of **San Leonardo** with its Romanesque clock tower stands on the highest point in the village. Inside are frescoes and an altar painting by Francesco Unterperger (1542). In the village itself, with its beautiful baroque town hall, Gothic parish church, façades decorated with frescoes and the Renaissance chapel of San Rocco, there are several wood carving workshops. A good time to visit is during Advent, for the 'Tèsero and its Cribs' festival, when both small and life-sized Nativity scenes are displayed in the village squares.

The peaks of **Lagorai**, one of the most isolated ranges in the Dolomites, rise up south of Cavalese. The many little lakes high up in the corries (and completely atypical of the Dolomites), are visited by very few walkers, since most of the range is uninhabited. Only the **Alpe Cermis** area south of Cavalese sees some visitors. You can get there from Cavalese by changing lifts twice: from **cable car to cable car to chair lift**; mid-Jun to Sep and in winter, from 09.00-13.00 and 14.00-17.30; up and back 21 €.

In summer there are some lovely **walking trails**, among them a 45-minute walk to three lakes teeming with char, the **Laghi di Bombasèl**. In winter it's popular on account of its slopes. But apart from a manned hut just by the lift, there are no other huts. To the south the Lagorai range borders the massive **Cima d'Asta group**, which is completely unlike other mountains of the Dolomites as it consists of a primitive crystalline rock.

Predazzo

In contrast to Cavalese, Predazzo lies along the valley floor. There are some fine old buildings tucked away off the main through road. The general impression is one of a completely Italian mountain village. The surroundings are worth seeing: Latemar, the whole Fassatal and **Val Travignolo**, which begins here and runs via the Rolle Pass into the Primiero Valley. Predazzo comes to life in winter: it is one of the most important cross-country skiing centres and has a well-equipped ski-jump centre.

Transport: The **bus station** is in the southeastern part of the village.

Events: Among the events staged here are the '**Dieci giorni equestri della Valle di Fiemme**' lasting 10 days in the first half of July, with 'Middle Ages' jousting tournaments, folklore, cultural programmes, concerts and the '**Giro dei 12 Masi**' on the first Saturday in August, an evening event in the old town with folk music, traditional costumes, and tastings.

Sights and excursions: The late gothic cemetery chapel of **San Nicolò** (somewhat west of the modern parish church) still has frescoes in the choir dating from the days of its founding.

The **Geological Museum** is also worth a visit: In the Mesozoic Era there were large volcanic eruptions in the southern part of Latemar, and the museum holds a collection of rare and interesting minerals and crystals (the **Dos Capèl geological nature trail** between the mountain station of the Predazzo cable car and Alpe di Pampeago give a good introduction). *Museum open Jun-Sep Mon-Sat from 10.00-12.30 and 16.00-19,00; in winter variable opening times. Entry 3.50 €, concessions 2.50 €.*

Cimone della Pala from Passo Rolle

A **cable car** runs from the ski centre on the Fassatal road north of Predazzo to an intermediate station, from where one takes a **chair lift** to the south slopes of **Latemar** (mid-Jun to mid-Sep and in winter 08.30-13.15 and 14.30-17.45. Combi-ticket one way 17 €, up and back 21 €). At the top it's an easy walk to the **Torre di Pisa Hut** on the south side of Latemar (from where you could continue down to Obereggen).

Val Travignolo and the Rolle Pass

The road to the Rolle Pass, San Martino di Castrozza and the Primiero Valley runs through Val Travignolo. While the Lagorai mountains in the south are little visited, the **Lusia group** in the north has various lift installations starting from the small meadows of Bellamonte.

You pass **Bellamonte**, beautifully sited on a plateau and, around the next bend, come into the thick **Paneveggio Forest**, the largest in Trentino. Then there is a long stretch beside a reservoir, the **Lago di Paneveggio (or Lago di Forte)**. A clearing introduces a visitors' centre for the **Paneveggio-Pale di San Martino Nature Park**, the main purpose of which is to protect this forest. *Open mid-Jun to mid-Sep, 09.00-12.30 and during the Christmas holidays 14.00-17.30, otherwise variable opening hours: check the website; entry fee 2 €. www.parcopan.org.*

The landscape changes completely at the **Passo Rolle**, where the unbelievably steep walls of **Pale di San Martino** fill the picture. The nearest peak is **Cimone della Pala**, the huge rock tooth shown below, reaching 3184m. A detour (on foot) to the **Baita Segantini** is recommended: take either the little road (closed to cars in summer) or the unmarked track which avoids some of the bigger bends in the road). In winter you can get there by chair lift. From the first-floor terrace of this hut (open 20 Jun to 20 Sep and Christmas till Easter; excellent rustic cooking) there is an unforgettable view to Cimone della Pala.

Walk 25: LAGHI DI COLBRICON

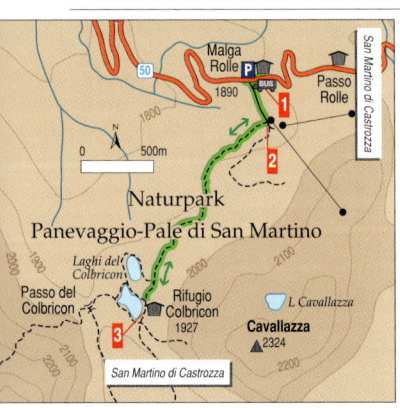

Distance/time: about 4.3km/ 2.7mi; 2h

Grade: ● easy woodland walk on well-built trails; ascent/descent 80m/260ft
Waymarking: red/white; Trail 14 throughout
Equipment: sturdy walking shoes or trainers
Refreshments: there's a restaurant at Malga Rolle; also the Rifugio Colbricon at 3
Walking map: Tabacco 022, Pale di San Martino, 1:25,000
Transport: 🚌 to Malga Rolle, at the Rolle Pass (46° 17.755'N, 11° 46.606'E); or infrequent 🚐 B122 from San Martino de Castrozza to the 'Malga Rolle' bus stop

This walk is an ideal leg-stretcher during a tour of the Fleimstal/Val di Fiemme. There are fine views to Cimone della Pala and the Paneveggio Forest as you walk an easy path back through history — from the horrors of World War 1 to the shores of the lakes, where settlers lived 10,000 years ago.

Begin the walk at **Malga Rolle** (1): take the track to the lift stations below the Rolle Pass that begins here. Before you get to the lifts, turn right on Trail 14 (2).

This well-graded trail rises gently through woods to the **Colbricon Lakes**. The two lakes lie in a landslip area, and there is a beautiful view across them to the north — to the south wall of Marmolada. There's a friendly little hut here, the **Rifugio Laghi di Colbricon** ... with just three beds(!) and good food (3; 1h).

Retrace your steps to **Malga Rolle** (2h) or, if you don't have to return to a car, you can take Trail 14 down to **San Martino di Castrozza**, although this does use some ski pistes and, lower down, follows an asphalted road.

One of the Colbricon lakes and the hut — a pleasant place to pause with a picnic

5 PRIMIERO VALLEY

San Martino di Castrozza • Paneveggio-Pale di San Martino Nature Park • Pale di San Martino • Fiera de Primiero • Val Canali

Walk: 21
Websites
www.sanmartino.com

Opening hours: see individual attractions

South of the Lagorai range, the Primiero runs south as a narrow valley dominated in the north by the rock needles of the Pale di San Martino. At the furthest northern point is the tourist centre of San Martino di Castrozza lying at almost 1500m; pretty Fiera di Primiero, only 14km away, lies at only about 700m. The difference in climate between these two villages is as great as the height difference would indicate.

Four places lie in the flat Primiero basin: Fiera di Primiero, Tonadico, Siror and Transaqua, of which the last three are villages. The many hay huts in the extensive meadows, often built closely together, are still used. In summer the cows and smaller cattle are up on the alms. Their return to the valley, called the *Desmontegada,* is the time of a big festival, celebrated with polenta from giant serving dishes, bratwurst and smoked alm cheese. Although tourists also come to the festivities, this is still essentially for the farmers who are happy that their animals are back down in the valley after the long summer.

San Martino di Castrozza

The setting of San Martino is fantastic — on a slope totally dominated in the north and east by vertical walls and the needles of Pale di San Martino 1500m higher up. In the west are the less severe eastern flanks of Lagorai, and in the south San Martino overlooks the Primiero.

Before the place was 'discovered' by English tourists, there was only a little hospice here; for hundreds of years it gave shelter to walkers crossing the Rolle Pass (its story is elaborated under 'Sights' opposite. Today San Martino has a large touristic infrastructure catering for almost all tastes, quite frenzied in high season but closed otherwise.

Transport: Buses stop at 16 Via Pezgaiart (near the Clinic); there are two a day to Trento and 10 to Feltre, as well as buses to Predazzo and Bolzano.

Sights: The **Via Passo Rolle**, the main street, runs past the **parish church** with its Romanesque campanile. The most important hotels and restaurants, shops and public services are concentrated here. The church tower is the last remains of a **Middle Ages hospice** that the monks deserted in 1418. At that time crossing the Rolle Pass was quite an undertaking, economically and strategically: the Habsburg interests in the Primiero were vital (in the south the Primiero borders Venice, thus foreign territory). So the Counts of Welsperg, the Habsburg's governors in the Primiero, took over the well-kept building and turned it into a fortress and toll point.

In the 19th century English

tourists started coming — the vanguard of the masses who now flood in during August and at Christmas. Four young men from San Martino worked for them as mountain guides, and an Irish mountaineer, John Ball, built an hotel to cater for them (the Cima di Ball is named after him). Called the 'Alpino', it was ready in 1883 and had 15 beds. In 1893, greatly enlarged, it opened as the 'Hôtel des Dolomites'. The one-time hospice became the 'Hotel Rosetta' in 1888, a predecessor of today's 'Hotel des Alpes' (opened in 1908, but not built on the same site). When in 1915 the Austrians pulled back to the Rolle Pass for strategic reasons, they burned the place down. Only the church is original; everything else you see today was built after 1919.

Paneveggio-Pale di San Martino Nature Park

The Paneveggio Forest, one of the largest forests in the region, and the Pale di San Martino, one of the most spectacular mountain groups in the Dolomites, come together here in one natural park. You can learn more about the park's climate, geology, archaeology, flora and fauna at the **park information centre** on Via Laghetto in the western part of San Martino *(open end Jun to beginning of Sep, daily from 09.00-12.30 and 15.30-18.30; entry free; www.parcopan. org).*

A lovely **nature trail** begins at this information centre; one of the highlights is a protected damp area called **Prà delle Nasse**. Damp areas are very rare in the karst Dolomites, so it is not surprising that the trail only touches on the edge of the protected area.

There are other visitors' centres for the park in Val Canali and Paneveggio, as well as a nature trail and the Prà de Madègo Ecological Museum in Caoria.

Pale di San Martino

The easiest way to climb the massif is to take the **cable car from San Martino** up to **Col Verde**, with connecting **Rosetta cable car** (mid-Jun to end Sep and in winter from 08.00-16.45, combi-ticket one way 17 €, up and back 28 €).

There are lovely views even from the col, and then it gets really wild: the little gondola cable car which runs from here up to **Cima di Rosetta** crosses a gorge, taking everyone's breath away. Up here you first have the impression that you can't walk a metre in any direction, but then you find yourself on a rolling plateau and the little walk over to the **Pedrotti Hut** is so easy you could take your auntie … *unless* it's snowing or freezing — which can even happen in August, since you're at 2600m!

The plateau is like a moon landscape as far as the eye can see, and you will only see any of the tiny plants that survive here if you look really hard. The plateau's highest reaches were once full of glaciers, but these have almost all melted since 1870.

What many people come here for is the fantastic climbing — peaks like Sass Maor, Schleier Edge, Cima di Ball, Pala di San Martino, and Cima Canali. As with so many peaks in the Dolomites, the first climbers to master them were the Viennese and English tourists, as the name 'Ball' reminds us.

Walk 26 is a magnificent hike round the Pala di San Martino.

Fiera di Primiero and surroundings

Mining and agriculture were the traditional occupations in the Primiero. With the breakdown of the mining industry after 1500 because of competition from the Spanish Habsburg holdings in America came centuries of poverty. Only tourism, which took hold in Fiera at the end of the 19th century, but really only got into its stride in about 1970, brought a new source of income. The number of hotels continues to rise, albeit more hesitantly and not so overwhelmingly as in San Martino. **Fiera di Primiero** and the three villages of **Tonadico**, **Siror** and **Transaqua** form a single world, cut off from the rest of Trentino. Ties with nearby Venetian Feltre are stronger than with those of Trento, to which the Primiero belongs administratively. The outside world can only be reached via passes or through the narrow **Cismon Gorge** in the south. While San Martino dances to the tourists' tune, in the Primiero itself life goes on unperturbed.

Transport: There are up to 10 buses a day to Feltre and San Martino (from where there are two buses a day over the Rolle Pass into Trentino).

Sights and excursions: Fiera's parish church with its high tower is Gothic, built on the site of earlier churches. The interior, with its complicated net vaulting, has a choir decorated with late Gothic frescoes. Behind the church is the little church of **St Martin**, with frescoes inside and out, and somewhat higher, an old house with a magnificent fresco portraying the Madonna of Charity.

Paneveggio Forest in Tonadico

On the road below is the **Palazzo delle Miniere**, built in Renaissance style by the Habsburgs during the heyday of copper, silver and iron mining in the Primiero. In the interior, the history and culture of the area is well documented. *Palazzo documentation centre open Jul/Aug 16.30-19.30, in Jun and Sep 20.30-22.30; entry about 3 €.*

Alm hut at the southern foot of Pala di San Martino in the Val Canali

Transaqua is the scene of the annual **Hay-cutting Festival** at the end of August. To commemorate how hay used to be brought down from the mountains on wooden sledges, several laden sledges are dragged through the village to the church, with attendant competitions like wood-sawing, etc — a programme lasting three days.

Another, important festival is celebrated in the whole area: the **'Gran Festa del Desmontegar'**. This takes place at the end of September and celebrates the animals' return from the mountain pastures with colourfully decorated animals, wagons and people dressed in local costume. Folk music groups start at **Siror** and pass through Fiera and Transaqua on their way to **Tonadico**, an old village with beautiful farmhouses and a hilltop Gothic church, where there is a folk festival and stock-breeding exhibition. All the restaurants in the area sell traditional dishes.

Val Canali

This valley reaches from Tonadico to halfway up the Pale di San Martino.

Lower down are the ruins of **Castel Pietra**, one of the most delightful pictures of Trentino — a castle built on a rock in the middle of a wood to protect the Passo Cereda-Agordino road. In 1377 it came into the hands of Tyrol and in 1401 became the seat of the Counts of Welsperg. It only fell in the 19th century, although it was burned many times; today it belongs to a branch of the Thun family. *Ask about opening times at the tourist office (entry with guided tour 5.50 €).*

The province of Trentino has established the main office of the Paneveggio-Pale di San Martino Nature Park in the old counts' **Villa Thun-Welsperg** nearby. The **visitors' centre** has all information about this natural park *(open daily all year: mid-Jun to early Oct from 09.00-12.30 and 15.00-18.00, Oct-Christmas Mon-Fri from 09.30-12.30 and 14.00-17.00, in winter times vary: see www.parcopan.org; entry fee 3 €).*

Walk 26: ROUND PALA DI SAN MARTINO

Distance/time: about 14km/ 8.7mi; 6h
Grade: ●❗ magnificent high-altitude hike for experienced mountain walkers. You must be sure-footed, with plenty of stamina, and have a head for heights. Ascent 300m/985ft overall; descent 1400m/4600ft. Only suitable in fine settled weather; the high plateau is prone to disorientating mists and fog; be sure to keep to the main paths, marked by cairns and paint!
Waymarking: red/white; Trail 707/709 from **2** to **3**, Trail 709 to **5**, Trail 715 to **7**, then Trail 702 to the end
Equipment: hiking boots, sun protection, walking pole(s)
Refreshments: available at the Ristorante Rosetta (**1**), Rifugio Pedrotti alla Rosetta (**2**), Rifugio Pradidali (**5**)
Walking map: Tabacco 022, Pale di San Martino, 1:25,000
Transport: 🚗 to the Col Verde cable car at San Martino di Castrozza (46° 15.838'N, 11° 48.306'E); or 🚌 B501 from Feltre to San Martino di Castrozza and alight at the valley station of the lift. Then cable car to Col Verde and another to Rosetta (mid-Jun to end Sep from 08.00-16.45, combi-ticket one way 17 €). You will walk back down to San Martino for your car or bus.
Short walk: Out and back from Rosetta (● easy; gentle ups and downs). Follow the main walk for a while, then retrace steps.

This is one of the most fascinating walks you can take in the Dolomites without being a mountain climber. You will come very close to the famous Sass Maor climb. And you'll have a little frisson of excitement, too, as you traverse a long exposed ledge secured with wire cables.

Start out at the top station of the **Rosetta** lift (**1**): walk left, to the **Rosetta Hut** ('Rifugio Pedrotti'; **2**; **15min**), which lies on the Altopiano di San Martino, the high karst plateau of the Pala massif which extends for about 20 square kilometres. Take Trail 707/709; further on, fork right on Trail 709 (**3**). Almost nothing grows here; rubble and rock cover the rolling landscape. It's a bleak landscape in summer, despite the bright peaks all around and views into forested valleys slicing off the plateau in deep gashes. The landscape is only enlivened by the bright colours of alpine flora.

Trail 709 leads south uphill, crosses snow fields (where until

The exciting cable car lift to Rosetta

6 AGORDINO

Arabba • Pieve de Livinallongo • Andraz • Porta Vescovo • Passo di Campolongo • Col di Lana • Passo di Falzàrego • Àgordo • Dolomiti Bellunesi National Park • Valbiois • Àlleghe • Monte Pelmo • Zoldano Valley

Walks: 27-29; *walking tips:* stroll through the *viles* (page 156); Col di Lana (page 157)
Websites
www.arabba.it
www.austro-hungarian-army.co.uk/battles/coldilan.htm (website about the battle for the Col di Lana)
www.dolomitipark.it (Dolomiti-Bellunesi National Park)
www.valdizoldo.net (Zoldano)
Opening hours: see individual attractions

The Cordevole rises in the district of Livinallongo del Col di Lana/Buchenstein, and its long valley, together with all its tributaries, is called Agordino (after the main town of Àgordo). Before the river emerges in the lowlands between Belluno and Feltre and runs into the Piave, it flows through a beautiful mountain landscape.

Coming from Sella, the Cordevole first runs past the Ladin farmland area of Livinallongo, then, at Caprile, it flows through Italian-speaking Agordino. Averau, Nuvolau, Croda da Lago, Pelmo, Civetta, Moiazza and Schiara rise to the left, Marmolada and the Pale di San Martino to the right. In Pieve and in the side-valleys there are still old farming villages with *tabià* (log cabin-style barns) — for instance in Rocca Piètore,

in the Zoldano Valley and in the hamlets above Canale di Àgordo. This Dolomite landscape *par excellence* has one surprising feature: except for a few key centres (Àlleghe, Selva di Cadore, Rocca Piètore, Falcade) one meets hardly any tourists, and then only during high season.

A whole array of passes link Trentino with the Agordino area: Pordoi, Fedaia, San Pellegrino, Passo di Valles (on a turn-off from the road to the Rolle Pass) and Passo di Cereda between Fiera di Primiero and Àgordo. There is also an easily-driven road without any passes (but not without bends!): the road between Fiera, Feltre and Belluno, along which you can drive to Àgordo through the valley straits called the Canale d'Àgordo.

Arabba

The Great Dolomite Road descends between the Pordoi Pass and the Passo di Campolongo into the Cordevole Valley and runs past the highest village in Livinallongo/Buchenstein, Arabba (called Reba, its Ladin name, by the inhabitants). It's the only large place in Livinallongo, but still only a village.

Transport: There is a large **car park** by the valley station of the Porta Vescovo lift (in winter it's a bit further downhill). In the school period there are up to five **buses** a day to Àgordo and Belluno, but only three otherwise (and none on Sundays). In summer up to five buses a day to the Pordoi Pass and Canazei, Wolkenstein/Selva and Corvara.

Sights and excursions: The **parish church** of **Saints Peter and Paul**, dedicated in 1664, is one of the few buildings to have survived the inferno of the First World War — the village itself was reduced to rubble and ashes by firing from the Italian emplacements higher up. Today Arabba is a tourist centre (the only really touristic place in the area) and a good base from which to explore the central Dolomites.

New apartment blocks flank the road up towards the Pordoi Pass — they are mostly owned by Italian families and only used in high summer and at Christmas.

Arabba, with a view west towards Passo Pordoi and the Padon ridge (setting for Walk 24) at the left.

● **Walking tip: stroll through the 'viles'.** To get to know some Ladin hamlets *(viles)*, you can stroll from Arabba along the road to the Campolongo Pass as far as **Varda** and from there take beautiful Trail 22 through meadows and woods: you will walk above **Mazarei** and come to **Cherz**. In the lower part of this hamlet there is a very attractive old holy statue (like a crucifix, but God the Father holds the crucifix on his knees). From there you *could* follow a path to the fort on the main road (with hotel), but since this is not easy to find, it's better to take the little road to **Renaz** and return from there by bus. Total time about 1h30min (Tabacco 1:25,000 map N° 07).

Pieve di Livinallongo/ Buchenstein village

On the village square in Pieve di Livinallongo (Ladin: Fodóm), in front of the church, is a memorial (1912) dedicated to **Caterina Lanz**, the 'Heroine of Spinges'. In 1797, in Spinges village (near Mühlbach/Rio di Pusteria in the Pustertal/Val Pusteria, see Book 1), this young woman used a pitchfork to fight the invading French, before spending the rest of her life cooking for the parish priest in Andraz. After her death, as nationalism bloomed in the second half of the 19th century, this fighting Ladin became the symbol for Austrian justice. She is still considered a heroine today, who defended the Ladins and Tyroleans against their enemies.

Andraz

It's hard to believe that this little roadside hamlet, just a handful of houses, was once the seat from which the bishops of Brixen/ Bressanone administered this district. But in fact their seat, **Andraz Castle**, is not located here, but further up the valley towards the Falzàrego Pass at Ciastèl ('Castle').

You reach the well-restored ruins via a little road that turns left off the pass road (sign: 'Castello'). Or you can take local walking Trail 26 that goes off the first hairpin bend past La Baita (an inn). There could hardly be a more beautiful setting for a castle: it stands on a gigantic isolated rock in the middle of a meadow; the old walls appear to grow out of the rock itself.

Porta Vescovo

Looking south from Arabba, the dark **Padon ridge** hides the Marmolada glacier, which can only be seen from points above Arabba. A **cable car** runs from Arabba (Jul-Sep and in winter 08.30-17.00 on the half hour; one way 12 €, up and back 16.50 €) to a pass on this ridge called **Porta Vescovo** ('Bishop's Gate'). Once you're up there, the whole Marmolada panorama opens up, the view is one of the most attractive on the whole Padon ridge — and best seen from the famous **Viel dal Pan/Bindelweg** (Walk 24). In winter Porta Vescovo is the starting point for magnificent ski runs which unfortunately have so disfigured the slopes that in summer this is not a worthwhile walking area.

Passo di Campolongo

The alm landscape around this pass into the Hochabteital is a most pleasant **walking area** with a whole array of manned alms and huts. In winter the terrain changes into a real *ski circus,* undemanding, and suitable for families and inexperienced skiers. Walking Route 636, one of the most attractive routes up to the base of Sella, begins just at the pass.

Col di Lana

This small grassy mountain in the centre of the Livinallongo/ Buchenstein district appears to be nothing special. But on the peak (2425m) is the huge cavity left by a 5000kg mine that the Italians exploded on April 17th, 1916 to take the peak from the Austrians. Col di Lana was a strategic point of the first order, overlooking four passes: Falzàrego, Valparola, Campolongo, and Pordoi — as well as the approach from Agordino, one of the most important Italian lines of aggression. (The story of the battle is movingly told, in English, at the website recommended on page 154.) A cross and chapel on the peak are a reminder that this will be the last war between neighbours on this **Col di Sangue** ('Blood Mountain', as the Italians call it).

● **Walking tip: Col di Lana.** Take Trail 23/21 from the **Rifugio Valparola** (only manned in high summer) at the **Valparola Pass**. The walk is straightforward (see Tabacco 1:25,000 map N° 07), but the ridge between Monte Sieg and Col di Lana is only recommended for sure-footed walkers who have a head for heights. Return the same way, allowing 2h30min-3h there and back (ascent/descent of 260m/850ft).

Passo di Falzàrego

Between Arabba and Cortina the Great Dolomite Road must cross a high pass — the Falzàrego at 2105m. There's a large **parking area**, bars, shops, and a restaurant.

On the left a steep block of rock towers over the pass, the **Sasso di Stria** (Witches' Stone).

From the Falzàrego a road runs over the Valparola Pass into the Gadertal/Val Badia to St Kassian/ San Cassiano; if you take this you will pass a most attractive Austrian fort, the **Forte Tre Sassi**. It is part of the **Open-air Museum** that takes in areas around the Falzàrego Pass, Monte (Piccolo) Lagazuoi in the north (with the Rifugio Lagazuoi) and the Cinque Torri (in Ampezzo). Much of this area is shown on the walking map on page 165. On one Sunday in August the museum comes to life, when volunteers dress in Austrian and Italian uniforms. *Open Jun to end Sep daily from 10.00-13.00 and 14.00-17.00; entry 8 €. www.cortinamuseoguerra.it.*

On **Lagazuoi** (reached via a **cable car** straight from the Falzàrego Pass, end May to mid-Oct and in winter, 09.00-17.00, one way 14.50 €, up and back 21 €), the Austrians and Italians were so close together that they had to dig themselves into tunnels, in order not to be constantly shot at. Most of these tunnels have been

> **Museo all'aperto del Monte Lagazuoi (Open-air Museum)**
> This museum has no boundaries; the entire area is an open-air museum and entry is free. The trails are generally well protected and well marked, with panels explaining individual sites. But be sure to wear suitable shoes for mountain walking, take a torch (and head protection!) for the tunnels. More information is available from the tourist offices in Arabba and Cortina, as well at www.cortinadelicious.it.

The main square in Àgordo, with Moiazza in the background

opened to the public — but without lights, so take a torch! Not only do the tunnels remain; there are also trenches and many ruined buildings. In some of the latter the conditions of 1917 have been reconstructed, right down to the potatoes and ration bowls which were warmed in field ovens.

The **Kaiserjägersteig** dates from the same time: a path/*via ferrata* for sure-footed, vertigo-free hillwalkers. It climbs in hairpins from Forte Tre Sassi (or you can park at the valley station of the lift and start there, both are signposted) and crosses a hangbridge over a ravine to the highest old emplacements at the Front. Once at the top (2h30min), a path signed 'Galleria' (behind the top lift station) leads to the entrance of the tunnel labyrinth. You proceed for over an hour down steep steps, in the dark (with a few holes for light) until you come out at the bottom of the escarpment and can continue to the valley lift station at the Falzàrego Pass (2h).

The area south of the Falzàrego Pass is an ideal starting point for **walks** on Averau and Nuvolau as well as the Cinque Torri, all wild

Dolomite peaks which rise out of green alm meadows (see Walk 28). Most of the walking routes here are also suitable for cycling.

Àgordo

What a picture! The two attractive side-towers of the parish church with the peak of Moiazza behind them. If you have a good wide-angle lens, you can even capture the second 'sight' of Àgordo in the picture — the Palazzo Crotta, with its statues on the wall. A Venetian villa with Dolomite peaks in the background — quite unusual!

Àgordo is also home to the world-famous Luxottica, Italy's largest manufacturer of sunglasses for the European luxury market: Armani, Chanel, Ferragamo, Moschino, Ungaro and Yves St Laurent. It's the town's main livelihood.

Transport: Àgordo has its own bus station and good **bus connections** to Belluno (12 a day) and Àlleghe/Caprile (3 a day); there's also one bus a day to Corvara and one serving Cortina and the Drei Zinnen/Tre Cime de Lavaredo.

Sights: The **parish church** with its wide front and side-towers was built between 1836 to 1852, but in the interior you will find paintings from the previous building, among them the works of the early baroque Venetian painter Palma il Giovane.

The **Palazzo Crotta-De Manzoni** is the most northerly Venetian villa and the only one in the mountains. It was built in the 18th century and enlarged in the 19th century; it is private and cannot be visited. But you *can* take a peek into the courtyard with its side arcades.

The **main square** lies between the church and the villa; there are beautiful arcades below which some cafés and shops have opened. The old part of town lies beyond this — two, three narrow streets, a couple of old houses with outdoor frescoes — and that's it.

Dolomiti-Bellunesi National Park

The most southerly reaches of the Dolomites lie in Belluno and are protected in a national park, one of the few national parks in Italy to encompass a mountain region. With the exception of the Schiara group southeast of Àgordo, the park lies in the pre-Alps, so can't hold a candle to the nearby mountain giants. But that's a blessing: this is a place to see rare plants and animals which otherwise have died out or are very rare in the southern Alps. There's a handful of rustic huts and many **walking** (and even mountain biking) opportunities.

Valbiois

The Valbiois begins at **Cencenighe Agordino** as a narrow gorge before opening up by **Tis** and then at **Canale d'Àgordo**. **Vallada**, north of Canale, is a monument to the agricultural past; its church (San Simón) has a cycle of frescoes from the Titian school. **Falcade**, in a sunny position high in the Valbiois, is a totally touristic sports centre. In summer this valley is a good base for cyclists who can't tackle the Dolomite passes.

Transport: There are five **buses** a day to Àgordo, one to Bolzano (via Vigo di Fassa), three to the Passo di San Pellegrino (summer only), and up to three a day from Falcade to the Fedaia Pass (via Caprile).

Àlleghe and Civetta

The setting, shown overleaf, could not be more beautiful: a lake on the doorstep and mountains behind the village. From the far side of the lake you can see the pointed spire of the parish church of San Biagio; behind it, mighty Civetta rises above a green apron.

Winter sports are writ large in Àlleghe; it's the centre for skiing on Civetta, and the ice-skating stadium is just five minutes from the centre of town. Mountain climbers and free climbers visit in summer, since not only is Civetta on the doorstep, but other colossal mountains of the central Dolomites are nearby — Marmolada, Sella, Pelmo. Since the number of beds is limited, you must reserve in high season.

Transport: There is a large **car park** in front of the ice skating rink; covered car park between the ice skating stadium and Via Monte Pape. Good **bus connections** to Àgordo, but for Arabba only two buses a day outside the school term; some buses to the Falzàrego Pass in the summer.

Sights and excursions: The **parish church of San Biagio** hides its Gothic origins rather feebly under its baroque façade. The adjacent **chapel** with its Loreto Madonna is an important goal for pilgrims and the oldest building in the valley.

Two little roads, Via Europa and Via Monte Pape, run from the church forecourt down to **Lago di Àlleghe** with its beautiful **lakeside promenade**. To photograph the famous view of Civetta, you have to drive south along the edge, round to the far side of the lake, to the small village of **Masarè**. On the western slopes above Masarè you can clearly see the results of a massive landslide in 1771, which resulted in the lake. Cross the Cordevole bridge and pass the Chalet am Lago, then you come to a footpath on your right from where the view sweeps over the lake and Àlleghe to Civetta. If you walk (or cycle) further, you can continue on an easy, well-marked track (mostly in woodland and by the banks of the river) to **Caprile**.

A **cable car** runs from Corso Venezia at the southern entrance to Àlleghe up to the **Piani Pezzè** (where the Fontanabona inn and pizzeria by the ski run serves up rustic food), and from there you can take another **cable car** to the **Col dei Baldi**. These two lifts operate from end Jun to mid-Sep and in winter, 08.30-17.30; combi-ticket one way 13.50 €, up and back 18 €. (Malga Boi Vescovà, an alm with hut below the Col dei Baldi, can be reached by a tarred road from the Forcella Staulanza; rustic cooking: grilled farm wurst, goats cheese, ricotta and smoked cheeses, wine).

Taking the lift to the Col dei Baldi and then doing Walk 29 makes a full day's outing. On the other hand, those up to following Route 565 with its unprotected climbs through the Val d'Antersass are *really* ready for refreshments when they get to the Tissi or Coldai huts!

Civetta (3220m) is a long strung-out reef, and its peaks are really the preserve of climbers. The most famous climbing route on Civetta is the extremely bold **Via ferrata degli Alleghesi**. You come to this if you take Route 557 south from the Coldai Hut, which then joins Route 559 to traverse the eastern flank of the ridge. If you

Agordino

can handle the first 40m without problems (vertical, sometimes overhanging drops, metal pins and grips), the worst will be behind you.

If it gives you the jitters, just turn back — there is another route perfectly suitable for hillwalkers — Walk 29: from the top lift station at the Col dei Baldi you can go over to the Forcella di Àlleghe, where the climb begins. It takes you to the Rifugio Coldai, from where Route 560/Dolomites High Route 1 runs along the west side of the main Civetta ridge.

North of Àlleghe, heavily built up **Caprile** lies at the turn-off to the Falzàrego Pass; its church is somewhat higher up. It is a good base for outings in upper Agordino, Livinallongo and Ampezzo — and an alternative to expensive and crowded Cortina!

Monte Pelmo

From Caprile you can drive via Selva di Cadore to **Forcella Staulanza**; alternatively you can get into the Zoldano Valley from Agordo via **Passo Duran**, but this route is quite poorly built.

The Zoldano Valley lies between rock giants: driving via Forcella Staulanza, Civetta is on your right; on the left **Monte Pelmo** offers a textbook picture of the Dolomites: steep rock walls all around, just a couple of flecks of snow in the gorges, and a flat area on top. The **Città di Fiume Hut** on its northern flank is a good starting point for the famous circuit of Monte Pelmo on Routes 472 and 480; both routes perfectly within the capabilities of 'normal' **mountain walkers** (a few short protected stretches). The peaks, including the karst plateau between the main peak and the eastern shoulder are, by contrast, the preserve of climbers.

Zoldano Valley

Whether up in **Zoldo Alto** or in the main village of **Forno di Zoldo**, the attractive villages and hamlets that stretch along the Zoldano Valley have one thing in common: in summer hardly anyone lives here, but it's very busy in winter when almost all the cars have German licence plates: that's when the ice-cream makers (Zoldano's speciality) return home from their shops in Germany! Most houses are north of the main road, including some very venerable ancient dwellings in grey or brown stone, four storeys high.

Àlleghe with its mountain lake and Civetta

Walk 27: FROM THE FALZÀREGO PASS TO LAGAZUOI

Distance/time: about 6.6km/4mi; 3h50min

Grade: ●❗ strenuous mountain hike with a very steep ascent/descent of 800m/2625ft on terrain covered with loose scree. Largely without shade, and hot in summer despite the high altitude. Slippery after rain. You must be sure-footed and have a head for heights, as well as being in tip-top shape. To enjoy the fantastic view from Lagazuoi at leisure, I recommend an overnight stay at the Rifugio Lagazuoi (**7**): book several months in advance!

Waymarking: red/white; the ascent trail is marked 'Kaiserjäger-steig M3'; the descent is trail 401 to Forcella Travenanzes and from there Trail 402.

Equipment: hiking boots, sun protection, walking pole(s); if descending via the tunnels (see 'Variation' below) helmet and headlamp

Refreshments: available at the valley station of the cable car and at Rifugio Lagazuoi (**7**; www.rifugiolagazuoi.com), but take drinking water and provisions with you for when you're on the go.

Walking map: Tabacco 07, Alta Badia-Arabba-Marmolada, 1:25,000

Transport: 🚗 free car parking at the valley station of the Lagazuoi cable car at the Falzàrego Pass (46° 31.171'N, 12° 0.517'E). Or 🚐465 that links Stern/La Villa with Corvara and usually runs every hour; alight at the pass. There is also a Dolomiti 🚐 from Cortina to the Falzàrego Pass. Last 🚐465 back at 17.55, last Dolomiti 🚐 back at 18.25.

Variation for the adventurous; descent through the tunnels

For the descent through the tunnels, *helmet, headlamp and walking poles are compulsory!* At **7** take the path immediately behind the **mountain station of the cable car** (sign 'Galleria'). After 15 minutes on a steep mountain path with a breathtaking panorama, you get to the **tunnel network**. This goes downhill on steep rock steps for about an hour and a half — very hard on the knees! Again and again, rock 'windows' afford spectacular views onto the rock wall. Info boards explain about the shelters and bunks. After the end of the tunnels, the trail descends for 10 minutes on a scree path. Beyond a short rock tunnel you meet the normal descent route at a fork. Pick up the main walk here at **11**.

The Kaiserjägersteig (named for the Austrian light infantry) is one of the most spectacular dolomite hikes ever! Part trail and part *via ferrata*, it rises on steep scree paths past old trenches to the summit of Lagazuoi Piccolo with its incom-

Walk 27: From the Falzàrego Pass to Lagazuoi

parable panorama. Your descent, partly through scree, passes some old gun positions and later follow a ski piste. But the adventurous can scramble down through the tunnels…

Start the hike at the northern end of the **Lagazuoi lift car park** (**1**): take the metal staircase down to a gravel path. A few metres further on, follow the signpost 'Galleria' up a wide gravel path. At the next fork (**2**) keep left with the sign 'Kaiserjägersteig M3'.

The trail goes steeply uphill through scree fields in a north-westerly direction. Soon you cross the route of the cable car and, after a total of 20 minutes' ascent, you can turn right at a junction (**3**) onto the **Kaiserjägersteig**.

Now you will repeatedly pass the remains of trenches, rusted hunks of metal and wooden beams. About 15 minutes on from the junction, the trail climbs in sweaty switchbacks; above you there's a mighty tangle of jagged edges, steps and overhangs that protrude into the sky. And high above, a suspension bridge swings boldly between the walls.

After about 10 minutes of ascent, the **Frote Tre Sassi**, a museum (see page 157 and panel at the right) can be seen far below on the pass road. Ten minutes later the switchbacks are behind you. And shortly afterwards you reach a crevice (**4**) which has been made accessible by means of wooden beams and iron steps. Conquer

---

The Grande Guerra trench warfare in ice and snow
Between 1915 and 1917, Austrians and Italians waged a senseless trench war on Little Lagazuoi and Sass di Stria opposite.

After above ground position gains largely failed to materialize, the warring parties turned to planting mines beneath their enemies. Five large mines exploded on Lagazuoi. In some cases they blasted considerable amounts of rock into the abyss. The largest blast by the Austrians on May 22nd, 1917, led to the demolition of a 200m/650ft-high and 136m/450ft-wide wall area with a volume of over 100,000m³. Its huge cone of rubble can still be seen today.

For the war, kilometre-long tunnels were driven into the mountain under unimaginable conditions (snowfall, ice, avalanches, extreme cold).

If you descend through this cool, damp labyrinth today and repeatedly pass observation posts, sleeping caves or shelters for weapons and equipment, you cannot help feeling uneasy and asking yourself — as with all wars — why all this had to be.

Panorama from Lagazuoi Piccolo

this passage and shortly after you get to the top, you reach the airy hangbridge shown below. Wow!

At the end of the bridge follow the cable-protected climb until you reach a **tunnel window** (**5**; 1h15min) after about 15 minutes. If you have a torch with you, you can go on a tour of discovery here! Above the window, your path leads uphill in five minutes to a trench and then past other remains of a moat and wall. Then you head north across a rugged rock face on a wide strip of gravel, partly stabilised with wooden planks.

About 25 minutes after the trench you come to a small rock platform, from which you spot the Lagazuoi Hut for the first time.

About 15 minutes later, on a knoll with the signpost 'Kaiserjägersteig' you have a fantastic view of **Big (Grande) Lagazuoi** and the **Conturines peaks**. The rugged ridge leads you southeast in about five minutes to the summit of **Little (Piccolo) Lagazuoi** (**6**; 2h05min), marked by a large cross and a memorial to those who died here during World War 1. Exhausted Kaiserjägersteig conquerors rest here next to relaxed cable car users…

After a 10-minute descent on a well-paved path, you reach the **Rifugio Lagazuoi** (**7**) with its incredible panoramic terrace. Sella and Marmolada in the west, Civetta and the Pale di San Martino in the south, Tofana and Monte Cristallo in the east — what more could you wish? Take a long break here, preferably with a hearty pasta or polenta and a good red wine. Then, if you're exhausted after the ascent, just hop on the cable car.

For the main walk, descend past the mountain station of the cable car towards 'Galleria/Forcella Lagazuoi/Travenanzes'. *(Those looking for adventure and with the*

The Kaiserjägersteig crosses a large ravine on a hangbridge. Wow indeed!

Walk 27: From the Falzàrego Pass to Lagazuoi

right equipment, can descend through the war tunnels, see Variation on page 162.)

A wide path take you to a tunnel window in a **rock wall**. Steep serpentines take you down *variation descent through the tunnels rejoins the main walk here.)* Head downhill on steep bends towards 'Passo Falzàrego'; the car park and the valley station of the cable car are already in view.

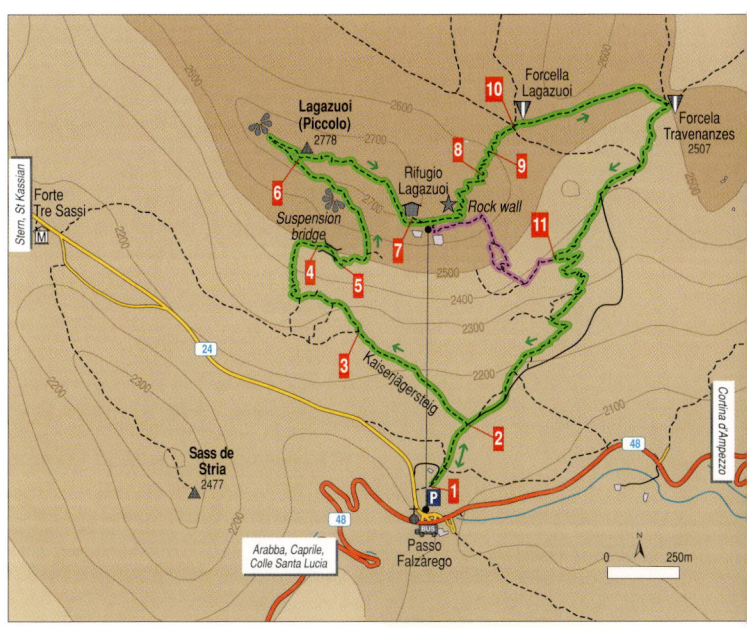

past a second tunnel entrance (**8**) and then a third (**9**; marked 'FW9'). They're only minutes apart, but obviously, if you explore here, you'll need more time.

After the end of the rock wall, follow the ski slope down into a depression, the **Forcella Lagazuoi** (**10**; **2h45min**), the pass separating Little Lagazuoi from its higher brother. Here the ski piste turns east. Trail N° 401 now takes you downhill to **Forcella Travenanzes**. From there, continue down the gravel trail (N° 402) with the signpost 'Falzàrego'.

About 35 minutes past Forcella Lagazuoi you reach a fork (**11**; **3h20min**) with the signposts 'Falzàrego' and 'Galleria'. (*The*

The Tre Sassi fortress on the Valparola Pass

Those who shy away from the route through the Lagazuoi tunnels can visit numerous relics of the war in the Tre Sassi Fortress built in 1897 on the nearby Valparola Pass and find out more about the historical background. In summer open daily from 10.00-13.00 and 14.00-17.00, www.cortinadelicious.it.

After about 25 minutes through scree and dwarf mountain pines, your path joins a wide motorable track that brings you back to starting point (**1**; **3h50min**) in a few minutes.

Walk 28: FROM THE FALZÀREGO PASS ROUND AVERAU AND NUVOLAU

Distance/time: about 9km/5.9mi; 4h
Grade: ● moderate mountain walk, with an ascent/descent of 400m/1300ft on generally good trails which nevertheless demand agility

Waymarking: red/white; Trail 441 to ▣, Trail 439 to ▣, and Trail 440 to finish
Equipment: hiking boots, sun protection, walking pole(s)
Refreshments: available at the Rifugio Averau (▣), with good rustic cooking and at the Rifugio Scoiattoli (▣)
Walking map: Tabacco 03, Cortina d'Ampezzo-Dolomiti Ampezzane, 1:25,000
Transport: 🚗 free car parking at the Falzàrego Pass (46° 31.125'N, 12° 0.571'E). Or 🚌 465 that links Stern/La Villa with Corvara and usually runs every hour; alight at the pass. There is also a Dolomiti 🚌 from Cortina to the Falzàrego Pass. Last 🚌 465 back at 17.55, last Dolomiti 🚌 back at 18.25.

While Walk 27 heads north to Monte Lagazuoi Piccolo, this walk climbs south for superb views to Lagazuoi and in all directions. The Cinque Torri (Five Towers), seen from above on this walk, form part of an open air museum encompassing the mountains surrounding this pass — a sad reminder of the War in the Dolomites.

Start out at the **Falzàrego Pass** (▣), where a sign behind the large shop indicates the way (Trail 441 to Nuvolau). You cross hilly, fairly damp terrain, rising to a rougher landscape. Behind you, the landscape is dominated by the Tofana massif, with the Lagazuoi, setting for Walk 27, to its west. Keeping to Trail 441 for Nuvolau and Averau, you arrive at a high valley; it appears to run to a pass, but you will suddenly be led to a crevice taking you out of the valley and back onto the slope. The *next* high valley leads to the pass, **Forcella Averau** (▣). Here you switch to the other side of the ridge and thus round the steep massif of **Mount Averau**.

The Open-air Museum (see page 157) is a reminder of the fighting that took place around the Falzàrego Pass during the First World War. The Cinque Torri, seen at close quarters on this walk, form part of the museum. All of these photos were taken on Walk 27 around Lagazuoi Piccolo: a trench (right), one of the many tunnels (below), and the path at the start of the tunnel network through the mountain (opposite).

After an easy climb in loose rubble you come to another pass, **Forcella Nuvolau**, with the **Averau Hut** (**3**; **1h50min**) — known for its good food and fine view to Marmolada. (It's possible to climb to the Rifugio Nuvolau from here in under 30 minutes, the oldest refuge in the Dolomites: once over some initial rock 'steps', the path is easy and not too steep.

Your walk now continues on the northern, Ampezzo side of the ridge (on Trail 439; also Dolomites High Route 1), with the strange rock formation called Cinque Torri ahead. Crossing mountain meadows, you descend to the **Scoiattoli Hut** (**4**; **2h30min**)

below the **Cinque Torri** — only about 200m away. The 'Five Towers' are a paradise for climbers; you may see them dangling precipitously from the rock as you relax on the hut's terrace. The 'Five Towers' form part of the **Lagazuoi/Cinque Torri Open-air Museum** (see page 157).

Retrace your steps from the hut a short way, then go right on Trail 440 (**5**; still Dolomites High Route 1). This descends towards the main SS48 road, but just before you get there (just before the steam), take the ascending route to the left. This takes you to the **Col Gallina Hut** (**6**) and the **Falzàrego Pass** (**1**; **4h**).

Walk 29: UNDER THE WALLS OF CIVETTA

Distance/time: 21km/13mi; 7h30min (best done as a 2-day hike, with an overnight stay at the Tissi Hut)
Grade: ● long, strenuous, but technically straightforward mountain walk; overall ascents of 500m/1640ft, descents of 1800m/5900ft
Waymarking: red/white; Trail 561, then 564 to **2**, Trail 556 to **4**, Trail 560 to **6**, N° 563 to **7**, and back to Trail 560 to the end
Equipment: hiking boots, sun protection, walking pole(s)
Refreshments: available at the Rifugio Coldai (**3**), Rifugio Tissi (**6**), Rifugio Vazzoler (**9**), Capanna Trieste (**10**) and Gasthof Monte Civetta in Listolade

Walking map: Tabacco 015, Marmolada-Pelmo-Civetta-Moiazza
Transport: 🚗 free car parking at the cable car at the southern entrance to Àlleghe (46° 24.352'N, 12° 1.334'E). Or 🚐 003 from Àgordo to Àlleghe, usually runs every hour; alight at the 'Àlleghe Impianti' bus stop close to the lift. Then cable car to the Piani Pezzè and from there another cable car to the Col dei Baldi (end Jun to mid-Sep, 08.30-17.30; combi-ticket one way 13.50 €). Take the same bus back from Listolade — to your car at Àlleghe, or back to base (last bus back at 17.42).

Passing Lake Coldai, a lovely setting for a picnic

Walk 29: Under the walls of Civetta

What looks so difficult from Àlleghe turns out to be a normal — but spectacular — traverse along the famous western wall of Civetta (the 'Little Owl'), known in the mountaineering world as 'the wall of walls'.

The walk starts at the **Col dei Baldi** (**1**). With Civetta in front of you and the huge bulk of Monte Pelmo to the left on the far side of the upper Zoldano Valley, head south on Trails 561, then 564 to the **Forcella di Àlleghe** (**2**). Your onward ascent path (Trail 556; please avoid short-cuts) winds up from the old alm at this pass to the **Coldai Hut** (**3**; **1h15min**) between **Cima di Coldai** (right) and **Civetta**'s northern ridge (left).

You cross a low pass and come to the basin of **Lago Coldai** (**4**), a typical karst lake with no surface inlet or outlet. Continuing left on Trail 560 (also Dolomites High Route 1), cross another low pass.

You then traverse below the wild west wall of the main Civetta ridge, avoiding the scree slopes at the foot of the wall by going right and slightly downhill. From the **Forcella Col Reàn** (**5**) it's half an hour up to the **Tissi Hut** (**6**; **3h15min**), on a rise up to the right. While the sanitation facilities at this old hut leave a lot to be desired, the views compensate, with the peaks 1000 metres above and Àlleghe 1000 metres below.

From here take Trail 563 back down to Trail 560 (**7**) and follow it along the western flanks of Civetta all the way to the ruined alm **Cason di Col Reàn** (**8**). Keep to Route 560, gently descending into woodland. There are spectacular views along the southern foot of Civetta, with the vertical **Torre Venezia** just above to the left.

The route continues as a forestry track, past the **Vazzoler Hut** (**9**; **5h15min**), with its alpine garden. Then it hairpins down into **Val Corpassa** and the **Capanna Trieste** (**10**; **6h15min**), from where you are on asphalt all the way to the main road in **Listolade** (**11**; **7h30min**). A **bus stop** is to the left.

7 AMPEZZO

Cortina d'Ampezzo • Passo Giau • Great Dolomite Road to Passo Falzàrego • Tofana group • Höhlensteintal and Monte Piana • Cristallo • Sorapis and Antelao

Walk: 30; *walking tip:* Monte Piana from the Bosi Hut (page 175)
Websites
www.cortina.dolomiti.org
www.infodolomiti.it
www.musei.regole.it
Opening hours: see individual attractions

Ampezzo lies in the highest valley of the river Boite between Dolomite giants. At its centre is Cortina d'Ampezzo at 1200m — a popular winter and summer sports centre for a century. The peaks around Cortina rise up to 2200m above the town: Tofana di Mezzo 3244 m, Cristallo 3216m, Sorapis 3205m. The *enrosadüra*, the pink Alpine glow of sunset, is most evident on the west wall of Sorapis.

Ladin Ampezzo and the adjacent Italian Cadore were separated until 1919, when Ampezzo belonged to Austrian Tyrol. Today both are part of the province of Belluno. But in principal Ampezzo has always had special rights: it's had autonomy since the Middle Ages, when it was ruled by Venice. These rights were given them in 1511 under Kaiser

Maximilian, when Ampezzo joined Austria of its own free will. Called the 'Regoles', they were last written down in 1971 as part of an agreement between Ampezzo and Italy. The people of Ampezzo are proud of their autonomy. Ladin is spoken by very few people here today, and you hardly ever see the old local dress — only amongst churchgoers and at festivals, when 'Schützen' (see page 17) come together. As an old Tyrolean region *of course* Ampezzo has 'Schützen'!

Cortina d'Ampezzo

All that is left of the tiny Cortina of 100 years ago is the parish church, the Ciasa de ra Regoles (seat of the autonomous government) and the church cemetery. Cortina is a modern tourist area *par excellence*, and the Tyrolean atmosphere of most other places in the Dolomites only surfaces in a few examples here.

Prices are high, *very* high. You are paying for the privilege of being in Cortina. The season is short; on September 15th most of the shops close down and don't reopen until the middle of December. If you want to see a farmhouse, you will have to go up to one of the places above Cortina, to the sunny slopes spreading out below Tofana.

Cortina is the place where Italian chic and money come together, with women in expensive designer dirndels, and some of the men in even more expensive lederhosen. Those who can afford it takes a villa while staying in Cortina, but you can also stay in a hotel, and four of the handful of five-star hotels in the Dolomites are located here.

Whether you come to enjoy yourself or you only come to be seen, there's a lot on offer — from the turbulent nightlife in high season (but *only* in high season) to the slickest sports. Restaurants are 'in' one minute and 'out' the next, so that one winter you'll meet at X, the next winter at Y, and the next who knows where… If you 'do' the *corso*, strolling along the Corso Italia early in the evening, you'll soon learn where to be seen and where not to be seen under any circumstances!

Transport: There are two large **car parks** near the old railway

Cortina d'Ampezzo — where the chic meet the sports enthusiasts

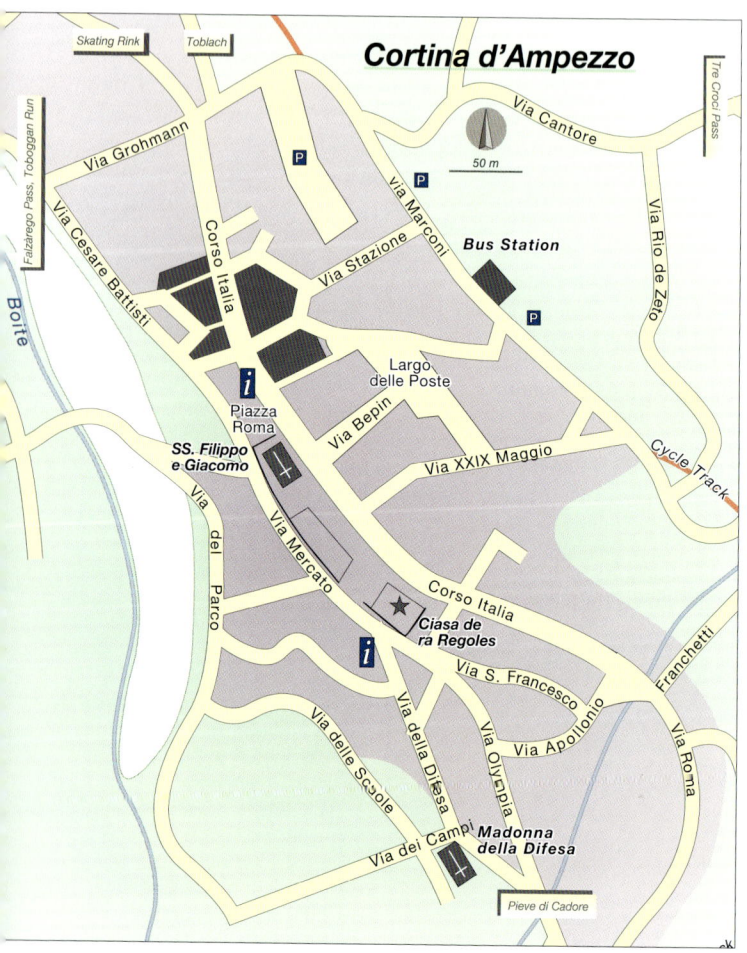

station; the Corso Italia and adjacent lanes are all pedestrian zones. The **bus station** is in the old railway station. **Cortina-express** operates a bus transfer to Venice, Bologna and Bolzano, in winter also to the Pustertal/Val Pusteria and Alta Badia. **Dolomitibus** operates to San Vito and Calalzo (from where trains run to Belluno and Treviso/Venice); in summer also daily to the Falzàrego Pass (6-8 buses), Corvara (3-4 buses) and the Trecroci Pass/ Auronzo Hut (5 buses). **SAD** has six services to Toblach/Dobbiaco and five to the Auronzo Hut (with a change of buses). For all bus information see www.servizi ampezzo.it. In winter there is a **free ski bus** between Borca, San Vito, Cortina, Misurina and the Falzàrego Pass. The nearest **railway** stations are Calalzo di Cadore and Toblach.

Events: Among the various events held are the **Cortina-Dobbiaco mountain bike race**

> **Cortina 1956: the year of Toni Sailer**
>
> The first time the Olympic Games were shown on television was in 1956, when the Winter Games took place in the then little-known Cortina d'Ampezzo. Italy had done all it could to get the games — built a new ice-skating stadium and toboggan run, and run a huge international publicity campaign. It was the first time a Russian team had attended the Olympics. Despite a shortage of snow — but a lot of ice — the outstanding performer was an Austrian skier named Toni Sailer. By winning the downhill, slalom and giant slalom, he became the first skier to sweep all three Alpine events. Triumph for Toni Sailer — and for Cortina, which gained world-wide fame.
>
> At the time of those Olympics Cortina already had a 60-year-old skiing tradition. In 1894 August Kolitsch from the Sudetenland, a teacher at the local art school, first brought a pair of skis to the Ampezzo — and used them, to the great astonishment of all. The Cortina Ski Club, founded in 1903, is the oldest in what is today Italy. The first skiing competitions took place here in 1907. Since 1924 there has also been an Ice Hockey Club. Cortina may be a wonderful destination for summer, but it really comes into its own in winter.

(31.5km) at the end of May/early Jun, the **Coppa d'Oro delle Dolomiti**, a classic car rally in July, and the **Festa de ra Bàndes**, when bands from Ampezzo get together in local costume (in August).

Sights: The **Corso Italia**, the middle stretch of which is a pedestrian zone, runs a long way through the town, taking in the **Via dell'Alemagna**, which was built by the Austrians in 1830 to link Venice (which at that time belonged to Austria) and Toblach in the Pustertal. This was, of course, a very old route, since the Fugger family sent their fabrics from Augsburg to Venice along the 'Alemagna'.

Some older buildings break through the front of the modern hotels and shops, including above all the **parish church SS Filippo e Giacomo** with its 71m high, Venetian-style campanile (1851-1858). The church itself is baroque, with a very beautiful Lady altar (the first side-altar on the left) decorated with wood carvings by Andrea Brustolon (1703); the ceiling paintings are the work of Franz Anton Zeiller. In the church square are the shell-shaped *Tribüne* for live performances and a memorial to Cortina's famous mountain guide, Angelo Dibona (1879-1956).

The large **Ciasa de ra Regoles** next to the church was the seat of the autonomous government of Ampezzo from 1511 to 1915, when Cortina came *de facto* under Italian rule (in the peace treaty of 1919). The building houses the **Museo delle Regole**, which comprises three sections. The **Rinaldo Zardini Paleontology Museum** is devoted to the geology of the Dolomites — the rocks, fossils and minerals. Good dioramas show the development of the Dolomites over the last 200 million years. The **Mario Rimoldi Pinacoteca** is dedicated to contemporary Italian and classical modern art. In the **Ethnographical Museum** there is information about the handicrafts and dress of the Ampezzo Ladins. *Museo delle Regole open daily (ex Mon) from 10.00-12.30 and 15.00-19.00 ; entry 9 €, concessions 6 €; www.musei.regole.it*

Passo Giau

Passo Giau (2233m) is an alternative connection to Livinallongo/Buchenstein and the Agordino; it has far more curves than the Falzàrego Pass road, so it's very popular with bikers. Two buses a day cross the pass (Cortina–Selva di Cadore route). Approaching the pass you have the jagged profile of **Croda da Lago** on your left, with **Becco di Mezzodì** in front of it — both isolated reefs in a green alm landscape. Becco means 'beak' — the beak-shaped peak rises just south of Cortina.

Below Croda da Lago there's a pretty little lake with a hut (Rifugio Croda da Lago), which can be reached **on foot** from the road to Passo Giau in 2h (Trails 437/434 from Ponte di Rucùrto at 1700m). From the hut it's 1h to the start of the climb to Becco di Mezzodì, a 45min ascent (Grade II).

At **Passo Giau** (shown on page 18) there are very fine views to the rock bastion of **Ra Gusela**, the southern spire of **Nuvolau** (which is also obvious from Cortina itself). A not especially difficult *via ferrata,* called Ra Gusela, runs to Nuvolau; it ends by the attractively-sited Nuvolau Hut on the peak (which can also be reached on a detour from Walk 28).

Great Dolomite Road to Passo Falzàrego

If you drive from Cortina on the Great Dolomite Road to the Falzàrego Pass (2105m), the **Tofana** massif dominates the panorama. (The Dolomitibus to Falzàrego and SAD bus to Wolkenstein/Selva also cover this route.) The famous **Cinque Torri** can be reached from the Rifugio Bai de Dines on this road, either on foot or by **chair lift** (early Jun to end Sep 09.00-17.00; one way 14.50 €, up and back 19.50 €). These massive rock lumps, looking like giants' toys, are one of the most-loved photographic images of the Dolomites. There are two very pleasant huts nearby, where you could spend the night, the Rifugio Scoiattoli (visited on Walk 28) and the Rifugio Cinque Torri.

With its countless, easy-to-difficult (2min- to 1h-long) climbs, the Cinque Torri make an attractive **climbing area**. The highest peak is Torre Grande at 2366m (normal climbs on its three needles of Grades I, II and III; note that sometimes a route may be closed due to rockfall). Or, if you like scrambling over boulders, you can do so to your heart's content in the **climbing garden** — even if you're a beginner. This is a good place to learn climbing techniques in straightforward surroundings.

In 1915-1917 the Cinque Torri were at the Front; the Italians dug in here. As at Lagazuoi, trenches, artillery posts and shelters have been restored, rebuilt and made accessible thanks to the **Open-air Museum**. *For details see page 157 and Walks 27 (page 162) and 28 (page 166).*

Only when you leave the pass to return to Cortina does the panorama over Ampezzo gradually open up — with Cristallo, Sorapis and Antelao on the horizon, as well as Pomagagnon towering over Cortina itself.

Tofana di Mezzo

Tofana group

Tofana di Mezzo (3244m) and **Tofana di Rozes** (3225m) dominate the horizon northwest of Cortina; the third Tofana, **Tofana di Dentro** (3238m) is hardly noticeable. The Tofanas are **climbing mountains** and, except for Tofana di Rozes, classed as moderate to difficult. If you take the Freccia di Cielo ('Heaven's Arrow') cable car to the Tofana di Mezzo peak, you will see that there's no room to fool around: except for the terrace of the hut at the top, there is not a single square metre of flat land.

Walkers take the road from **Gilardon** (on the Falzàrego road) to the **Baita Piè Tofana** at the end of the road (1557m, rustic restaurant with terrace), then take **two chair lifts**: Piè Tofana to Duca d'Aosta (with hut), and Duca d'Aosta to Pomedes. These run from end Jun to mid-Sep, combi-ticket one way 13.50 €, up and back 17.00 €. In winter the lightning-fast Canalone Run dives down into the valley (red, with a black alternative); this was the run used in the 1956 Olympics. From the Pomedes Hut at the mountain station (2300m) they take Route 421 down to the Dibona Hut (more good food) and from there Route 412 to the Falzàrego Pass, all the while with views to Averau, Nuvolau and the Cinque Torri.

Höhlensteintal/Valle di Landro and Monte Piana

The southern approaches to the Fanes and Sennes groups begin in the Höhlensteintal north of Cortina. From **Lake Dürren** in the valley an old, eroded military road runs up to isolated Monte Piana, where the plateau was the front line in 1915-1917. During the War in the Dolomites the north peak, **Monte Piano** (2321m), was in Austrian hands, the south peak, **Monte Piana** (2325m) in Italian. There are many remains of emplacements, tunnels and shelters.

A **walking/climbing circuit** (you must be sure-footed, with a head for heights) has been laid out round the old fighting area and can be done in about 2h30min. You can get there on foot — for instance from the Höhlensteintal/Valle di Landro — or (much less strenuously) by taking the **shuttle** (private cars and mountain bikes are not allowed!) from Misurina up to the **Bosi Hut** on the plateau.

● *Walking tip: Monte Piana from the Bosi Hut.* For something tamer than the trail mentioned above, take the shuttle to the **Bosi Hut** and just do the first part of

the yellow- and black-waymarked route; it's easy; you don't need a head for heights and you don't even have to climb 100m (Tabacco 1:25,000 map N° 010).

Cristallo and Cadin

One of the best drives (or cycle tours) from Cortina is the circuit round Cristallo. Take the Great Dolomite Road to the **Passo di Tre Croci** (1809m) and down to idyllic **Lake Misurina** (1735m). The view from its northern bank across the lake to Sorapis is one of the most famous mountain motifs in the world. From the lake you can continue along the road to the **Auronzo Hut** (toll) and explore around the Drei Zinnen (Walk 30) or the wild landscape of the **Cadin peaks**.

The national road runs further downhill into the Höhlensteintal and meets the Toblach–Cortina road in **Schluderbach/Carbonin** (from where those with bikes could take the cycle path back to Cortina or Toblach).

From the south the **Rio Gere chair lift** runs up to the Rifugio

Monte Piana — a memorial to the bloody War in the Dolomites

Son Forca (end Jun to mid-Sep, 08.30-16.30, one way 13.20 €, up and back 18 €). From there a legendary basket lift used to go up to the **Forcella Staunies** with the Lorenzi Hut, under the neighbouring peak of **Cristallino**, but this has been closed.

The climb to Cristallino, which begins at the hut, requires mountaineering expertise. But more famous is the **Via Ferrata Dibona** (often photographed with its suspension bridge) which also begins at this hut. Named for the great Angelo Dibona, this runs over into Valgrande between Cristallo and Pomagagnon and then to Ospitale in the Höhlensteintal (medium difficulty; walking time without stops 6h).

Sorapis and Antelao

When Cortina's first cable car to Faloria opened in 1939, it was a sensation — the latest in technology. Today's **cable car to the Faloria Hut** (2123m, mid-Jun to end Sep and, in the winter season, half hourly from 08.30 to 16.30, one way 17/19 €, up and back 20/22 €), on a ridge in the **Sorapis** massif, is just one of many. But what's nice about it is that it starts in Cortina itself (in the part of town called Pecol). Once you get up to the top, however, it's tricky: only properly equipped expert mountaineers can tackle the crossing.

That's even more true for **Antelao**, somewhat further south (by San Vito di Cadore). You get a good look at Antelao's profile from the west side of the Ampezzo: it is completely asymmetric. There is not even one hut on Antelao, only two bivouacs to protect you from the loneliness of the heights.

Walk 30: ROUND THE DREI ZINNEN/ TRE CIME DI LAVAREDO

Distance/time: about 9.4km/ 5.8mi; 3h
Grade: ● straightforward mountain walk with magnificent views; ascent/descent 350m/ 1150ft
Waymarking: red/white; Trail 105 to the Drei Zinnen Hut/Rifugio Locatelli (**5**), and from there Trail 101 to the end
Equipment: hiking boots, sun protection, walking pole(s)
Refreshments: available at the Langalm (**4**), Drei Zinnen Hut/ Rifugio Locatelli (**5**; open end Jun-end Sep), and the Auronzo Hut (**9**)
Walking map: Tabacco 010, Sextener Dolomiten-Dolomiti di Sesto, 1:25,000
Transport: 🚗 free car parking at the end of the (toll) road from Lake Misurina, near the Auronzo

Hut (46° 36.761'N, 12° 17.632'E). Or 🚌 445 from Cortina to the Auronzo Hut, usually runs every two hours from Jun to Sep; return on the same bus.

This is an easier approach to the Drei Zinnen/Tre Cime than the trail in Book 1, which approaches from the north. And it looks at these iconic peaks from all angles. As you round the mountain triptych you'll take photos galore!

View to Rautkofel from the Col de Medo

Begin at the end of the toll road (**1**) from Lake Misurina up to the Drei Zinnen. At this point 98% of visitors make for the Auronzo Hut, then head east on Route 101. Do *not* join them. Instead, take Trail 105 from the end of the car park (**2**), heading west — with superb views to the Cadin peaks, Monte Cristallo and Hohe Gaisl.

The route rises very gently below the southern walls of the Drei Zinnen to the **Forcella del Col de Medo** (**3**), where you have a new view: the alm landscape on the floor of the Rienztal/Valle dell'Acqua (the river has its source up here) and the fearful ridges of Rautkofel/Monte Rudo and Bullköpfe/Cima Bulla.

A scree slope is crossed on a good path and beyond a pretty little lake you come to the hut on **Langalm** (**4**; **45min**), where there's fresh milk and cold drinks to be had. At this point the panorama of the Drei Zinnen has unfolded (the most famous view of it is this one from the north).

To carry on to Patternkofel/ Monte Paterno and the Drei Zinnen Hut, you now cross the alm — 100m down, then 200m back up (keep right at two forks, then head left on the motor track). On this steep ascent your attention will be drawn to rusted barbed wire from World War II. At the top, head right to the **Drei Zinnen Hut/Rifugio Locatelli** (**5**; **1h40min**) and the famous view, with the peaks of the Sexten Dolomites rearing up on the far side of the pass.

To return, take the motor track to the **Paternsattel/Forcella Lavaredo** (**6**; **2h20min**) east (left) of the Drei Zinnen, then a short-cut trail. Above the **Lavaredo Hut** (**7**) you're back on the track: pass a **chapel** (**8**) and reach the **Auronzo Hut** (**9**), then the **car park/bus stop** (**3h**).

Drei Zinnen/Tre Cime de Lavaredo from the south

14 CADORE

San Vito di Cadore • Cibiana • Museu delle Dolomiti • Pieve di Cadore and surroundings • Auronzo di Cadore and surroundings • Marmarole group

Walks: none
Websites
www.infodolomiti.it

Opening hours: see individual attractions

You'll see Cadore if you look south from Monte Cristallo at Cortina, from the Kreuzberg/Monte Croce di Comelico Pass at Sexten/Sesto or from the main Carnic ridge on the Austrian border. The three valleys that run from the old main town of Pieve ('Parish') — the Boite, Ansiei and Piave — are collectively called Cadore.

Cadore was in Venetian hands from 1420. For centuries, since early modern times, the area was the main supplier of timber for this seafaring republic; the wood was floated down the Piave River to its mouth. But there are still forests in Cadore; the republic and later the Habsburgs made sure there was reafforestation.

While in Cortina you're tripping over people all the time, in Cadore it is supremely peaceful. Maybe too peaceful: in the lonely Marmarole group there are days, even in high season, when you will meet no one at all. Cadore has only two large settlements lying within the Dolomites — San Vito di Cadore in the Boite Valley (Valboite), just near Cortina d'Ampezzo, and Auronzo di Cadore, the main town of the Ansiei Valley. Both make good bases if you want somewhere quieter than Cortina.

San Vito di Cadore

After Cortina, San Vito is the most important tourist centre in the Valboite. It is prettily situated at the foot of **Antelao**.

Sights and excursions: The **parish church** is worth a visit; the painting on its high altar is by Francesco Vecellio, one of the brothers of Titian, who came from Pieve di Cadore. San Vito is a good base for climbing Antelao and Sorapis — and Monte Pelmo on the other side of the valley. The same is true for nearby **Borca di Cadore** 2km away, but accommodation there is limited. You can swim at tiny **Lake San Vito** at 1000m, but it's *cold, cold, cold!*

Cibiana

This little place lies on the pass road from Valboite to Zoldano. It was one of the Italian villages decorated in the last century with **outside frescoes**. The villagers (all 500 souls) gave artists a free hand in 1980, with only one stipulation: the paintings should as far as possible have some connection with Cibiana — the buildings and the occupants. So on one house you will see two women with wooden clogs and backpacks ('Zocui e Zestoi'). Another is 'La Botega': the door on the fresco is the door to the house. One wall depicts two street musicians; 'L'Emigrante' shows one of the emigrants who left to find work decades ago.

Transport: 7 **buses** a day from the railway station at Calalzo di Cadore.

Museo delle Dolomiti

From **Forcella Cibiana** (pass) you can take an old military road up to an Italian fortress on **Monte Rite** at 2181m. The extremely well-preserved stronghold has been made into '**Dolomiti**', a **Messner Museum** (see www.messner-mountain-museum.it/en). Using glass and metal, they've transformed the old artillery positions with shafts of light. It opened in 2002 — the 'International Year of the Mountain'.

On display among other things is Reinhold Messner's large collection of Alpine paintings dating over the past 150 years — including mountain 'portraits' by **E T Compton** (1849-1921), who pioneered a very romantic interpretation of realism. Another part of the collection is devoted to **Deodat de Dolomieu** and geology (see page 5). The museum (sometimes called Museo della Montagna or 'Museum in the Clouds') is 2h on foot from the pass, but from 1/6 to 30/9 there is a daily minibus service from 09.00-18.00 ('Servizio Navetta'): one way 10 €, return 14 €. There is also the Dolomitibus service up to 6 times a day from the Valboite to Cibiana and Forcella Cibiana. *Museum open daily Jun to Sep 10.00-17.00 (18.00 from Jul to mid-Sep); entry 9 €, children 4.50 €.*

Pieve di Cadore and surroundings

Pieve lies on a slightly hilly terrace at the exit of the Valboite; it's the main parish of Cadore.

Transport: Pieve (and Calalzo) are linked by **train** and frequent **buses** with Belluno (14 buses a day to Cortina, 15 towards Auronzo). The railway station is at Calalzo di Cadore, 2km away.

Sights and excursions: The house where Tiziano Vecellio, better known as **Titian**, was born in 1490 is today a small **museum**, although it has none of his paintings. *Daily May-Oct from 09.30-*

Lake Misurina and the Sorapis group

12.30 and 15.30-18.30; entry 4 €.

Pieve's main square is named after Titian, and a memorial to him stands there. But the most important building in the Piazza Tiziano by far is the **Palazzo della Magnifica Comunità Cadorina**. Today it is only the town hall, but earlier it was the seat of government for all of Cadore. It has a **local museum**, displaying among other things some paintings by the Vecellios, like the beautiful 'Dedication of Cadore to the Madonna' by Cesare Vecellio. In the **parish church of Santa Maria Nascente** there is a large 'Last Supper', clearly inspired by Leonardo, and also the work of Cesare Vecellio, a relation of Titian.

If you make the effort to go up to the village of **Pozzale** on Monte Tránego above Pieve, you'll find that its church has the only Titian that remains in the area where the artist was born — a Madonna with Child (on the left).

Pieve has virtually merged with neighbouring **Calalzo di Cadore**; the railway from Belluno up into Cadore ends here. In **Tai di Cadore**, on the other side of Pieve, the **San Candido Church** holds more works by Cesare Vecellio, for example a beautiful St Apollonia. This village also has a worthwhile **optical museum** (Museo dell' Occhiale) with spectacles, lenses, magnifying glasses and optical instruments from the 16th century to today. *Museum open daily (incl holidays) Jul-Sep 09.30-12.30 and 15.30-18.30; Oct-Jun Tue-Sat only, same hours; entry 5.50 €.*

Longarone lies at the junction of the Zoldano and Piave valleys. The village was in the 'line of fire' when the **Lago di Vajont** dam burst on 9th October 1963, killing up to 2500 people. Longarone was rebuilt on the other side of the valley, although they say the dam is now safe. The Longarone council runs 'Informatori del Vajont', which allows you to visit the famous dam with a guide. For information about the dam, see www.vajont.net (Italian and French only) or Wikipedia.

Auronzo di Cadore and surroundings

Like the other large lakes in Cadore, **Lake Auronzo** is a reservoir. That does not stop it from being very attractive when the sun is shining and one or two sailboats are plying the waters. This lake is also the largest single expanse of water in the Dolomites where swimming and angling are allowed. It also has a very pretty beach for sunbathing. But if you came to climb a mountain, you have a large choice nearby — from Marmarole to Cadin with its protected but not very difficult **Bonacossa Trail**, Cristallo and the Drei Zinnen/Tre Cime di Lavaredo.

Transport: Auronzo can be reached by up to 15 **buses** a day to Calalzo/Pieve di Cadore (from where there are **train** connections); there are also buses to the Kreuzbergsattel in summer and up to three buses a day to Misurina.

Marmarole group

No group of mountains in the Dolomites is more isolated than the Marmarole, which culminates in the **Cimone della Foppa** at 2932m. The only huts are at the south foot; on the mountain itself there are only two bivouacs. The crossing of the group from east to west (from Auronzo), is a strenuous undertaking of three to four days demanding climbing skills.

Index

Bold type indicates a photograph; *italic type* indicates a map or plan; both may be in addition to a text reference on the same page.

Alta Badia *see* Hochabteital
Abtei/Badia (combined villages of Pedratsches and St Leonhard) 96, 97, 95-98, 106, *108-9*
Abteital/Val Badia *see* Gadertal
Agordino 7, 27-8, 126, 129, 154-5, 157, 159, 161, 174
Agriturismo 14
Airports 9
Alpe di Siusi *see* Seiser Alm
Alta Badia *see* Hochabteital
Altopiano di San Martino 151, *152-3*
Ampezzo 7, 12, 14, 18, 22, 26, 28, 40, 95, 102, 157, 161, 167, 170-4, 176, 179
Andraz 154, 156
Antelao 170, 176
Antermoia (peak, lake, pass, hut) 99, *138-9*, **139**
Antersass (peak, pass) 77, 79, 82
Arabba **154-5**
Auronzo di Cadore (and lake) 181
Auronzo Hut 176, *177*, 178
Averau (peak, pass, hut) 158, *166*, 167, 175
Avisio (stream) 124, **128**, 131
Agordo 154, **158-9**
Alleghe (village, lake, pass) 159, **160-1**, 168, *169*
Badia *see* Abtei
Badia Valley *see* Gadertal
Belluno 8, 12, 154-5, 158-9
Biella Hut *see* Seekofel Hut
Bindelweg/Viel dal Pan (trail, hut) 28, 133-134, *141*, **140-1**, 156
Boè (peak, hut, lake. lift) 76, **77**, 78-9, 82, **83**, 95, 114, 133
Boite (river, valley) 102, 170, *172*, 179
Bolzano (German: Bozen) 9-10, **12**
Bosi Hut 175
Bozen *see* Bolzano

Brenner Pass 10-11, 24
Brenta Dolomites 6
Bressanone *see* Brixen
Brixen/Bressanone 10, 12
Brogles (alm, hut, stream) 55, *56*, 57
Buchenstein/Pieve de Livinallongo 7, 14, 26, 156
Buses 11-12
Cadin group 176
Cadore 7-8, 170, 179-81
Campilltal/Val de Longiarü 92, 97, 99
Camping 14
Campitello 135
Campolongo Pass 156-7
Canazei 129-31
Town plan 130-1
Capanna Alpina 110, *112*, 113, *116-7*, 118
Capanna Piz Fassa **82**, 83, 134
Capanna Trieste *169*
Carezza *see* Karer
Cason Hut 55, *56*
Catinaccio *see* Rosengarten
Catinaccio d'Antermoia *see* Kesselkogel
Cavalese **142**, 143-4
Christomannos monument **5**, *136-7*, **137**
Ciablun 97, *122*, 123
Ciampàc (peak, lift) 132
Ciampedié (lift, hut) 127, *136-7*
Ciampëi Pass (Puez-Geisler Nature Park) *86-7*
Ciampëi (north of Wengen) *122*-123
Ciampinoi (peak, lift) 45, 65, *66*, 69, *70-1*, **71**
Cibiana 179-80
Cimone della Pala **144-5**
Cinque Torri (peaks, hut) 158, *166*, 167, 174-5
Cinque Torri Open-air Museum *166*, 167
Cir (peaks, pass) *86-7*
Cisles (stream, valley) 42-3, *49*, *75*
Civetta group 28, 159, **160-1**, 168, *169*
Climate and Weather 16
Col di Lana 154, 157

Col de Locia *116-7*, 118
Col de Medo *177*, **177**
Col dei Baldi 168, *169*
Col Raiser **27**, 36, 43, **48**, *49*, 51, *52*, 53, **54**, 57, *75*
Col Reàn (peak, pass, alm) *169*
Col Rodella (peak, hut) 69, *70-1*, 135
Col Verde 148, 151, *152-3*
Colbricon (lakes, hut) **146**, *146*
Coldai (peak, pass, hut, lake) 160-1, **168**, *169*
Colfosco *see* Kolfuschg
Comici Hut **65**, *66*, 69, *70-1*, 72, **73**, 135
Communications 16
Contrin (alm, dairy) 89, *91*
Cordevole Valley 154-5, 160
Cortina 27, 28, 40, **170-1**, 172-4
Town plan 172
Corvara **93-4**, *114*
Crep de Munt *82*, 83
Crespëina (peak, hut, lake) 84-5, *86-7*
Cristallo 170, *176*
Cuisine 14-5
Cycling 13, 23, 41, 99, 102, 131, 158

Dantercepies (lift, lodge) 45, 62, 84, *86-7*
Daunëi *58*, **59**, *75*
Dlacè (lake, peak) *82*, 83
Dolomites
Great Dolomite Road 25, 124, 137, 155, 157, 170, 174, 176
High Route 45, 76, 80, 93, 102, 118-21, 140
Dolomiti SuperSummer Card 12, 22, 93
Dolomiti Superski 8, 22-23
Drei Zinnen/Tre Cime di Lavaredo (peaks, hut) **1**, 6, 28, 176, *177*, **178**, **cover**
Driving 9-11
Eisack/Isarco Valley 6, *27*, 29
Eissee, Eisseespitze *see* Dlacè
Emergencies 33

Index 183

Enneberg/Marebbe 92, **100-1**
Events 16
Falcade 129, 158
Falzàrego Pass 109, 157, 162-3, *165*, **166**, *166*, 167, 170, 174
Fanes (alm, group, hut) 28, 32, 92-3, 101, **102**, *116-7*, **117**, 118
Fassa Valley 27-8, 40, 124-36
Fauna 31-2
Fedaia (pass, lake) 28, 124, 132-134, 140, *141*
Fermeda (peaks, hut) 43, **49**, 51, *52*
Fiera de Primiero 147, 149-50
Firenze Hut *see* Regensburger Hut
First World War 23, 25, 28, 39-40, 102, 131, 140, 155, **166**, **167**
Fleimstal/Val di Fiemme 7, 15, 17, 22, 124, 142-143, 145-146
Flora 30-1
Fodara Vedla 102, 119, **120**, *120-1*, **121**
Forcella Lavaredo *see* Paternsattel
Forte Tre Sassi 157-8, *165*
Franzensfeste 9, 12
Frara Hut 45, 76, **77**, *80-3*
Franz Kostner Hut *82*, 83
Friedrich August (hut, trail) 69, *70-1*, 135
Gadertal (or Abteital)/Val Badia 6, 27, 76, 92-123
Gardeccia Hut *138-9*
Gardenaccia 84, *86-7*
Geisler/Odle group 48, **49**, 51, **52**, 55, *56*, **74-5**, *75*
Giau Pass **18**, 170, 174
Grasleitenpass Hut/Rifugio Passo Principe *138-9*
Gries 126, 130, **132**
Grödner Joch/Passo di Gardena 45, 76, **77**, 79, *80*, *82*-3, 84-5, *86-7*
Grödner Tal (or just 'Gröden')/Val Gardena 6, 22, 27, 36-91
Heiligkreuz *see* Holy Cross
Heiligkreuzkofel/Sasso della Croce **106-7**, *108-9*
History 24
Hochabteital/Alta Badia 92-3, 95, 156
Holy Cross (hospice, pilgrimage church) **106-7**, *108-9*
Höhlensteintal/Valle di Landro 175-6

Horse-riding 23
Huts, mountain 14
Illness 19
Insom **21**, 51, *52*, 54
Isarco *see* Eisack
Jimmi Hut 45, 84-5, *86-7*
Juac Hut 58, *59*, 74, *75*
Kaiserjägersteig 158, 162, **164**, *165*
Karer/Carezza (pass, lake) 124-7, *136-7*
Kesselkogel/Catinaccio d'Antermoia *138-9*
'Krampus' 18
Kolfuschg/Colfosco 45, 92-5
La Ciajota 62, 64, *86-7*
La Pli de Mareo **100**, 101
La Val *see* Wengen
La Valle *see* Wengen
La Villa *see* Stern
Lace 20
Ladin, Ladins 38, 40, 64, 92, 98, 126, 133; *see also* Fassatal, Buchenstein, Ampezzo
Lagazuoi Lake (in the Fanes-Sennes-Prags Nature Park) 110, **111**, *112*, **112-3**
Lagazuoi Piccolo (peak, pass, hut, war museum) 28, 102, 157, **162-163**, *165*, **166**, **167**
Lagorai group 142-5
Lake Misurina 176-7, **180**
Lake Sant 51, *52*, 53, *75*
Langental/Vallunga **32**, 44, *59*, **60-1**, *62*, **63**, *64*, 84-7
Langkofel/Sassolungo 27, 39, 43, 45, **50**, **54**, 55, *66*, 67, 69, *70-1*, **71**, 72-4
Langkofel Hut *70-1*, 72
Latemar 144-5
Lavaredo Hut *177*, **178**
Lavarella Hut 102, *116-7*, 118
Legends Trail 46, **47**, *47*
Lifts 6-8, 12, 22-3, 27; *see also* individual areas and walks
Limo (pass, lake) *116-7*, **117**, 118
Listolade 168, *169*
Livinallongo *See* Buchenstein
Locatelli Hut *see* Drei Zinnen Hut
Longarone 181
Lunz **100**, *122*
Mahler, Gustav 17
Maps 7, 19, 35
Marebbe *see* Enneberg
Marmarole 179, 181

Marmolada 124, **134**, 140
Mazzin 128, 131, *138-9*
Medésc (valley, pass) *116-7*, 118
Mesdi, Val de *82*, **83**, *114*
Messner Museum 180
Misci *103*
Moèna 126, **128**, 131
Moiazza (peak) **158**
Money, Banks 20
Mont de Sëura 43
Mont Sëuc 41, 89-90, *91*
National Park Dolomiti-Bellunesi National Park 154, 159
Nature Parks
Fanes-Sennes-Prags Nature Park 92, 101, *108-9*, *112*, *116-7*
Paneveggio-Pale di San Martino 145, 147-8, 150, *152-3*
Puez-Geisler 44, **49**, 61, **62**, **84-5**, *86-7*, **94-5**
Sexten Dolomites *177*
Nigritella Hut *136-7*
Nuvolau (peak, pass, hut) 154, **158**, *166*, 167, 174-5
Odle *see* Geisler/Odle group
Odles Hut 48, **49**, 51, *52*
Padon ridge **140-1**, *141*
Pala di San Martino (peak) **150**, 151, *152-3*
Pale di San Martino (group) 28, 145-8
Panascharte/Forcella Pana 55, *56*, 57, 74, *75*
Paneveggio Forest 145-6, 148, **149**
Paolina Hut 127, *136-7*
Passo Principe Hut *see* Grasleitenpass Hut
Paternsattel/Forcella Lavaredo *177*, **178**, **cover**
Pederoa 97, *122*
Pederü 101-2, 119, *120-1*
Pedratsches 92, 96-7, *116-7*
Peitlerkofel/Sass de Pútia 96, 98, **100**, 103
Pelmo, Monte (peak) 161
Penìa 127, **130**, 131
Piana, Monte (peak) 175, **176**
Piave di Cadore 154, 179, 180-1
Piave River 154, 179
Pic (knoll) *52*, *75*
Pieralongia Hut **48**, *49*, *52*
Pieve di Livinallongo *see* Buchenstein
Pisciadù (hut, lake, peak) 76, **77**, *78*, *80*, **81**, *82*, 93
Pisciadù (stream, waterfalls) *114*, **115**

184 Dolomites, Book 2: Centre and East

Piz Boè 77, *82*-3, 95, 133
Plattkofel/Sassopiatto (peak, alm, hut) 49, 53, **54**, 55, 57, 69, *70-1*, **72-3**
Pordoi (pass, hut) 76, *77*, **78**, 79, 124, 129, 133, 140, *141*, **154-5**
Porta Vescovo 140, *141*, 156
Pozza 28, 127-8, 131-2
Prà da Ri *86-7*
Pradidali (peak, pass, hut) 151, **152-3**, *152-3*
Pralongià ridge 96
Pramulin Hut *49*, 50
Preuss Hut *138-9*
Primiero Valley 147-53
Puez group (and plateau) 27, 32, 41, 43, 45, 49, 55, 74, *75*, **84-5**, *86-7*, **88**, **94-5**
Puez Hut 45, 84, *86-7*, **88**
Pustertal 8-9, 12, 27
Ra Gusela **18**, 174
Rail travel 9, 12
Raschötz/Rasciesa (peak, hut, lift) *38*, 39, 55, *56*, 57
Rasciesa *see* Raschötz 52, 55, 70
Regensburger Hut/Rifugio Firenze 43, 48, *49*, 74, *75*
Roda di Vael (peak, hut) 127, *136-7*
Roda daes Viles (trail) *122*, 123
Rodella 69, *70-1*, **125**, 135
Rolle Pass **144-145**, *146*, 147
Rosengarten/Catinaccio 28, 89, 124, 127, 135, *136-7*
Rosetta (peak, lift, hut) 148, **151**, *152-3*
Rotwand/Roda di Vael *136-7*
Runch 97, *122*, 123
Rü *116-7*, 118
Rü de Ciampló Valley 97, *122*
S[ain]t Christina/Cristina/Crestina 36, 41, **42**, 43, 46, *47*, **47**, 48, *49*, 51, *52*, 53, *75*
St Jakob/San Giacomo 39, 46, *47*, 53
St Kassian/San Cassiano (village, stream) 92, *108-9*, *116-7*, **118**
St Leonhard/San Leonardo **18**, 92, 96, **97**, *108-9*, *116-7*
St Martin in Thurn/San Martino 92, 96-7, 99
St Ulrich/Ortisei 22, 27, 36, **37**, 38-41, *56*
Town plan 38-39

St Vigil/San Vigilio 92, 95, 101
Saltria 89-90, *91*
San Cassiano *see* St Kassian
San Giacomo *see* St Jakob
San Leonardo *see* St Leonhard
San Martino de Castrozza 142, 146-7, *152-3*
San Pellegrino (pass, valley) 124, 128-9
San Vito di Cadore 179
Sandro Pertini Hut *70-1*
Santa Crestina *see* St Christina
Santa Cristina *see* St Christina
Sass de Pútia *see* Peitlerkofel
Sass Maor 151, *152-3*
Sass Songher 92, **93**, 95
Sasso della Croce *see* Heiligkreuzkofel
Sassolungo *see* Langkofel
Sassopiatto *see* Plattkofel
Schlern/Sciliar **84-5**, 89
Schloss Thurn 97-8
Sciliar *see* Schlern
Scotoni Hut 110, *112*, 113, *116-7*
Seasons 29
Seceda (peak) 40, 43, *52*, 55, **56-7**, **74-75**, *75*
Seekofel (peak, pass, hut) 102, 119, *120-1*
Seiser Alm/Alpe di Siusi **84-5**, 89, **90-1**, *91*
Sella (group, pass, resort) 27, 36, 44-5, 65-7, *66*, **68**-69, 72-73, 76, *82*, **94-5**, 124, 129, 134
Sella Ronda 22, 36, 45
Selva *see* Wolkenstein
Sennes/Ladin: Sénes (group, hut, lake) 100-102, 119, *120-1*
Seres 28, **99**, *103*, 105
Seurasas Alm 51, *52*, 53
Sexten Dolomites 6, 8, *177*
Shopping 20, 37-38, 42
Sofie Hut 55, *56*, 57
Soraga 126, 128
Sorapis group 170, 176, 179, **180**
Souvenirs 20
Spina da Lèch *138-9*
Sports 6, 20-3
Steinerne Stadt ('Stone City') 65, *66*, **66-7**, 68, *70-1*, 73, 135
Stern/La Villa 92-3, 95, 106-7, *108-9*, *116-7*
Stevia (plateau, alm, hut) 49, 58, **59**, *59*, 60, 61

'Stone City' *see* Steinerne Stadt
Tèsero 142-3
Tissi Hut 168, *169*
Titian (Tiziano Vecellio) 180-1
Tofana group 170, **175**
Tolpëi 97, *122*, **122-123**
Tonadico 147, **149**, 150
Törggelen 15
Transaqua 147, 149-50
Transhumance 17-18
Tre Cime de Lavaredo *see* Drei Zinnen
Trenker, Luis (and Promenade) **37**
Troier Hut 43, 48, *49*, 74
Vajolet (valley, towers, hut) 127-8, *138-9*, **139**
Val Badia *see* Gadertal
Val Canali 147-8, **150**
Val Contrin 124, 132
Val de Longiarü *see* Campilltal
Val de Mesdi 79, **83**, *114*, **115**
Val di Fiemme *see* Fleimstal
Val Gardena *see* Grödner Tal
Val Pusteria *see* Pustertal
Val de Udai *138-9*
Valle di Landro *see* Höhlensteintal
Valle Isarco *see* Eisacktal
Valley of the Mills 96, *103*, **104, 105**
Valón de Rü 119, *120-1*
Valparola (pass and hut) 96, 109, 157, *165*
Vazzoler Hut *169*
Via ferrata 21-22, 83, 93, 114, 158, 160, 162, 174, 176
Viel dal Pan trail *see* Bindelweg
Viel dal Pan Hut 140, *141*
Vigo di Fassa 28, 124, **125**, 126, **127**, *136-7*
'Viles' 27, 92, 96-9, **100**, 101, **122-3**, 154, 156
Walking 6-7, 27-35
Wengen/La Valle 27, 92, 96-7, *122*, 123
Wolkenstein/Selva 22, 27, 36, 39, 43, *49*, 51, 58, *59*, *62*, 63-5, *66*, 68-69, 74, *75*, 84, *86-7*
Town plan 44
Wood carving 42
Zoldano Valley 154-5, 161, *169*, 179, 181